The Stoics Reader

The Stoics Reader

Selected Writings and Testimonia

Translated, with Introduction, by
Brad Inwood
and
Lloyd P. Gerson

Hackett Publishing Company, Inc.
Indianapolis/Cambridge

Copyright © 2008 by Hackett Publishing Company, Inc.

14 13 12 11 10 09 08   1 2 3 4 5 6 7

For further information, please address:
    Hackett Publishing Company, Inc.
    P.O. Box 44937
    Indianapolis, IN   46244-0937

    www.hackettpublishing.com

Cover design by Listenberger Design and Associates
Text design based on a design by Dan Kirklin
Composition by William Hartman
Printed at Edwards Brothers, Inc.

Library of Congress Cataloging-in-Publication Data
The stoics reader: selected writings and testimonia / translated, with
introduction by Brad Inwood and Lloyd P. Gerson.
        p. cm.
    Includes bibliographical references and index.
    ISBN-13: 978-0-87220-952-7 (pbk.)
    ISBN-13: 978-0-87220-953-4 (cloth)
    1. Stoics. I. Inwood, Brad. II. Gerson, Lloyd P.
    B528.S6825 2008
    188—dc22
                                                    2008016794

Contents

Preface

We are delighted that Hackett Publishing Company asked us to produce *The Stoics Reader* on the model of *The Epicurus Reader*. This book bears roughly the same relationship to *Hellenistic Philosophy: Introductory Readings*, Second Edition, as that one did. To a great extent, we have reproduced and rearranged the texts from the Stoicism section of that book and made only a few improvements and corrections to the original translations. We have also taken the opportunity to consolidate related texts into larger, more continuous selections, a feature of our original plan that has proven to be useful to students. We have also added material originally appearing in the Skepticism section of *Hellenistic Philosophy*, where the skeptical attack on Stoicism provides unique or particularly good evidence for Stoic theory; naturally, this material has been regrouped and occasionally expanded as well.

Further, we have added a modest amount of wholly new material, which falls into two parts. The evidence for two post-Chrysippean Stoics, Panaetius and Posidonius, has been enhanced, though it is of course by no means adequate to give a full picture of their thought any more than the rest of our texts provide a full picture of earlier Stoicism. These two thinkers were treated rather stingily in the book as we first conceived it, because the generally prevailing view in the early 1980s was that they represented a quite distinct period in the history of the school, one that would inappropriately complicate the picture of early Stoicism that we aimed to provide. But research over the past twenty-five years has convinced us that the distinctiveness of what used to be called 'middle Stoicism' was seriously overstated, and it makes more sense now to regard Panaetius and Posidonius as part of the range of varying opinion that prevailed among Stoics of the Hellenistic period. Readers with a particular interest in Posidonius may now consult the volume of translations by Ian Kidd.[1] Those interested in Panaetius face a greater challenge: not only is there no complete translation of van Straaten's collection of fragments,[2] but they must also wrestle with the intractable question of how much of the material in Cicero's *On Duties* books 1 and 2 can legitimately be treated as evidence for Panaetius. We have tried to be both critical and conservative on this issue,

---

1. *Posidonius Volume III: The Translation of the Fragments* (Cambridge: Cambridge University Press, 1999).

2. M. van Straaten, ed., *Panaetii Rhodii fragmenta*, 3rd ed. (Leiden, The Netherlands: E. J. Brill, 1962).

but the entire work is now available in a fine modern translation by Margaret Atkins,[3] and we encourage our readers to study it with care. Indeed, much of Cicero's evidence for Hellenistic Stoicism is now more readily accessible than it was previously, with the appearance of excellent new translations of *De Finibus* by Raphael Woolf,[4] of *Tusculan Disputations* books 4 and 5 by Margaret Graver,[5] and of the *Academica* by Charles Brittain.[6] Our translations here do not aim to replace these fine works, and we have concentrated on maintaining consistency with the style and terminology used for the rest of the evidence for Hellenistic Stoicism.

The other principal change is the addition of a short section which introduces the reader in a very limited way to some of the more interesting texts on Stoic ethics from the Roman imperial period. Previously we included such texts only as evidence, where we thought it helpful, for Hellenistic Stoicism; but the growth of philosophical interest in the later period has encouraged us to provide just enough to whet the reader's appetite. Short extracts from Musonius Rufus, Seneca the Younger, and Epictetus give an indication of what this later phase of the school's thinking has to offer in the field of ethics. Readers may also want to study *The Handbook* of Epictetus in the translation by Nicholas White.[7] However, no attempt is made here to cover later Stoic physics or logic, and it is worth noting that Marcus Aurelius is not included here at all. Though deeply affected by Stoicism in many respects, he was not a self-described Stoic, either as a teacher or as a writer. His brilliant philosophical diary, *To Himself* (better known as the *Meditations*) is available in many translations, including those by Grube and Hard.[8] A figure of political as well as philosophical interest, the emperor Marcus Aurelius deserves to be studied in his own right.

There is one further set of revisions, the effect of which will, we hope, be apparent even to the casual reader, and this concerns the use of gender-marked terminology. Both ancient Greek and Latin have distinct words for male human beings (*anēr, vir*), female human beings (*gunē, femina*), and human

3. M. T. Griffin and E. M. Atkins, eds., *Cicero: On Duties* (Cambridge: Cambridge University Press, 1991).

4. J. Annas, ed., R. Woolf, tr., *Cicero: On Moral Ends* (Cambridge: Cambridge University Press, 2001).

5. M. R. Graver, tr. and comm., *Cicero on the Emotions: Tusculan Disputations 3 and 4* (Chicago: University of Chicago Press, 2002).

6. C. Brittain, tr. with introduction and notes, *Cicero: On Academic Scepticism* (Indianapolis: Hackett Publishing, 2006).

7. *Epictetus: The Handbook (The Encheiridion)* (Indianapolis: Hackett Publishing, 1983).

8. G. M. A. Grube, tr. with introduction, *Marcus Aurelius: The Meditations* (Indianapolis: Hackett Publishing, 1983); R. Hard, tr., and C. Gill, introduction and notes, *Marcus Aurelius: Meditations* (Ware, UK: Wordsworth Editions Limited, 1997).

beings regardless of gender (*anthrōpos, homo*). Normally the gender-marked terms are used when biological gender is significant, and very often *anthrōpos* and *homo* are used when referring to the human species or to humans in contrast to animals, or even merely when biological gender is not particularly significant in context. Yet in both languages actual usage is in fact quite complex. For example, both languages (like many modern languages) have a convention governing pronoun and adjective use: mixed groups or generic references are indicated with the masculine grammatical gender. It is notoriously difficult to take full account of these facts when translating into English (which has its own evolving conventions), and in the first version of these translations the generic 'man' and 'men' were used far more often than would be considered normal today. Hence, there has been a thorough but context-sensitive revision of the translations of these terms, yielding significant rewording in many cases and minor, transparent changes in others. Terms like 'humans', 'human beings', 'people', 'humankind' now appear where it would have been misleading to retain the term 'man', 'men', or 'mankind'. At the same time, where the male-gendered Latin or Greek term is used or where the context indicates that masculine gender is important, 'man' or 'men' are naturally used in our translations. There is one systematic feature of this revision of which readers should be aware. In Stoicism the ideal human being is the 'wise man' or 'sage' (*sophos, sapiens*), and the masculine gender is always used in our Greek and Latin sources. Wisdom is not the only trait idealized in this way: all the virtues and their opposites are attributed to people in a strongly normative manner. Although it was tempting to convert all these to gender-neutral translations, we did not do so, and so 'wise man', 'base man', 'virtuous man', 'prudent man' and so forth persist as indicators of this normative use. One reason for this decision is the fact that even though Stoics themselves were often relatively enlightened about gender roles in their philosophical theory, they frequently used gendered attributes to indicate the ideals of human virtue. As progressive as they were, the ancient Stoics were still integral parts of an essentially sexist culture, and their thought as well as their language often reflect that fact. Rather than discriminate among such contexts in a way that could only mislead the readers of this book, we have retained the now somewhat dated generic masculine usage in contexts where idealized traits, both positive and negative, are invoked.

We would like to renew our thanks to Oxford University Press for its permission to include here several translations first published in Brad Inwood's *Ethics and Human Action in Early Stoicism* (Oxford: Oxford University Press, 1985). Emily Fletcher has done a wonderful job in adapting and updating the indexes, Glossary, and list of sources; for that and for other excellent editorial assistance, we are most grateful.

Introduction

Socrates was the most inspirational figure in the history of ancient philosophy. Of all those who fell under his influence, Plato is the best known and ultimately the one with the greatest impact. But there were many others as well. Directly or indirectly, Socrates was the ancestor of the most important schools of thought in the ancient world, perhaps of all schools except for those in the atomist tradition. And of the philosophical traditions inspired by Socrates, three stand out above all: Plato's Academy, Aristotle's Peripatetic school, and the Stoic school founded by Zeno, son of Mnaseas, from the town of Citium on Cyprus. Plato was a member of one of Athens' most powerful families. Aristotle was not only the student of Plato but also the son of the court physician to the royal house of Macedon and tutor to the young Alexander the Great. Zeno began his philosophical career as a nobody, and yet the school he founded was for centuries the most widespread intellectual movement in the Greco-Roman world. It only gradually succumbed to the revival of Platonism in late antiquity, which ultimately provided the dominant pagan philosophical legacy to the medieval world which followed. During the period of Stoicism's greatest influence and for long after, it continued to have an astonishing impact on Platonism, Aristotelianism, other philosophers, and educated culture generally.

History, even the history of philosophy, is written by the winners, and ultimately Stoicism lost its central place in the philosophical landscape of antiquity. One result of this is that its major thinkers and their books were cast into the shadows. Very little of their philosophical output survived the drastic cull of pagan literature and philosophy at the end of antiquity. The works of Stoicism which survived did so for various peculiar reasons, not all of which were likely to leave us with a clear and balanced representation of the school's doctrines and intellectual methods. Some, like the *Discourses* of Epictetus, survived because they were of tremendous importance to Platonists. Others, such as the prose works of Seneca, survived because of their unique literary qualities and their inspirational value for Christian writers. The one work by an early Stoic author, the *Hymn to Zeus* by Cleanthes, the second head of the school, survived in a single source, one manuscript of a Byzantine anthology. Others, such as the homilies of Musonius Rufus, were salvaged for their alleged moral uplift. Virtually all the rest of our information about ancient Stoicism comes down to us either in the sketchy outlines characteristic of philosophical encyclopedias or because the ideas were discussed by hostile critics only in order to be rejected.

That is why *The Stoics Reader* is necessary and is composed of a rather eclectic collection of texts. We have tried to gather in a form amenable to use by students and university teachers alike the most important evidence about Stoic thought surviving from the ancient world, including even some selections from the few authors (such as Seneca and Epictetus) whose texts survive relatively intact. This material ranges from summaries of doctrine—the most extensive of which are preserved in the *Lives of Eminent Philosophers* compiled by Diogenes Laërtius in late antiquity and in Cicero's philosophical dialogues—to snippets of dismissive criticism and attempts at sympathetic but thoughtful refutation.

Socrates' philosophical impact flowed through many channels, and the stories we have about Zeno's early life reveal which aspects of Socrates first caught his attention. According to Diogenes Laërtius (TEXT 1), he had already been attracted by Socratic literature when he was at home in Cyprus. At the age of thirty, he came to Athens, heard a reading from book 2 of Xenophon's *Memorabilia of Socrates,* and on the basis of that chose to study first with the Cynic philosopher Crates—the Cynics being a group that championed some of the more radical aspects of Socrates' thought, in particular his challenges to the social and political norms of conventional Greek society. But Zeno's philosophical talent and commitment were too great to be limited to one school, and he also apprenticed himself to Academics, dialecticians, and others and devoted considerable effort to the study of 'the ancients', that is, philosophers whom we know as Presocratics, in particular Heraclitus, and poets such as Hesiod and Homer. Although he was critical of Plato's philosophy in many ways, there is abundant evidence that Plato's dialogues were very influential on Zeno and his early followers. The impact of Aristotle and his school is a more controversial issue, but we take the view that either directly or indirectly the published and even the unpublished, more technical work of Aristotle played an important role in the formation of Stoicism.

After his years of apprenticeship, Zeno came into his own as a philosopher, challenging in debate and argument the traditions from which he had learned and developing a distinctive philosophy. He began teaching in a public space, the Painted Porch (or Stoa) in the Athenian marketplace, and attracted an impressive array of talented followers. At first they called themselves Zenonians, but eventually their habitual meeting place gave the group the name we still use for it, the Stoics. As far as we can tell, in Zeno's lifetime the school was the locus of considerable internal debate among his followers as well as the source of considerable challenge to the more established schools, especially the Academy, which in the course of Zeno's career had transformed itself from a school devoted to working out the implications of Plato's mature, dogmatic philosophy into a hotbed of skepticism. The critical epistemology of Arcesilaus the Academic was a powerful stimulus for the development of Stoic thought, just as the teleological approach to physics characteristic of Plato and Aristotle and the Cynic version of Socratic ethics had been.

It was the work of two or three generations to meld these varied influences into a philosophical system that was authoritative and relatively stable. Chrysippus, the third head of the school (after Zeno's student Cleanthes), was responsible for this synthesis, and his version of Stoicism became more or less standard. But even the authority of Chrysippus, one of the most creative and insightful philosophers in the ancient world, could not dampen the creative impulse for change within the school, and in the second century B.C. leading Stoics continued to find stimulus for innovation in debates with other traditions. The most famous (though not necessarily the most important philosophically) of these confrontations occurred in 155 B.C. when representatives of Aristotle's school, the Academy, and the Stoa were sent to Rome on a diplomatic mission. The Peripatetic Critolaus, the Academic Carneades, and the Stoic Diogenes all lectured in public as well as doing their political duty, and the event was symbolic not only of the ongoing and creative debate among the three major Socratic schools but also of the growing importance of Greek philosophy to Roman culture—and vice versa. The rise of Roman political influence in the Mediterranean world accelerated the already established trend of philosophers to meet, debate, and do their creative work in major cities throughout the Greco-Roman world, but Athens remained the intellectual heartland of philosophy for a while longer. Eventually, though, in the first century B.C. the political upheavals that accompanied Rome's expansion led to military action in Athens itself; as far as we can tell, the major schools closed, at least temporarily. The leading philosophers of all traditions, including Stoicism, moved on to Rome, Rhodes, Alexandria, and other cities; more of them taught privately or in the households of wealthy oligarchs. The highly focused world of face-to-face debate in Athens of the fourth century B.C. was gone. For the next three centuries Stoicism would flourish in the complex world of the Roman Empire, a world in which Latin joined Greek as a language of intellectual debate and teaching, in which philosophers from all traditions engaged with influential figures in politics and literature, medicine, mathematics, the other sciences, and eventually Christian theology. In all these areas Stoicism either took the lead or stood respectably alongside the other philosophical schools. Hence in the later history of Stoicism we see political leaders like Seneca who are also major philosophical authors, teachers like Epictetus who have an impact at the highest levels of elite political culture, and eventually even an emperor, Marcus Aurelius, who exemplifies in his personal philosophical journal the deep impact of Stoic thinking on the most powerful levels of Greco-Roman society.

The doctrines that characterize Stoicism throughout its long history can be grouped naturally under the three headings used to categorize so much of later ancient philosophy: logic, physics, and ethics. Logic includes the theory of knowledge, and in that area the Stoics are dedicated defenders of the view that human beings can achieve genuine knowledge about the physical world. Indeed, in their view this is the only world that exists; there are no incorporeal entities for us to know. Everything we know comes to us directly or indirectly through sense-perception; the cognitive powers of the human mind, itself a physical entity, are the product of a providential and purposive plan by the creative deity, so it is no wonder that our senses are adequate to the task. In the area of logic proper, the analysis of the structures of inference, proof, and discovery, the Stoics (Chrysippus in particular) were second to no one in the ancient world, not even Aristotle. Stoic logic surpassed Aristotle's, exploring and systematizing the relationships among propositions; the Stoics sought to analyze all valid inferences in terms of five basic and self-evidently valid argument forms. Stoic logicians also made important contributions to what we would call semantics, to the study of logical puzzles and paradoxes, and to the analysis of language. The importance of Stoicism in the development of formal grammatical theory cannot be overestimated.

In physics the Stoics were materialists of a sort, influenced deeply by the insight that causal interactions could take place only between physical objects. This corporealism did not, however, mean that their account of the natural world was crudely or reductively materialist; void, place, time, and *lekta* (roughly, intelligible content; the literal meaning is "things said") were all held to be non-bodily and therefore causally inefficacious, though nevertheless subsistent as features of the real world. But they did not think that things like the soul, god, and the formal structures that make particular objects what they are could possibly be incorporeal, as Platonists and Aristotelians did. They therefore rejected Platonic Forms and incorporeal gods, including Aristotle's Unmoved Mover, and they denied that immanent forms should be thought of as opposed to body. This meant that Aristotelian hylomorphism had to be rethought and that Aristotle's system of categories could not play a role in the analysis of the world. Instead, the Stoics developed an analysis that rested on two principles and four 'categories', the details of which are complex and controversial (see TEXT 25.134 and TEXT 55). What is clearer is that their physics and cosmology were in the mainstream of ancient physical thought. Like Empedocles, Plato, and Aristotle, they held that there are four basic kinds of matter in the world (earth, air, fire, and water), but they rejected an Aristotelian fifth element as the substance of heavenly and divine bodies. The earth lies at the center of a spatially bounded cosmos and has no void within it—though Stoicism does claim that there is an unlimited amount of emptiness outside the cosmos. Like Plato and Aristotle, Stoics held that the world and everything in it is teleologically organized; their version of the history of the cosmos and its relation to the divine is closer to Plato's vision in the *Timaeus* than to Aristotle's theory. Their doctrine of cyclical creation and destruction of the world is indebted to an Empedoclean vision, though no doubt supported by considerations more pertinent to the fourth century B.C. than to the Presocratics. The Stoics' decision to align the element fire with the pervasive rational force in the cosmos is part of their debt to Heraclitus. In keeping with their intense interest in causation, the Stoics embraced determinism along with their providential teleology, thus preparing the way for later debates about theodicy and the challenge of justifying the existence of defects within a world designed to be good. Stoic determinism also led them, necessarily, to take a strong and clear line on moral responsibility; they were the first to develop the stance we know today as compatibilism, the view that human choice is real though ultimately determined by causal factors.

In ethics the Stoics were perhaps at their most innovative *and* most conservative. The Socratic commitment to the role of rationality in determining the best human life is developed with an unswerving emphasis; they rejected completely the suggestion that human beings have in their souls an essentially irrational part. They were committed, like Plato, Aristotle, and even Epicurus, to the notion that happiness (*eudaimonia*) is the goal of human life and that it can be achieved by cultivation of our distinctively human attributes. When perfected, such excellence of our soul is virtue, and the Stoics were adamant in their view that true virtue is all one needs to be happy, regardless of whether bodily or external circumstances are favorable. It can be argued that their stringent claims in ethics (the self-sufficiency of virtue, the need to eliminate all irrational passions, the unity of virtues, the impossibility of *akrasia*) are the purest and most rigorous expression of an original Socratic stance in ethics. Although the outlandish content of some of these theories (which some Stoics emphasized for pedagogical purposes) certainly reduced the breadth of their appeal, the sharp focus and rational coherence of their ethics ensured that their doctrines continued to influence and challenge philosophers throughout antiquity and into the modern world.

Perhaps the key idea of Stoic ethics is the injunction that as rational animals our job is to follow nature, that is, to live in accordance with the way nature is; this will assure our fulfillment and success in the world. This doctrine makes excellent sense within ancient Stoicism because the Stoics held that nature is rational and indeed structured by the same sort of rationality that we humans possess. It is one of the strengths of Stoicism that the ideal of living according to the best possible understanding of the natural world is something that still has considerable appeal today, even among those who do not share the Stoics' now outmoded and essentially anthropocentric cosmology.[9]

9. See the stimulating book by Lawrence Becker, *A New Stoicism* (Princeton, NJ: Princeton University Press, 1998).

A good human life is possible if we follow nature. Following nature means figuring it out, which means that the study of physics requires a mastery of logic, epistemology, and scientific method. The Stoics embraced the division of philosophical activity into logic, physics, and ethics (see TEXTS 2–6), but this does not mean that these were independent branches of knowledge, each to be pursued in its own sphere by its own canons and for its own reasons. They are all parts of a single activity, philosophy, the love for and pursuit of wisdom. The wisdom they sought was (and still is) an intensely rational thing, based on the uncompromising search for the most adequate knowledge of how the world (including us humans) actually works; it demands a great deal of us. But, or so the Stoics thought, it also promises a great deal; indeed, it promises all that a rational person could want—happiness in a mortal world. Stoic philosophy is based on the exhortation to follow nature; but this is essentially an updated and generalized version of the exhortation which Socrates delivered to his fellow citizens in Athens, that they should take care to make their souls as good as possible, to cultivate virtue. Zeno seems to have learned from his Cynic teachers that his 'fellow citizens' actually included all human beings, in all places and times, not just those living in Athens or Citium; and so the Stoic exhortation is directed to everyone. It is that universal vision which made Stoicism so effective in the ancient world and which sustains its appeal today. We hope *The Stoics Reader* will help modern students, in a very distant place and time, to appreciate the challenges and opportunities, intellectual and moral, that Stoicism still offers to each and every human being.

Abbreviations and Conventions

CIAG: *Commentaria in Aristotelem Graeca*
Dox. Gr.:   *Doxographi Graeci,* ed. H. Diels
M: Sextus Empiricus *Adversus Mathematicos*
PH: Sextus Empiricus *Outlines of Pyrrhonism*
Prep. Ev.:   Eusebius *Preparatio Evangelica*
W-H: C. Wachsmuth and O. Hense, eds., Stobaeus *Anthology*

Square brackets [ ] are used to indicate words added to the translation to make the sense clearer than it would be in a strictly literal translation or for brief explanations by the translators. Parentheses ( ) are normal punctuation marks. Angle brackets < > represent material supplied by the editors of the original Greek and Latin texts to repair a gap in the ancient text caused by damage or omission by scribes in the course of transmission; words in angle brackets should be regarded as part of the original ancient text. Where a gap is longer and has not been filled, even conjecturally, by editors, we add a brief note in square brackets indicating where the gap (or lacuna) lies. An ellipsis . . . indicates omission of material by the translators for the sake of brevity.

Lives of the Stoics (Zeno, Ariston, Herillus, Cleanthes, Sphaerus, Chrysippus)

TEXT 1: Diogenes Laërtius 7.1–38 (selections), 160–89 (selections)

1. Zeno, the son of Mnaseas or Demeas, was a citizen of Citium on Cyprus, a Greek town that had Phoenician settlers. . . .

2. As was said above, he studied with Crates; then they say that he also studied with Stilpo and Xenocrates for ten years, according to Timocrates in his *Dion;* but he also [is said to have studied with] Polemo. Hecaton says (and so does Apollonius of Tyre in book 1 of his *On Zeno*) that when he consulted the oracle to find out what he should do to live the best life, the god answered [that he would live the best life] if he were to join his flesh with that of the dead. Seeing what this meant, he read the works of the ancients.

He met with Crates as follows. On a commercial voyage from Phoenicia to sell purple dye, he shipwrecked near the Piraeus. He went into Athens (he was thirty years old at the time) and sat down by a certain bookseller. The bookseller was reading the second book of Xenophon's *Memorabilia;* he enjoyed it and asked where men like that [i.e., like Socrates] spent their time. **3.** Fortuitously, Crates came by and the bookseller pointed to him and said, "Follow this man." From then on he studied with Crates, being in other respects fit for and intent on philosophy but too modest for Cynic shamelessness. . . .

4. So he studied with Crates for a while; that is when he wrote the *Republic* too, and some people said in jest that he had written it "on the tail of the dog." . . . In the end he left [Crates] and studied with those already mentioned for twenty years; hence, they also say that he said, "I have had a good voyage this time, now that I have been shipwrecked." But some say he said this about Crates. **5.** And others say that he was spending time in Athens when he heard about the shipwreck and [then] said, "Fortune does me a big favor by driving me to philosophy." Some say that he disposed of his cargo in Athens and so turned to philosophy.

He used to set out his arguments while walking back and forth in the Painted Stoa, which was also named for Peisianax but [called] 'painted' because of the painting by Polygnotus. He wanted to make sure that his space was unobstructed by bystanders; for under the Thirty Tyrants 1,400 citizens had been slaughtered in it. Still, people came to listen to him, and for this reason they were called Stoics; and his followers were given the same name although they had previously been called Zenonians, as Epicurus also says in his letters. . . .

1

15. . . . He was devoted to inquiry and reasoned with precision on all topics. . . . **16.** He pursued his disputes with Philo the dialectician with great care and studied along with him. Hence, [Philo] was admired by Zeno (who was younger than he) no less than his teacher Diodorus [Cronus]. . . .

20. When someone said that he thought that philosophers' arguments were brief, he said, "You're right; but if possible even the syllables in the arguments should be short." . . . He said that one should converse vigorously, as actors do, and that one should have a loud voice and great strength but not distort one's mouth—which is what people do who chatter about a lot of impossible things. . . .

23. He used to say that there was nothing more alien to the grasp of [various branches of] knowledge than [mere] opinion and that we are in need of nothing so much as time. Someone asked him what a friend is; he said, "Another me." They say that he beat a slave for stealing. And when he [the slave] said, "It was fated for me to steal," [Zeno] said, "And to be flogged." . . .

24. Apollonius of Tyre says that when Crates dragged him away from Stilpo by the coat, [Zeno] said, "Crates, the sophisticated way to get a hold on philosophers is by the ears. So persuade me and drag me away by *them;* but if you use force on me, my body will be with you and my soul with Stilpo."

25. He also studied together with Diodorus, according to Hippobotus; it was in his company that [Zeno] worked his way through dialectic. When he was already making progress he came into Polemo's [lectures] (a result of his freedom from arrogance); so they say that [Polemo] said, "Zeno, I caught you sliding in by the garden gate to steal my doctrines and dress them up in Phoenician style." He asked the dialectician, who showed him seven dialectical patterns in the Reaper argument, how much he charged for them. When he was told [that the price was] a hundred drachmas, he gave him two hundred—so great was his love for learning. They also say that he was the first to use the term 'appropriate act' [*kathēkon*] and to have developed a theory of it. . . .

27. . . . He had already become a kind of proverbial figure; anyway, it was he who inspired the line, "more temperate than Zeno the philosopher." . . .

28. In fact, he surpassed everyone in this form of virtue and in gravity and, Yes by Zeus!, in blessedness. For he died at the age of ninety-eight, free of disease and healthy to the end. But Persaeus says in his *Ethical Studies* that he died at the age of seventy-two and that he came to Athens at the age of twenty-two. And Apollonius says that he headed his school for fifty-eight years. This is how he died: on leaving his school he stumbled and broke his toe; he struck the earth with his hand and uttered the line from the *Niobe:*[1] "I am coming. Why do you call me?" and immediately died by suffocating himself. . . .

---

1. Of Timotheus, 787 Page.

31. . . . Demetrius of Magnesia says in his *Men of the Same Name* that his father Mnaseas often came to Athens as a merchant and brought back many Socratic books to Zeno when he was still a boy; hence, he got a good training while still in his homeland. **32.** And that is how he came to Athens and joined Crates. . . . They say that he swore by the caper as Socrates did by the dog.

But some people, including the followers of Cassius the skeptic, criticize Zeno for many things, and first of all they say that he claimed, at the beginning of his *Republic,* that general culture was useless; and second that he said that all those who are not virtuous are hostile and enemies and slaves and alien to each other, parents to children and brothers to brothers <and> relatives to relatives. **33.** Again, in the *Republic* he claimed that only virtuous men are citizens and friends and relatives and free men, so that, in the eyes of the Stoics, parents and children are enemies since they are not wise. Similarly, in his *Republic* he takes the position that wives are [held] in common and at about line 200 [he holds] that they do not build temples or law courts or gymnasia in their cities. He writes as follows about coinage: "They do not think that one should produce coinage either for the sake of exchange or for the sake of foreign travel." And he orders that men and women should wear the same clothes and that no part [of the body] should be hidden. **34.** In his work *On the Republic* Chrysippus says that the *Republic* is [indeed] by Zeno. And he wrote about erotic matters at the beginning of the book entitled *Art of Sexual Love;* but he also writes similar things in the *Diatribes.*

That is the sort of thing [one finds] in Cassius and also in [the works of] the rhetor Isidor of Pergamum; he also says that the parts criticized by the Stoics were excised by Athenodorus the Stoic, who was entrusted with the library in Pergamum; then they were restored when Athenodorus was exposed and put in jeopardy. So much about the passages of his work that have been marked as spurious. . . .

36. There were many students of Zeno, but the well-known ones include the following. Persaeus of Citium, son of Demetrius; some say he was his follower, others that he was a member of his household, one of those sent by Antigonus to help him with his library, having been a tutor to Antigonus' son Halcyoneus. Antigonus once wanted to put Persaeus to the test and so had a false message announced to him to the effect that his lands had been sacked by the enemy; when he frowned, Antigonus said, "Do you see that wealth is not an indifferent thing?" . . .

37. [Another student of Zeno was] Ariston of Chios, the son of Miltiades, the one who introduced [the doctrine of] indifference. And Herillus of Carthage, the one who said that knowledge was the goal. And Dionysius, the one who went over to hedonism; for because of a severe inflammation of the eye, he became reluctant to say any longer that pain was an indifferent thing; he came from Heraclea. And Sphaerus from the Bosporus. And Cleanthes, son of Phanias from Assos, the one who took over the school; Zeno compared him to writing tablets made of hard wax, which are hard to write on but which retain what is written. Sphaerus also studied under Cleanthes after Zeno's death, and we shall mention him in our discussion of Cleanthes. **38.** The following too were students of Zeno, according to Hippobotus: Philonides of Thebes, Callippus of Corinth, Posidonius of Alexandria, Athenodorus of Soli, and Zeno of Sidon. . . .

160. Ariston of Chios, the Bald, [also] nicknamed the Siren. He said that the goal was to live in a state of indifference with respect to what is intermediate between virtue and vice, acknowledging no distinction whatsoever in them but treating them all alike. For the wise man is like a good actor, who plays either role fittingly whether he takes on the role of Thersites or Agamemnon. He abolished the topics of physics and logic, saying that the one was beyond our powers and that the other was nothing to us and that only ethics mattered to us.

161. [He said] that dialectical arguments were like spiderwebs: although they seem to indicate craftsmanlike skill, they are useless. He did not introduce many virtues, as Zeno did, nor did he say that there was one called by many names, as the Megarians did; rather, he appealed to relative dispositions. By philosophizing thus and conversing in Cynosarges, he became important enough to be called the leader of a school. Thus Miltiades and Diphilus were called Aristonians. He was a persuasive fellow and just what the crowd liked to hear. . . .

162. He met Polemo and, as Diocles of Magnesia says, went over [to his school] when Zeno became afflicted with a long illness. He was most attached to the Stoic doctrine that the wise man is undogmatic. Persaeus opposed him on this point and had one of a set of twins deposit money with him and the other then get it back. Thus he perplexed and refuted him; and he opposed Arcesilaus. When he saw a deformed bull with a womb, he said, "Woe is me! Arcesilaus has been given an argument to use against [trusting] clear facts." **163.** To the Academic [Skeptic] who said that he grasped nothing, he said, "Do you not see the man sitting next to you?" And when the other said no, he said, "Who blinded you, who took away the brightness of your eyesight?"[2] . . .

165. Herillus of Carthage said that knowledge was the goal—i.e., always living by referring everything to a life with knowledge and not being discredited by ignorance—and knowledge is a condition concerned with the reception of presentations, which is immune from being upset by argument. He once said that there was no one goal, but that it changed in accordance with the circumstances and the facts, just as the same bronze becomes a statue of Alexander or of Socrates. The goal and the subordinate goal are different; for

2. Cratinus, fr. 459 (Kassel and Austin).

even men who are not wise aim at the latter, whereas only the wise man aims at the former. And the things between virtue and vice are indifferent. His books are short but are full of vigor and include some counterarguments aimed at Zeno. . . .

168. Cleanthes of Assos, son of Phanias. He was a boxer at first, according to Antisthenes in his *Successions*. He arrived in Athens with four drachmas, as some say, and meeting Zeno he began to philosophize most nobly and stayed with the same doctrines. He was famous for his love of hard work; since he was a poor man, he undertook to work for wages. And by night he labored at watering gardens, whereas by day he exercised himself in arguments. . . .

171. . . . When someone said that Arcesilaus did not do what he ought to do, he said, "Stop it and do not blame the man; for even if he abolishes appropriate action by his argument, at least he supports it by his deeds." And Arcesilaus said, "I am not flattered." In response to which Cleanthes said, "Yes, I am flattering you by claiming that you say one thing and do another." . . .

174. . . . When someone criticized him for his old age, he said, "I too want to make my exit. But when I consider everything and see that I am completely healthy and able to write and to read, I continue to wait." . . .

175. . . . And he died as follows. He got badly swollen gums, and on the orders of his doctors he abstained from food for two days. And somehow he got so much better that the doctors allowed him to eat his customary diet, but he would not agree to this, instead saying that the way was already prepared for him; and so he abstained for the rest of his days and died, according to some, at the same age as Zeno did. He had studied with Zeno for nineteen years. . . .

177. As we said above, **Sphaerus** from the Bosporus also studied with Cleanthes after [studying with] Zeno; he had made considerable progress in argumentation and then went off to Alexandria to the court of Ptolemy Philopator. Once, when a discussion arose about whether the wise man will form opinions, Sphaerus said that he did not. The king wanted to refute him and ordered wax pomegranates to be set out. Sphaerus was fooled and the king shouted that he had assented to a false presentation, to which Sphaerus nimbly replied by saying that what he had assented to was not that they were pomegranates but that it was reasonable that they were pomegranates and that there was a difference between a graspable presentation and a reasonable one. . . .

179. Chrysippus, son of Apollonius, from Soli (or from Tarsus, as Alexander says in the *Successions*), was a student of Cleanthes. He had previously been in training as a long-distance runner. Then he studied with Zeno, or Cleanthes according to Diocles and the majority [of authorities], and left his school while he [Cleanthes] was still alive and became a significant philosophical figure. He was a man of natural ability and so extremely clever in all parts [of philosophy] that in most points he differed with Zeno and even with Cleanthes, to whom he frequently said that he only needed to be taught the doctrines and he himself would discover the demonstrations. Nevertheless, whenever he resisted Cleanthes he regretted it, so that he constantly quoted this, "I was born blessed in all else, except with respect to Cleanthes; in this I am not happy."[3]

180. So famous did he become in dialectic that most people thought that if there were dialectic among the gods, it would be none other than Chrysippus'. He had abundant material, but he did not get his style right. He worked harder than anyone else, as is shown by his writings; for there are more than 705 of them. . . .

183. . . . He was so arrogant that when someone asked, "To whom should I send my son to study?" he said, "To me; for if I thought there were anyone better than I, I would be philosophizing with him myself." Hence they say that it was said of him, "He alone has wits, and the [others] rush around like shadows"[4] and "If there were no Chrysippus, there would be no Stoa."[5]

In the end he philosophized with Arcesilaus and Lacydes, attending [their meetings] in the Academy, according to Sotion in book 8. **184.** That is the reason why he argued both for and against [the reliability] of ordinary experience and used the standard Academic technique when discussing magnitudes and pluralities.

Hermippus says that he was holding his session in the Odeon when he was called to a sacrifice by his students. There he drank sweet, unmixed wine, and losing his head left the realm of men on the fifth day at the age of seventy-three in the 143rd Olympiad [208–204 B.C.], as Apollodorus says in his *Chronology.* . . . **185.** But some say that he died after being seized with a fit of laughter; for when an ass had eaten his figs, he said to the old woman, "So give the ass some unmixed wine to swill," at which he cackled so heartily that he died. . . .

186. . . . The philosopher also used to put forth arguments of this sort: "He who tells the mysteries to the uninitiated is impious; but the high priest tells <the mysteries> to the uninitiated; therefore, the high priest is impious." Another one: "That which is not in the city is not in the house; but a well is not in the city, so it is not in the house." Another one: "There is a head; and

---

3. Euripides *Orestes* 540–41, adapted.

4. Homer *Odyssey* 10.495.

5. Compare the rejoinder by the Academic philosopher Carneades in the next generation, as recorded by Diogenes Laërtius at 4.62: "Carneades of Cyrene was the son of Epicomus or, according to Alexander in his *Successions*, of Philocomus. He read carefully the books of the Stoics, particularly those of Chrysippus. He countered these so persuasively and acquired thereupon so much renown that he remarked, 'If there were no Chrysippus, I would not be.'"

you do not have it; there is indeed a head <which you do not have>; therefore, you do not have a head." **187.** Another one: "If someone is in Megara, he is not in Athens; but a person is in Megara; therefore, there is not a person in Athens." And again: "If you say something, this comes out of your mouth; but you say 'wagon'; therefore, a wagon comes out of your mouth." And: "If you have not lost something, then you have it; but you did not lose horns; therefore, you have horns." But others say that this argument is by Euboulides.

Some people assail Chrysippus for having written much that is shameful and indecent. For in his work *On the Ancient Natural Philosophers*, he reinterprets the story about Hera and Zeus,[6] saying at line 600 or so things that no one could say without defiling his mouth. **188.** For, they say, he reinterprets this story into something extremely shameful, even if he does praise it as being a contribution to physics; still, it is more fitting for cheap hookers than for gods. The story, moreover, is not recorded by the professional bibliographers; for [they say that] it is not found in Polemo or Hypsicrates and not even in Antigonus but that it was made up by him. In *On the Republic*, he says [that one may] lie with mothers and daughters and sons, and he says the same thing right at the beginning of his *On Things Not Worth Choosing for Their Own Sakes*. And around line 1,000 of book 3 of *On the Just*, he urges that [people] should eat the dead. And in book 2 of *On Life and the Making of Money*, he says that he is planning for how the wise man will make money. **189.** And yet, why must he make money? For if it is for the sake of life, life is an indifferent; if for the sake of pleasure, this too is indifferent; and if for the sake of virtue, then [virtue] is self-sufficient for happiness. And the means of making money are ridiculous, such as [receiving it] from a king—for one must yield to him; and [so too] for [making money] from friendship—for then friendship will be on sale for profit; and [so too] for [making money] from wisdom—for then wisdom will be put to work for wages.

These are the criticisms of his work.

---

6. The seduction of Zeus, in book 14 of the *Iliad*, was portrayed in a famous painting that represented Hera performing fellatio on Zeus. Chrysippus allegorized this as a reference to key doctrines of Stoic physics (the presence of spermatic principles in the passive element). See below TEXT 25.136, etc.

On Philosophy

38. . . . It seemed a good idea to me to give a general account of all the Stoic doctrines in the life of Zeno since he was the founder of the school. . . . The common doctrines are as follows. Let a summary account be given, as has been our custom in the case of the other philosophers.

39. They say that philosophical theory [*logos*] is tripartite. For one part of it concerns nature [i.e., physics], another concerns character [i.e., ethics], and another concerns rational discourse [i.e., logic]. Zeno of Citium first gave this division in his book *On Rational Discourse* [*logos*] and so did Chrysippus in book 1 of *On Rational Discourse* and book 1 of his *Physics* and so did Apollodorus and Syllos in the first books of their respective *Introductions to Doctrine;* and so too did Eudromus in his *Outline of Ethics;* and so too did Diogenes of Babylon and Posidonius. Apollodorus calls these parts 'topics'; Chrysippus and Eudromus call them 'species'; others call them 'kinds'.

40. They compare philosophy to an animal, likening logic to the bones and sinews, ethics to the fleshier parts, and physics to the soul. Or again, they compare it to an egg; for the outer parts [the shell] are logic, the next part [the white] is ethics, and the inmost part [the yolk] is physics. Or to a productive field, of which logic is the wall surrounding it, ethics is the fruit, and physics is the land and trees. Or to a city which is beautifully fortified and administered according to reason. And, as some Stoics say, no part [of philosophy] is separate from another, but the parts are mixed. And they taught [the three parts] mixed together. Others put logic first, physics second, and ethics third; Zeno (in his *On Rational Discourse*) and Chrysippus and Archedemus and Eudromus are in this group.

41. Diogenes of Ptolemais, though, begins with ethics, and Apollodorus puts ethics second; Panaetius and Posidonius start with physics, as Phaenias the follower of Posidonius says in book 1 of his *Posidonian Lectures*. But Cleanthes says there are six parts: dialectic, rhetoric, ethics, politics, physics, and theology. Others say that these are not the parts of [philosophical] discourse but of philosophy itself, as, for example, Zeno of Tarsus. Some say that the logical part is divided into two sciences: rhetoric and dialectic. And some say it is also divided into the species concerned with definitions and the one concerned with canons and criteria. Others omit the definitional part.

TEXT 3: Aëtius 1, preface section 2 (Pseudo-Plutarch *On the Doctrines of the Philosophers* 874e = *Dox. Gr.* p. 273)

So, the Stoics said that wisdom is the knowledge of divine and human things and that philosophy is the exercise of the craft of the 'suitable' and that virtue is the highest and indeed the only thing which is suitable. At the highest level there are three virtues: the one that deals with nature (*phusikē*), the one that deals with ethics (*ēthikē*), and the one that deals with discourse (*logikē*). And that is why philosophy is tripartite, one part being physical, one ethical, and one logical—the physical whenever we inquire about the cosmos and the things in the cosmos, the ethical being the one preoccupied with human life, and the logical is the one concerned with discourse (*logos*), which they also call 'dialectic'.

TEXT 4: Sextus Empiricus *M* 7.19

And Posidonius held that since the parts of philosophy are inseparable from each other whereas the plants are seen to be different from their fruit and the walls are distinct from the plants, one should rather compare philosophy to an animal: physics is like the flesh and blood, logic is like the bones and sinews, and ethics is like the soul.

TEXT 5: Plutarch *On Stoic Self-Contradictions* 1035a–d

(1035a) Chrysippus thought that young men should study logic first, ethics second, and afterward physics; and likewise he thought that they should acquire theology as their final study. Since he made these comments frequently, it will suffice to adduce verbatim what is found in *On Lives* book 4: "It is my opinion, first of all, in accordance with the correct claims made by the ancients, that there are three kinds of philosophical theorems, logical, ethical, and physical; next, that of these logic should be placed first, ethics second, and physics third; and that theology is the final topic in physics; (1035b) and that is why they called the teaching of this topic the 'final revelation'."

But in practice he usually puts this topic, which he says ought to be put last, at the beginning of his every ethical inquiry. For manifestly he never utters a word on any topic—the goal of life, justice, good and bad things, marriage, child rearing, law, citizenship—without prefacing his remarks (just as those who introduce decrees in public assemblies preface their remarks with invocations of Good Fortune) with references to Zeus, fate, [and] providence and stating that the cosmos is one and finite, being held together by a single power. And none of this can be believed (1035c) except by someone who is thoroughly immersed in physics. So listen to what he says about these matters in book 3 of *On Gods:* "For one can find no other starting point or origin for justice except the one derived from Zeus and that derived from the common nature; for everything like this must take that as its starting point, if we are going to say anything at all about good and bad things." And again in his *Propositions in Physics:* "There is no other, and certainly no more appropriate, way to approach the discussion of good and bad things or the virtues or happiness <except> on the basis of common nature and the administration of the cosmos." **(1035d)** A bit further on again: "For the discussion of good and bad things must be linked to them since there is no better starting point or reference point and since the study of physics is not to be taken up for any other reason than to distinguish good from bad."

TEXT 6:   Plutarch *On Common Conceptions* 1069e

[Chrysippus] says, "So, where shall I start from? And what am I to take as the principle of appropriate action and the raw material for virtue if I give up nature and what is according to nature?"

Logic and Theory of Knowledge

TEXT 7: Diogenes Laërtius 7.42–83

42. So they include the [study] of canons and criteria in order to discover the truth. For it is in this study that they straighten out the differences among presentations; and similarly [they include] the definitional part for the purpose of recognizing the truth. For objects are grasped by means of conceptions. And rhetorical knowledge is about speaking well in expository speeches, whereas dialectical knowledge is about conversing correctly in speeches of question and answer form. And that is why they also define it thus, as a knowledge of what is true and false and neither.

And they say that rhetoric itself is tripartite. For part of it is deliberative, part forensic, part encomiastic. **43.** It is divided into invention, diction, organization, and delivery. And the rhetorical speech [is divided] into the introduction, the exposition, the counterargument, and the conclusion.

And dialectic is divided into the topic about the signified and [the topic about] the utterance. And the topic about the signified is [divided] into that about presentations and [that about] the *lekta* [things said] which subsist in dependence on them: propositions and complete [*lekta*] and predicates and the active and passive [*lekta*] similar [to them] and genera and species, and similarly arguments and modes and syllogisms and fallacies caused by [the form of] utterance or by the facts. **44.** These include the arguments about the Liar and the Truth-Teller and the Denier; and sorites and arguments like these, incomplete, puzzling, and conclusive; and the [ones about] the Hooded Man and Nobody and the Reaper.

The aforementioned topic concerning the utterance itself is also proper to dialectic. In it they explain the [kind of] utterance which is articulated in letters and [also] what the parts of rational discourse are. It also concerns solecism and barbarism and poems and ambiguities and harmonious utterance and music, and, according to some, definitions and divisions and [the study of different forms of] speech.

45. They say that the study of syllogisms is extremely useful; for it indicates what is demonstrative, and this makes a big contribution toward correcting one's opinions; and orderliness and good memory indicate attentive comprehension. And an argument itself is a complex [made up of] premises and a conclusion; and a syllogism is a syllogistic argument [made up] of these. And demonstration is an argument which by means of things more [clearly] grasped concludes to something that is less [clearly] grasped.

11

A presentation is an impression in a soul, the name being appropriately transferred from the imprints in wax made by a seal-ring.

46. Of presentations, some are graspable, some non-graspable. The graspable presentation, which they say is the criterion of facts [*pragmata*], is that which comes from an existing object and is stamped and molded in accordance with the existing object itself. The non-graspable presentation is either not from an existing object or from an existing object but not in accordance with it; it is neither clear nor well stamped [i.e., distinct].

Dialectic itself is necessary and is a virtue which contains other virtues as species. And freedom from hasty judgment is knowledge of when one ought to assent and when not. And levelheadedness is a strong-minded rationality with respect to what is likely, so that one does not give in to it.

47. And irrefutability is strength in argument, so that one is not swept away by it to an opposite opinion. And intellectual seriousness is a disposition which refers presentations to right reason. Knowledge itself, they say, is either a secure grasp or a disposition in the reception of presentations not reversible by argument. And the wise man will not be free of error in argument without the study of dialectic. For truth and falsity are distinguished by it, and persuasive and ambiguous statements are properly discerned by it. And without it, methodical question and answer are impossible.

48. Hasty judgment in assertions has an impact on events, so that those who are not well exercised in handling presentations turn to unruliness and aimlessness. And there is no other way for the wise man to show himself to be sharp, quick witted, and, in general, clever in arguments. For the same person will be able to converse properly and reason things out and also take a position on issues put to him and respond to questions—these are characteristics of a man experienced in dialectic.

So, this is a summary of their doctrines in logic; and in order to give a detailed account also of those of their views which pertain to an introductory textbook, <I shall report> verbatim exactly <what> Diocles of Magnesia includes in his *Survey of Philosophers,* writing as follows.

49. The Stoics choose to put first the account of presentation and sense-perception, insofar as the criterion by which the truth of facts is known is, generically, the presentation; and insofar as the account of assent and the account of grasping and conception which is basic to other accounts cannot be given without presentation. For the presentation is first, and then the intellect, which is verbally expressive, puts into rational discourse what it experiences because of presentation.

50. Presentation and phantasm are different. For a phantasm is a semblance in the intellect of the sort that occurs in sleep, and presentation is an impression in the soul, i.e., an alteration, as Chrysippus supposes in book 2 of his *On Soul.* For one should not interpret 'impression' as [being like] the stamped outline made by a seal-ring since it is impossible for there to be many outlines in the same respect and on the same substance. One conceives of a presentation which is from an existing object and is molded, outlined, and stamped in accordance with the existing object, such as could not come from a non-existing object.

51. According to them, some presentations are sensible, some are non-sensible. Those received through one or more sense organs are sensible; non-sensible are those which come through the intellect, for example, presentations of incorporeals and the other things grasped by reason. Of sensible presentations, those which come from existing objects occur with yielding and assent. But [representational] images which are 'as if' from existing objects are also [counted] among the presentations. Again, of presentations, some are rational, some are non-rational. The presentations of rational animals are rational; those of non-rational animals are non-rational. The rational, then, are thoughts, and the irrational have been given no special name. And some presentations are technical, some non-technical. For an image is considered differently by a technical specialist and by a non-specialist.

52. According to the Stoics, 'sense-perception' refers to [a] the *pneuma* that extends from the leading part to the senses and [b] the 'grasp' that comes through the senses and [c] the equipment of the sense organs (which some people may be impaired in), and [d] their activation is also called 'sense-perception'. According to them, the grasp occurs [a] through sense-perception (in the case of white objects, black objects, rough objects, smooth objects) and [b] through reason (in the case of conclusions drawn through demonstration, for example, that there are gods and that they are provident). For of conceptions, some are conceived on the basis of direct experience, some on the basis of similarity, some on the basis of analogy, <some on the basis of transposition,> some on the basis of composition, and some on the basis of opposition.

53. Sensibles are conceived on the basis of direct experience. On the basis of similarity are conceived things [known] from something that is at hand—as Socrates is conceived of on the basis of his statue. On the basis of analogy things are conceived by expansion, for example, Tityos and the Cyclops, and by shrinking, for example, a Pygmy. And the center of the earth is conceived through analogy with smaller spheres. On the basis of transposition, for example, eyes in the chest. On the basis of composition, the Hippocentaur is conceived of, and death on the basis of opposition [to life]. Some things too are conceived of on the basis of transference, for example, the things said [*lekta*] and place; and there is a natural origin too for the conception of something just and good; also on the basis of privation, for example, a person without a hand. These are their doctrines on presentation, sense-perception, and conception.

54. They say that the graspable presentation, i.e., the one from what exists, is a criterion of truth, as Chrysippus says in book 2 of the *Physics* and

Antipater and Apollodorus too. For Boethus says that there are a number of criteria: mind, sense-perception, desire, and knowledge. But Chrysippus, disagreeing with him in book 1 of *On Rational Discourse*, says that sense-perception and the basic grasp are criteria. (A basic grasp is a natural conception of things that are universal.) And other older Stoics say that right reason is a criterion, as Posidonius says in his *On the Criterion*. **55.** Most of them are agreed that the study of dialectic should begin from the topic of utterance. An utterance is air that has been struck or the proper sensible of hearing, as Diogenes of Babylon says in his *Treatise on Utterance*. An animal's utterance is air struck by an impulse, whereas a human [utterance] is articulate and emitted from the intellect, as Diogenes says; and this [the intellect] is completed from the age of fourteen on. And utterance is a body, according to the Stoics, as Archedemus says in his *On Utterance* and Diogenes and Antipater, and Chrysippus in book 2 of his *Physics*. **56.** For everything which acts is a body, and voice does act when it comes to the listeners from the utterers. As Diogenes says, speech, according to the Stoics, is an utterance in letters, for example, 'day'. Rational discourse [*logos*] is an utterance that signifies, emitted from the intellect, <for example, 'It is day'>. And dialect is speech marked both as Greek and as distinctive of a [specific] ethnic group or speech from a particular region, i.e., which is peculiar in its dialect. For example, in Attic [one says] *thalatta* [for *thalassa*], and in Ionic *hēmerē* [for *hēmera*].

The elements of speech are the twenty-four letters. Letter is used in three senses: <the element,> the character, and the name, for example, 'alpha'. **57.** There are seven vowels among the elements: alpha, epsilon, eta, iota, omicron, upsilon, omega; and six mutes: beta, gamma, delta, kappa, pi, tau. Utterance and speech differ in that utterance also includes echoes, whereas only what is articulate [counts as] speech. And speech differs from rational discourse in that rational discourse is always significant, and speech [can] also [be] meaningless—like the 'word' '*blituri*'—whereas rational discourse cannot be. There is a difference between saying and verbalizing. For utterances are verbalized, whereas what is said are facts (which [is why they] are also 'things said' [*lekta*]).

There are five parts of rational discourse, as Diogenes says in *On Utterance* and also Chrysippus: name, noun, verb, conjunction, article. And Antipater also adds the participle in his *On Speech and Things That Are Said*. **58.** According to Diogenes, a noun is a part of rational discourse which signifies a common quality, for example, 'person', 'horse'. A name is a part of rational discourse that reveals an individual quality, for example, 'Diogenes', 'Socrates'. A verb, as Diogenes says, is a part of rational discourse which signifies an incomposite predicate, or as others [say], it is an undeclined element of rational discourse which signifies something put together with [lit., of] some thing or things, for example, 'write', 'speak'. A conjunction is an undeclined part of rational discourse which joins together the parts of rational discourse. An article is a declined element of rational discourse which distinguishes the genders and numbers of names, for example, *ho, hē, to, hoi, hai, ta*.[1]

59. There are five virtues of rational discourse: good Greek, clarity, brevity, propriety, elaboration. Good Greek, then, is diction which is in conformity not with any random usage but one sanctioned by art. Clarity is speech which presents what is thought in a recognizable fashion. Brevity is speech which includes exactly what is necessary for the revelation of its object. Propriety is speech which is appropriate to its object. Elaboration is speech which has transcended ordinariness. Of the vices, barbarism is a [form of] speech which violates the normal usage of reputable Greeks. Solecism is rational discourse which is put together incongruently.

60. According to Posidonius in his *Introduction to Speech,* a poem is metrical speech or rhythmical speech together with elaboration that escapes being prosaic. The rhythmical is[2]

Greatest Earth and Zeus' sky.

But a *poiēsis* is a poem that signifies in virtue of containing an imitation of divine and human affairs.

A definition is, as Antipater says in book 1 of his *On Definitions,* an analytical statement [*logos*] expressed precisely, or as Chrysippus says in his *On Definitions,* the rendering of what is proper [to the thing]. An outline is a statement which introduces [us] to the objects by a [general] impression, or a definition which introduces the force of the definition [proper] in simpler form. A genus is a conjunction of several inseparable concepts, for example, 'animal'; for this includes the particular animals.

61. A concept is a phantasm of the intellect and is neither a something nor a qualified thing, but [rather] a quasi-something and a quasi-qualified thing; for example, there arises an impression of a horse even when no horse is present.

A species is that which is included by a genus, as human is included in animal. The most generic is that which, being a genus, does not have a genus, i.e., being; the most specific is that which, being a species, does not have a species, for example, Socrates.

Division is the cutting of a genus into its immediate species; for example, of animals, some are rational and some are irrational. Counterdivision is a

1. The six nominative forms of the Greek article 'the', given in singular and plural numbers and masculine, feminine, and neuter genders.
2. The meter of the Greek (fr. 839 of Euripides in Nauck) cannot be reproduced in translation.

division of the genus into a species in virtue of its opposite, as when things are divided by negation; for example, of beings, some are good and some are not good. Subdivision is a division following on a division; for example, of beings, some are good and some are not good, and of things not good, some are bad and some are indifferent.

62. A partitioning is an arrangement of a genus into its topics, according to Krinis; for example, of goods, some belong to the soul and some belong to the body.

Ambiguity is a speech which signifies two or even more things linguistically and strictly and in virtue of the same usage, so that by means of this speech several things are understood at the same time,[3] for example, *aulētrispeptōke;* for by means of this [speech] are indicated something like this, 'A house fell three times' and something like this, 'A flute girl fell'. According to Posidionius, dialectic is a knowledge of what is true, what is false, and what is neither. And, as Chrysippus says, it is concerned with signifiers and what is signified. This, then, is the sort of thing said by the Stoics in their study of utterance.

63. In the topic of objects and things signified are placed the account of *lekta* [things said]—complete ones and propositions and syllogisms—and the account of incomplete [*lekta*] and predicates both active and passive. And they say that a *lekton* is what subsists in accordance with a rational presentation. And of *lekta* the Stoics say that some are complete and some are incomplete. Incomplete are those which are unfinished in their expression, such as 'writes'; for we go on to ask, "Who?" Complete are those which are finished in their expression, such as 'Socrates writes'. So predicates are placed among the incomplete *lekta,* and propositions and syllogisms and questions and inquiries are placed among the complete.

64. A predicate is what is said of something or a thing put together with [lit., about] some thing or things, as Apollodorus says, or an incomplete *lekton* put together with a nominative case to generate a proposition. Of predicates, some are events, . . . [There is a lacuna here.] such as 'to sail through the rocks'. And some predicates are active, some passive, some neither. Active are those put together with one of the oblique cases to generate a predicate, such as 'hears', 'sees', 'discusses'. Passive are those put together with the passive form, such as 'am heard', 'am seen'. Neither are those which fit in neither group, such as 'to be prudent', 'to walk'. Reflexive passives are those which, being passive, are [nevertheless] actions, such as 'gets his hair cut'. For the man

---

3. Speech is utterance articulable in letters (§ 56 above). Our translation has been improved by reflection on ch. 4 of Catherine Atherton's excellent book *The Stoics on Ambiguity* (Cambridge: Cambridge University Press, 1993). The ambiguity in the example which follows is untranslatable but stems from alternate divisions into words of the same syllables.

getting his hair cut includes himself [in his action]. **65.** The oblique cases are the genitive, the dative, and the accusative.

A proposition is that which is true or false or a complete object which can be asserted on its own, as Chrysippus says in his *Dialectical Definitions:* "A proposition is what can be asserted or denied on its own, for example, 'It is day' or 'Dion is walking.'" The proposition gets its name [*axiōma*] from being accepted;[4] for he who says 'It is day' seems to accept [*axioun*] that it is day. So when it is day, the present proposition becomes true, and when it is not [day], it becomes false. **66.** There are differences among propositions, questions, inquiries, imperatives, oaths, curses, hypotheses, addresses, and objects similar to a proposition. For a proposition is what we say when we reveal something, and it is this that is true or false. A question is a complete object, like the proposition, that asks for an answer, for example, 'Is it day'? This is neither true nor false; so that 'It is day' is a proposition and 'Is it day'? is a question. An inquiry is an object to which one cannot give an answer with a gesture as one can to a question [by indicating] 'yes', but [in response to which one must] say [for example], 'He lives in this place'.

67. An imperative is an object which we say when we give an order, for example,[5]

> You, go to the streams of Inachus.

An oath is an object . . . [There is a lacuna here.] <and an address is an object>, which if one were to say, one would be addressing [someone], for example,[6]

> Noblest son of Atreus, lord of men Agamemnon!

[An object] similar to a proposition is what has a propositional [form of] utterance, but, because of the excessiveness or emotional quality of one part of it, falls outside the class of propositions, for example,

> Fair is the Parthenon!

<and>

> How similar to Priam's sons is the cowherd![7]

---

4. The words that follow, "or rejected," seem wrong and we omit them, following (among others) Richard Goulet in *Diogène Laërce: vies et doctrines des philosophes illustres* (Paris: Le Livre de Poche, 1999), who follows the proposal of Urs Egli in *Zur stoischen Dialektik* (Dissertation, Basel, 1967). The words are retained by Marcovich in the Teubner edition.

5. A fragment of an unknown Greek tragedy, fr. 177 Kannicht-Snell.

6. Homer *Iliad* 2.434.

7. A fragment of an unknown Greek tragedy, 286 Kannicht-Snell.

68. There is also a dubitative object, which is different from a proposition, and if one were to say it, one would be expressing puzzlement:[8]

Are pain and life somehow akin?

Questions, inquiries, and things like these are neither true nor false, whereas propositions are either true or false. Of propositions, some are simple, some not simple, as the followers of Chrysippus and Archedemus and Athenodorus and Antipater and Krinis say. So, the simple are those which are <not> composed of a proposition which is doubled,[9] such as 'It is day'. The not simple are those composed of a doubled proposition or of propositions. **69.** From a doubled proposition, for example, 'If it is day, it is day'; from propositions, for example, 'If it is day, it is light'.

Among simple propositions are the contradictory and the negative and the privative and the predicative and the predicational and the indefinite. And among the non-simple propositions are the conditional and the para-conditional and the compound and the disjunctive and the causal and that which indicates the more and that which indicates the less[10] . . . and a contradictory, for example, 'It is not the case that it is day'. A species of this is the double contradictory. A double contradictory is the contradictory of a contradictory, for example, 'It is not the case that it is <not> day'. It posits that it is day.

70. A negative [proposition] is that which is composed of a negative particle and a predicate, for example, 'No one is walking'. A privative is that which is composed of a privative particle and a potential proposition, for example, 'This [man] is unphilanthropic'. A predicative is that which is composed of a nominative case and a predicate, for example, 'Dion is walking'. A predicational is that which is composed of a demonstrative nominative case and a predicate, for example, 'This [man] is walking'. An indefinite is that which is composed of an indefinite particle or indefinite particles <and a predicate>, for example, 'Someone is walking' and 'That [man] is in motion'.

71. Of the non-simple propositions, a conditional is, as Chrysippus says in his *Dialectics* and Diogenes in his *Art of Dialectic,* that which is compounded by means of the conditional conjunction 'if'. This conjunction indicates that the second [proposition] follows the first, for example, 'If it is

---

8. Fr. 1 line 8 of Menander *Citharista* (Körte).

9. On the text here, see Goulet, p. 835, nn. 3–4. The negation supplied ("<not>") is based on a comparison with parallel material in Sextus Empiricus *M* 8.93. The reading *diphoroumenou,* which yields this sense, is found in Alexander of Aphrodisias (H. von Arnim, ed., *Stoicorum Veterum Fragmenta* 2.261, 263). See TEXT 11.112 (*PH* 2.112).

10. For the lacuna here, see Goulet, p. 836.

day, it is light'. A paraconditional [inference] is, as Krinis says in his *Art of Dialectic,* a proposition which is bound together by the conjunction 'since' and which begins with a proposition and ends with a proposition, for example, 'Since it is day, it is light'. The conjunction indicates that the second [proposition] follows the first and that the first is the case. **72.** A compound is a proposition which is compounded by certain compounding conjunctions, for example, 'Both it is day and it is night'. A disjunctive is that which is disjoined by the disjunctive conjunction, for example, 'Either it is day or it is night'. This conjunction indicates that one of the two propositions is false. A causal proposition is one put together by means of 'because', for example, 'Because it is day, it is light'. For the first is, as it were, the cause of the second. A proposition which indicates the 'more' is one put together by means of the conjunction which indicates 'more' and the [conjunction] 'than' put between the propositions, for example, 'It is more day than it is night'. **73.** The proposition indicating the 'less' is the opposite of the preceding, for example, 'It is less night than it is day'.

Again, among propositions, those are opposed to each other with respect to truth and falsehood where one is the contradictory of the other, for example, 'It is day' and 'Not: It is day'. A conditional is true if the opposite of the conclusion conflicts with the antecedent, for example, 'If it is day, it is light'. This is true; for 'It is not light', being the opposite of the conclusion, conflicts with 'It is day'. A conditional is false if the opposite of the conclusion does not conflict with the antecedent, for example, 'If it is day, Dion is walking'; for 'It is not the case that Dion is walking' does not conflict with 'It is day'.

74. A paraconditional is true if it begins with a true [proposition] and concludes with one which follows [from it], for example, 'Since it is day, the sun is over the earth'. A false [paraconditional] is one which either starts with a false [proposition] or concludes in one which does not follow from it, for example, 'Since it is night, Dion is walking', if it is said when it is day. A true causal [proposition] is one which begins from a true [proposition] and concludes in one which follows from it but whose first [proposition] does not follow from the conclusion, for example, 'Because it is day, it is light'; for 'It is light' follows from 'It is day', and 'It is day' does not follow from 'It is light'. A false causal [proposition] is one which either [1] begins from a falsehood or [2] concludes in a [proposition] which does not follow from it or [3] one whose first [proposition] follows from the consequent. **75.** A persuasive proposition is one which leads to assent, for example, 'If someone gave birth to something, she is its mother'. But this is false; for the bird is not the mother of the egg.

Again, some [propositions] are possible and some are impossible; and some are necessary and some are not necessary. That [proposition] is possible which admits of being true, if external factors do not prevent it from being true, for example, 'Diocles is alive'. That [proposition] is impossible which does not admit of being true, for example, 'The earth flies'. The necessary is that which, being true, is not receptive of being false or is receptive of being false but external factors prevent it from being false, for example, 'Virtue is beneficial'. The non-necessary is that which both is true and is able to be false, with external factors not opposing it at all, for example, 'Dion is walking'.

76. A reasonable proposition is one which has more chances at being true [than not], such as 'I will be alive tomorrow'. And there are other differences among propositions and changes of them from true to false and conversions; these we discuss in a general fashion.

As the followers of Krinis say, an argument is what is composed of a premise, an additional statement, and a conclusion. For example, something like this:

> If it is day, it is light.
> It is day.
> Therefore, it is light.

For the premise is 'If it is day, it is light'; the additional statement is 'It is day'; and the conclusion is 'Therefore, it is light'. A mode is a sort of schema for an argument, such as this:

> If the first, the second.
> But the first.
> Therefore, the second.

77. An argument mode is what is compounded of both [the argument and the schema], for example,

> If Plato is alive, Plato breathes.
> But the first.
> Therefore, the second.

The argument mode was added in order to avoid having to repeat the long additional statement and the conclusion in a somewhat lengthy series of arguments, so that the conclusion can be given briefly: The first; therefore, the second.

Of arguments, some are non-conclusive, others are conclusive. Non-conclusive are those where the opposite of the conclusion is not in conflict with the conjunction of the premises, for example, arguments like this:

> If it is day, it is light.
> It is day.
> Therefore, Dion is walking.

78. Of conclusive arguments, some are called conclusive homonymously with the genus. Others are syllogistic. Syllogistic arguments, then, are those which are either indemonstrable or reducible to the indemonstrables by one or more of the *themata,* for example, ones like this:[11]

> If Dion is walking, <Dion is moving.
> But Dion is walking.>
> Dion is, therefore, moving.

Those conclusive in the specific sense are ones which reach a [valid] conclusion non-syllogistically, for example, ones like this:

> It is false that it is day and it is night.
> It is day.
> Therefore, it is not night.

Unsyllogistic are those which are persuasively similar to syllogistic arguments but do not conclude [validly], for example,

> If Dion is a horse, Dion is an animal.
> But Dion is not a horse.
> Therefore, Dion is not an animal.

79. Again, of arguments some are true, some false. True arguments, then, are those which conclude [validly] by means of true premises, for example,[12]

> If virtue is helpful, vice is harmful.
> <But virtue is helpful.
> Therefore, vice is harmful.>

False arguments are those having at least one false premise or those which are non-conclusive, for example,

> If it is day, it is light.
> It is day.
> Therefore, Dion is alive.

---

11. The textual supplement by von Arnim is widely accepted.

12. The textual supplement by von Arnim is widely accepted.

And there are possible arguments and impossible and necessary and non-necessary. And there are indemonstrable arguments because they do not need demonstration, different ones being given by different authors. In Chrysippus there are five through which every argument is formed. These are used in conclusive arguments, in syllogisms, and in mode-arguments.

80. The first indemonstrable is that in which every argument is made up of a conditional and the antecedent from which the conditional begins and concludes to the consequent, for example,

> If the first, the second.
> But the first.
> Therefore, the second.

The second indemonstrable is that which, through a conditional and the opposite of the consequent, draws as its conclusion the opposite of the antecedent, for example,

> If it is day, it is light.
> But it is not light.
> Therefore, it is not day.

For the additional statement is formed from the opposite of the consequent and the conclusion from the opposite of the antecedent. The third indemonstrable is that which, through a negated conjunction and one of the elements in the conjunction, concludes the opposite of the other element, for example,

> It is not the case that Plato is dead and Plato is alive.
> But Plato is dead.
> Therefore, Plato is not alive.

81. The fourth indemonstrable is that which, through a disjunction and one of the disjuncts, has as its conclusion the opposite of the other, for example,

> Either the first or the second.
> But the first.
> Therefore, not the second.

The fifth indemonstrable is that in which every argument is formed from a disjunction and the opposite of one of the disjuncts and concludes the other, for example,

Either it is day or it is night.
It is not night.
Therefore, it is day.

According to the Stoics a truth follows from a truth, as 'It is light' follows from 'It is day'. And a falsehood follows from a falsehood, as 'It is dark' follows from the falsehood 'It is night'. And a truth follows from a falsehood, as 'The earth exists' follows from 'The earth flies'. A falsehood, however, does not follow from a truth; for 'The earth flies' does not follow from 'The earth exists'. **82.** And there are certain puzzling arguments, the Hooded Man, the Hidden Man, the Sorites, the Horned Man, and the Nobody. And the Hooded Man is like this . . . [There is a lacuna here, which includes the introduction of the sorites.] 'It is not the case that two are few and that three are not [few]; and it is not the case these are [few] but four (and so on up to ten) are not [few]; but two are few; therefore, so is ten'. . . . [There is a lacuna here, which no doubt gave an example of the Horned Man.] The Nobody is an argument which draws a conclusion and is composed of an indefinite and a definite, having an additional statement and a conclusion, for example, 'If someone is here, that [someone] is not in Rhodes; <but someone is here; therefore, there is not someone in Rhodes>'.[13]

83. And this is what the Stoics are like in logical matters, so that they can maintain that the wise man is always a dialectician. For *everything* is seen through consideration of it in arguments: both what belongs to the topic of physics and again what belongs to ethics. For if the logician is supposed to say something about the correct use of terms, how could he fail to say what are the proper names for things? There are two customary facets of the virtue [i.e., dialectic]: one considers what each existent thing is, the other what it is called. And this is what their logic is like.

TEXT 8: Porphyry *De Anima* in Stobaeus *Anthology*
            1.49.25 (vol. 1, pp. 349.23–27 W-H)

The Stoics did not make sense-perception consist in presentation alone but made its substance depend on assent; for perception is an assent to a perceptual presentation, the assent being voluntary.

TEXT 9: Sextus Empiricus *M* 8.275–76

275. . . . The dogmatists are silenced by each of these arguments, and in their effort to prove the opposite they say that humans differ from the irrational

13. The textual supplement by von Arnim is widely accepted.

animals not in virtue of verbalized reason (since crows and parrots and jays verbalize articulate utterances) but in virtue of internal reason; **276.** and not in virtue of just a simple presentation (since they too receive presentations) but in virtue of a presentation which is based on transference and composition. And that is why, having a conception of logical consequence, humans immediately derive a conception of a sign as a result of the logical consequence. For the sign itself is something like this: 'If this, this'. Therefore, the existence of a sign follows on the nature and constitution of human beings.

TEXT 10: Sextus Empiricus *PH* 1.62–69 (selections)

62. As an extra, we also compare the so-called non-rational animals and human beings with respect to their presentations; for after [relating] our effective arguments we do not disapprove of ridiculing these pompous and boastful dogmatists. So our side customarily makes a simple comparison between the many non-rational animals and humans. **63.** But since the dogmatists contrive to say that the comparison is unfair, we shall add another extra and ridicule them even more, basing our argument on one animal, the dog for instance, if you like, which is held to be the lowest [animal]. For we shall find in this way too that the animals, which are our topic, are not inferior to us with respect to the trustworthiness of what appears to them.

64. So, the dogmatists agree that this animal is superior to us with regard to sense-perception; for it has a keener sense of smell than we do and by means of this can track down animals which it cannot see, and it also has keener vision than we do and a sharper sense of hearing. **65.** So let us proceed to the faculty of reason. There are two kinds: internal and verbalized. So let us first consider the internal. So, according to the dogmatists who now hold the opinions which are most opposed to us, i.e., the Stoics, it seems to be occupied with the following: the choice of things to which we have an affinity and the avoidance of things alien to us, the knowledge of the crafts which contribute to this, the grasp of the virtues which accord with one's own nature, <and> the matters connected to the passions. **66.** So the dog, which it was decided would make a good example for our argument, makes a choice of things to which it has an affinity and avoids harmful ones since it pursues food and cringes from a raised whip; but it also has a craft for providing itself with things to which it has an affinity, namely, hunting. **67.** Nor does it lack virtue since justice, at least, is concerned with rendering to everyone what he deserves, and the dog is not without justice in that it fawns on those with whom it has an affinity, does good to them, and guards them, whereas it wards off those with whom it lacks an affinity and who do it wrong. **68.** And if the dog has justice, then since the virtues [all] follow upon each other it also has the other virtues too—which the wise men say that the majority of people lack. And we see that the dog is heroic in warding off attackers and intelligent. Homer[14] too testifies to this when he has Odysseus recognized only by [his dog] Argos and unrecognized by all the members of his household since the dog was not deceived by the change in its master's physical appearance and had not lost its graspable presentation [of its master], which it seems to have had more [clearly] than the human beings. **69.** And according to Chrysippus, who has a special interest in the non-rational animals, [the dog] also participates in their famous 'dialectic'. At any rate the fellow just mentioned says that [the dog] attends to the fifth indemonstrable with several [disjuncts] when it comes to a three-way intersection; for the dog sniffs at the two roads which the quarry did not go down and immediately charges off down the third without stopping to sniff it. In effect he says that its reasoning was this: either the quarry went here or here or here; but it [the quarry] did not go here or here; therefore it went here. . . .

Perception, Knowledge, and Skeptical Attack

TEXT 11: Sextus Empiricus *PH* 2.70–159 (selections)

70. Let us consider next the criterion 'according to which' they say matters are to be judged. First, therefore, there is this to say about it, namely, that the presentation is inconceivable. For they say that the presentation is an impression in the leading part of the soul. Since, therefore, the soul and its leading part are *pneuma* or something more subtle than *pneuma*, as they say, someone will not be able to conceive of an impression in it either in terms of depressions and elevations, as we see in the case of wax seals, or in terms of their fantastic 'alteration'. For no one could retain the memory of all theoretical propositions that constitute a craft since the previously existing [alterations] are wiped out by the subsequent alterations. Even if, however, the presentation were able to be conceived, it would be ungraspable. **71.** For, since it is a state of the leading part of the soul and its leading part is not grasped, as we have shown, we shall not be able to grasp its state either.

72. Further, even if we were to grant that the presentation is grasped, it will not be possible to judge matters according to it. For the intellect, as they say, does not apply itself to external objects and have them presented to it through itself, but rather by means of sense-perceptions; and the senses do not grasp externally existing objects, but only their own states, if that. And, therefore, the presentations will be of the state of the senses, which differs from the externally existing object. For honey is not the same thing as a sweet sensation, nor is wormwood the same as a bitter sensation, but they differ. **73.** And if this state differs from the externally existing object, the presentation will be not of the externally existing object but of some other thing different from it. If,

14. *Odyssey* 17.300.

therefore, the intellect judges according to the presentation, it judges badly and not according to the external object. So, it is absurd to say that external objects are to be judged according to the presentation.

74. But one cannot even say that the soul grasps the externally existing objects by means of the states of the senses on the basis of the similarity of these states to the externally existing objects. For on what basis will the intellect know if the states of the senses are similar to the sensibles when it has not encountered the external objects themselves and the senses do not reveal to it the nature of the sensibles but only their own states, as I argued on the basis of the modes leading to suspension of judgment?[15] **75.** For just as someone who, not being acquainted with Socrates and seeing a picture of him, does not know if the picture resembles Socrates, so, the intellect, when it observes the states of the senses but does not see the external objects, will not know if the states of the senses resemble the external objects. So, it will not be able to judge these according to the presentation on the basis of similarity.

76. But let us grant as a concession that in addition to being conceived and grasped, the presentation admits of having matters judged according to it, even though our reasoning suggested entirely the opposite. And so either we shall have confidence in every presentation <and we shall decide on the basis of it or on the basis of some [one] presentation. But if we have confidence in every presentation, it is clear that we shall have confidence in the presentation of Xeniades>[16] according to which he says that all presentations are untrustworthy, and the argument will be turned around into holding that it is not the case that all presentations are such that we are able to judge matters according to them. **77.** But if we have confidence [only] in some, how shall we decide that it is appropriate to have confidence in these presentations and not those? For if this decision is made without a presentation, they will be granting that the presentation is superfluous for judging since they will actually be saying that we are able to judge matters apart from it. But if the decision is made with a presentation, how will they grasp the presentation which they are bringing forward for the judgment of the other presentations? **78.** Or again, they will need another presentation for its judgment, and a third for the second, [and so on] to infinity. But it is impossible to make an infinite number of decisions. So, it is impossible to discover what sorts of presentations ought to be used as criteria and what sorts should not. Since, therefore, even if we grant that one ought to judge matters on the basis of presentations, whether having confidence in all as criteria or only in some, the argument is overturned in either case, and the conclusion must be that presentations ought not to be brought forward as criteria for the judgment of matters. . . .

15. Sextus *PH* 1.100 ff.
16. Sextus *PH* 2.18.

80. Even if we should grant hypothetically that there is some criterion of the truth, it is discovered to be useless and pointless if we suggest that, as far as concerns what the dogmatists say, the truth is non-existent and the true is non-substantial. **81.** We suggest the following. The true is said to differ from the truth in three ways: in substance, in composition, and in power. [It differs] in substance, since the true is incorporeal (for it is a proposition and a thing said [*lekton*]), whereas truth is a body (for it is knowledge capable of revealing all true things, and knowledge is the leading part of the soul in a certain state, just as the hand in a certain state is a fist) and the leading part of the soul is a body, for according to them it is *pneuma*. **82.** [It differs] in composition, since the true is simple, for example, 'I converse'; whereas truth is composed of many true cognitions. **83.** [It differs] in power, since truth depends on knowledge, but the true does not altogether do so. Therefore, they say that the truth exists only in the virtuous man, whereas the true exists even in the base man, for it is possible for the base man to say something true. . . .

104. . . . The Stoics, who seem to have described [the indicative sign] accurately and who wish to present the conception of the sign, say that a sign is "the antecedent proposition in a sound conditional revelatory of the consequent." They say that a proposition is a complete *lekton* [thing said] which makes an assertion on its own; and a sound conditional is one that does not begin with a truth and end with a falsehood. **105.** For either the conditional begins with a truth and ends with a truth, as in 'If it is day, it is light', or it begins with a falsehood and ends with a falsehood, as in 'If the earth is flying, the earth is winged', or it begins with a truth and ends with a falsehood, as in 'If the earth exists, the earth is flying'. They say that of these only the one that begins with a truth and ends with a falsehood is unsound, whereas the others are sound. **106.** They say that the antecedent is the first clause in the conditional that begins with a truth and ends with a truth. It is revelatory of the consequent, since 'She has milk' seems to reveal that 'She has conceived' in the conditional 'If she has milk, she has conceived'.

107. These are the Stoics' doctrines. We, however, say first that it is non-evident whether a *lekton* [thing said] exists. For since the Epicureans say that the thing said does not exist and the Stoics say that it does, either they are making a bare assertion or they have a demonstration. But if it is just a bare assertion, the Epicureans will oppose them with the assertion that the thing said does not exist. If they adduce a demonstration, since the demonstration is composed of propositions which are said, it will not be able to be adduced for the purpose of confirmation that the thing said exists, since it is composed of things said. For how will one who does not grant [the existence of] the thing said allow that a complex of things said exists? **108.** So, he who tries to establish the existence of a thing said on the basis of a complex of things said is someone who wants to confirm a matter under investigation by means of the matter under investigation. If, therefore, it is not possible to show either simply or by means of a demonstration that a thing said exists, it is non-evident. The case is similar for the existence of a proposition. **109.** For a proposition is a thing said. And perhaps even if it should be granted for the sake of hypothesis that a thing said exists, the proposition is found to be non-existent, being composed of things said not existing at the same time as each other. For example, take 'If it is day, it is light'. When I say 'It is day' the 'It is light' [part] is not yet in existence, and when I say 'It is light' the 'It is day' [part] is no longer in existence. If, therefore, the composite cannot possibly exist without the parts themselves existing at the same time as each other and [the parts] of which the proposition is composed do not exist at the same time as each other, the proposition will not exist.

110. To pass over this problem, the sound conditional will be found to be ungraspable. Philo says that a sound conditional is one that does not have a true antecedent and a false consequent, for example, 'If it is day, I am conversing' when it is day and I am conversing, whereas Diodorus [Cronus] [says that a sound conditional] is that of which it neither was nor is possible that it should have a true antecedent and a false consequent. According to him, the conditional just mentioned seems to be false since it has a true antecedent and a false consequent if it is day and I am silent; **111.** whereas 'If the partless elements of things do not exist, the partless elements of things do exist' is true, for according to him, the false antecedent 'The partless elements of things do not exist' is followed by the true consequent 'The partless elements of things do exist'. Those who introduce the notion of logical connectedness say that a conditional is sound whenever the contradictory of the consequent is in conflict with its antecedent. So, according to them, the above-mentioned conditionals will be unsound, but 'If it is day, it is day' is true [i.e., sound]. **112.** Those who judge [the correct answer] by implicit [entailment] say that the conditional is true where the consequent is contained virtually in the antecedent. According to them, 'If it is day, it is day' and all such doubled[17] conditionals will probably be false, for it is impossible for something to be contained [virtually] in itself.

113. So, it would perhaps seem impossible to decide this disagreement. For we shall not be trusted if we express a preference for one of the positions either without a demonstration or with a demonstration. For a demonstration seems to be sound whenever the conclusion follows from the conjunction of its premises as a consequent follows from its antecedent, for example, 'If it is day, it is light; but it is day; therefore, it is light'. **114.** But since what we are investigating is how we may judge the following of a consequent from an antecedent, the circular mode is adduced. For, in order that the judgment

---

17. Reading *diphoroumenon*. See TEXT 7.68 above.

about the conditional should be demonstrated, the conclusion [must] follow the premises of the demonstration, as we said before. And, again, in order that this should be confirmed, one must have already decided about the conditional and [logical] following [or consequence], which is absurd. **115.** Therefore, the sound conditional is ungraspable.

But even the antecedent is subject to doubt. For the antecedent, as they say, is the principal [i.e., first] part of the conditional that begins with a truth and ends with a truth. **116.** But if the sign reveals the consequent, that consequent is either self-evident or non-evident. If, then, it is self-evident, it will not need something to reveal it, but will be grasped along with it and will not be signified by it, for which reason [the antecedent] is not a sign of [the consequent]. If, however, it is non-evident, since there has been an undecided disagreement regarding which of these are true and which false and, in general, whether any of them are true, it will be non-evident whether the consequent of the conditional is true. With this follows that it is non-evident whether the principal [i.e., first] part [of the conditional] is the antecedent. . . .

134. It is clear then from these considerations that demonstration too is not a matter agreed upon. For if we suspend judgment regarding the sign and demonstration is a type of sign, it is necessary to suspend judgment regarding demonstration. And indeed we shall find that the arguments regarding the sign can be adapted for use against demonstration, since demonstration is supposed to be relative and revelatory of the conclusion, and practically everything said by us regarding the sign followed from this [line of argument]. **135.** If, however, we must speak specifically regarding demonstration, I shall concisely treat of the argument regarding it, first attempting to provide a little clarification regarding what they say a demonstration is.

Demonstration, as they say, is an argument which by means of agreed upon premises, according to conclusive deduction, reveals a non-evident conclusion. What they mean will be made clearer by means of the following. An argument is a complex of premises and a conclusion. **136.** The premises of the complex are said to be the propositions taken for the establishment of the conclusion, and the conclusion is the proposition established by the premises. For example, in the argument 'If it is day, it is light; but it is indeed day; therefore, it is light', the proposition 'Therefore, it is light' is the conclusion and the rest are premises. **137.** Some arguments are conclusive and some are non-conclusive; they are conclusive whenever the conditional which starts from the conjunction of the premises and ends with the conclusion of the argument is sound. For example, the above argument is conclusive since, from the conjunction of its premises 'If it is day, it is light' and 'It is day', 'It is light' follows in this conditional 'It is day, and if it is day, it is light; <therefore,> it is light'. Arguments that do not have this [structure] are non-conclusive.

138. Some conclusive[18] arguments are true and some are not true; they are true whenever not only the conditional formed from the conjunction of the premises and the conclusion is sound, as we said before, but also the conjunction of the premises, which is the antecedent of the conditional, is true. A true conjunction is that which has all its conjuncts true, as, for example, in 'It is day, and if it is day, it is light'. **139.** Those which are not like this are not true. For this argument 'If it is night, it is dark; but indeed it is night; therefore, it is dark' when it is day is conclusive since the conditional 'It is night and if it is night it is dark; therefore, it is dark' is sound, but the argument is not true. For the antecedent conjunction is false, namely, 'It is night and if it is night it is dark' since it contains the falsehood 'It is night'. For a conjunction which contains a false conjunct is false. Hence, they also say that a true argument is one in which true premises conclude to a true conclusion.

140. Again, some true arguments are demonstrative and some are non-demonstrative; the demonstrative ones are those which conclude to a non-evident conclusion by means of self-evident premises; those that do not have this characteristic are non-demonstrative. For example, the argument 'If it is day, it is light; but it is indeed day; therefore, it is light' is non-demonstrative. For the conclusion 'It is light' is self-evident. But this argument 'If sweat flows through the surface [of the skin], there are intelligible [i.e., non-sensible] pores; but sweat indeed pours through the surface [of the skin]; therefore, there are intelligible pores' is demonstrative, for the conclusion 'There are intelligible pores' is non-evident.

141. Some of the arguments concluding to a non-evident conclusion are only progressive, leading us to the conclusion by means of the premises. Some do so both progressively and by revelation. For example, those that are [merely] progressive that seem to depend on trustworthiness and memory, for example, 'If some god tells you that this man will become wealthy, this man will become wealthy; but this god (assume I am pointing to Zeus) tells you this man will become wealthy; therefore, this man will become wealthy'. For we assent to the conclusion not so much because the premises necessitate it as because we trust the pronouncement of the god. **142.** Among the arguments that lead us to the conclusion not only progressively but also by revelation are, for example, 'If sweat flows through the surface [of the skin], there are intelligible pores; but indeed the first; therefore, the second'. For the fact that sweat flows is revelatory of the existence of the pores because it is already understood that moisture is not able to be conducted through a solid body.

143. So, demonstration should be an argument which is both conclusive and true with a non-evident conclusion, revealed by the force of the premises; and because of this a demonstration is said to be an argument which, based on

18. See TEXT 7.77–78.

agreed premises according to conclusive deduction, is revelatory of a non-evident conclusion.

So these are the terms in which they customarily clarify the conception of demonstration. . . .

149. For this reason, therefore, the argument that deduces the conclusion from the conditional and the antecedent is said to be syllogistic—and so is that which deduces the contradictory of the antecedent of the conditional from the [positing of the] conditional and the contradictory of the consequent. The argument, as in the case of the above, that deduces the antecedent from the conditional and its consequent is non-conclusive, so that even though its premises are true, it deduces something false [i.e., it is day] when it [i.e., it is light] is said by lamplight at night. For 'If it is day, it is light' is a true conditional, but the additional statement 'But indeed it is light' is true, but the conclusion 'It is day' is false.

150. The argument is improper by omission in which something is left out which is needed for the conclusive deduction of the conclusion. For example, this is a sound argument, as they think, in 'Wealth is either good or bad or indifferent; but it is not bad or indifferent; therefore, it is good'; but the following is a bad argument on the grounds of omission: 'Wealth is either good or bad; it is not bad; therefore, it is good'. **151.** If, then, I show that on the basis of what they say it is not possible to discern a difference between non-conclusive and conclusive arguments, I have shown that the conclusive argument is ungraspable, so that their limitless treatises on dialectic are superfluous. I show this in the following way.

152. The argument that was said to be non-conclusive because of logical disconnectedness is understood to be so from the fact that there is no logical connection between the premises and between the premises and the conclusion. Since, therefore, the judgment about the conditional ought to precede the understanding of these logical connections and the conditional is undecidable, as I have argued, the non-conclusive argument based on logical disconnectedness will be indiscernible from a [conclusive argument]. **153.** For he who is stating that some argument is non-conclusive because of logical disconnectedness, if he is merely making an assertion, will have contradicting him an assertion opposed to what he previously said; whereas if he demonstrates by means of an argument, he will be told that this argument must first be [shown to be] conclusive, and then he can use it to demonstrate that the argument said to be logically disconnected has premises that are without logical connections. But we shall not know if it is demonstrative, not having an agreed upon means of judging the conditional by which we can judge if the conclusion is logically connected to the combination of the premises. And, therefore, on this basis we shall not be able to discern the difference between an argument that is improper because of logical disconnectedness and conclusive ones.

154. We shall say the same things to someone who states that some argument is improper because of being asserted in improper form. For he who is trying to establish that a form is improper will not have an agreed upon conclusive argument by means of which he will be able to deduce what he states. **155.** And by means of these criticisms, we have implicitly refuted those who attempt to show that arguments are non-conclusive by omission. For if the complete and finished argument is indiscernible [from a non-conclusive argument], the argument defective by omission will also be non-evident. And further, he who desires to show that some argument is defective by omission by means of an argument, since he does not have an agreed upon procedure for judging the conditional by means of which he will be able to judge the logical consequence of the argument he is speaking about, will not be able to say correctly and with judgment that it is defective by omission.

156. Further, the argument said to be improper because of redundancy is indiscernible from demonstrative arguments. For with respect to redundancy, even the arguments touted by the Stoics as 'indemonstrable' will be found to be non-conclusive. And when these [the indemonstrables] are abolished, the whole of dialectic is overturned. For these are the ones they say are not in need of demonstration to establish themselves but seem to demonstrate the conclusiveness of the other arguments. That they are redundant will be clear when we have set out the 'indemonstrable arguments' and thus provided arguments for what we have said.[19]

157. They dream up many indemonstrables but set forth these five above all others, and the other arguments are thought to be reduced to them. The first is that which concludes from the conditional and the antecedent to the consequent, for example, 'If it is day, it is light; but it is day; therefore, it is light'. The second is that which concludes from the conditional and the contradictory of the consequent to the contradictory of the antecedent, for example, 'If it is day, it is light; but it is not light; therefore, it is not day'. **158.** The third is that which concludes from the denial of a conjunction and one of the conjuncts to the contradictory of the other, for example, 'not: It is day and it is night; but it is day; therefore, it is not night'. The fourth is that which concludes from a disjunction and one of the disjuncts to the contradictory of the other, for example, 'Either it is day or it is night; but it is day; therefore, it is not night'. The fifth is that which concludes from a disjunction and the contradictory of one of its disjuncts to the other, for example, 'Either it is day or it is night; but it is not night; therefore, it is day'.

159. These then are the much-touted indemonstrables, all of which seem to be non-conclusive by reason of redundancy. So, for instance, starting with the first, either it is agreed that 'It is light' is logically connected to its antecedent

19. Text 7.80–81.

'It is day' in the conditional 'If it is day, it is light' or it is non-evident. But if it is non-evident, we will not grant that the conditional is agreed upon. But if it is self-evident that given that 'It is day' it is also necessarily the case that 'It is light', then when we say, 'It is day', it is also concluded that 'It is light'; so that the argument 'It is day; therefore it is light' is sufficient and the conditional 'If it is day, it is light' is redundant.

TEXT 12: Sextus Empiricus *M* 7.38–442 (selections)

38. Some, and especially the Stoics, think that truth differs from the true [or what is true] in three ways: in substance, composition, and power. In substance, in that truth is corporeal and the true is incorporeal. And reasonably so, they say; for the true is a proposition and a proposition is a thing said [*lekton*]; a thing said is incorporeal. And again truth is a body in that it seems to be knowledge which declares all which is true. **39.** And all knowledge is the leading part of the soul in a certain state (as the hand in a certain state is thought of as a fist). And the leading part of the soul, according to them, is a body. Therefore, truth too is corporeal in kind. **40.** In composition, in that the true is conceived of as something single and simple in nature, such as 'It is day' and 'I am speaking' and truth is thought of in the opposite way as systematic and a collection of several things, in that it is knowledge. . . .
42. In power, these things differ from one another since the true is not always connected to truth (for a fool and an idiot and a madman sometimes say something true but do not have knowledge of the true) and truth is contemplated in knowledge. Hence, he who has this is a wise man (for he has knowledge of true things) and never lies even if he says something false since he utters it not from a bad disposition but from a good one. . . . **44.** . . . In this way the wise man, i.e., the one who has knowledge of the true, will sometimes say what is false but will never lie since his mind will not assent to a falsehood. . . . **45.** . . . Saying a falsehood is very different from lying in that the former comes from good intention, whereas lying comes from bad intention. . . .
150. Arcesilaus and his followers in the Academy did not in the proper sense define a criterion, whereas those who seem to have defined one offered it as a move in their argument against the Stoics. **151.** For they hold that there are three things linked to each other: knowledge, opinion, and, placed between these, grasping. Of these, knowledge is sure and stable grasping unalterable by reasoning; opinion is weak and false assent; and grasping is what is between these, assent to a graspable presentation. **152.** According to the Stoics, a graspable presentation is true and such that there could not be a false one just like it. They say that knowledge is present only in the wise, opinion is present only in base men, but that grasping is common to both groups, and that this is the criterion of truth. **153.** These being the Stoics' views, Arcesilaus countered them

by showing that grasping is in no respect a criterion midway between knowledge and opinion. For that which they call grasping and assent to a graspable presentation occurs either in a wise man or in a base man. But if it occurs in a wise man, it is knowledge, and if in a base man, it is opinion, and there is nothing else left besides these two but a name. **154.** And if grasping is assent to a graspable presentation, it is non-existent, first, because assent occurs not with respect to a presentation but with respect to a statement, for assents are given to propositions; second, because there is no true presentation such that there could not be a false one just like it, as is shown by many and varied examples. **155.** Since there is no graspable presentation, grasping will not occur either, for the assent has to be to a graspable presentation. And if there is no grasping, everything will be ungraspable. Everything being ungraspable, it will follow, even according to the Stoics, that the wise man suspends judgment.

   156. Let us consider the matter in this way. Since everything is ungraspable because of the non-existence of the Stoic criterion, if the wise man gives assent, the wise man will opine; for since nothing is graspable, if he gives assent to something, he will give assent to the ungraspable, but assent to the ungraspable is opinion. **157.** So, if the wise man is one of those who give assent, the wise man will be one of those who opines. But the wise man is surely not one of those who opines; for, according to them, opining is a mark of imprudence and the cause of [moral] mistakes. Therefore, the wise man is not one of those who gives assent. If this is the case, he will have to refuse to give assent to everything. And refusal to give assent is nothing else but suspension of judgment. Therefore, the wise man will suspend judgment about everything. **158.** But since it was necessary after this [argument] to inquire into the conduct of life, which naturally cannot be directed without a criterion upon which happiness too—i.e., the goal of life—depends for its reliability, Arcesilaus says that he who suspends judgment about everything regulates choices and avoidances and, generally, actions by reasonableness and, proceeding according to this criterion, will act correctly [perform morally perfect actions].[20] For happiness arises because of prudence, and prudence resides in correct [morally perfect] actions, and a correct [morally perfect] action is that which, having been done, has a reasonable defense. Therefore, he who adheres to reasonableness will act correctly and will be happy. . . .

   227. Since the Stoic doctrine remains, let us next speak of it. These men, then, say that the graspable presentation is a criterion of truth. We shall know this if we first learn what presentation is according to them and what its specific differentiae are. **228.** So, according to them, a presentation is an impression in

---

20. It is important that Arcesilaus, as reported by Sextus, is here using a Stoic technical term, *katorthōma,* in a non-Stoic sense although the Stoic meaning (given in square brackets) is, we think, supposed to be in the reader's mind.

the soul; and they differed immediately about this. For Cleanthes took 'impression' in terms of depression and elevation—just like the impression on wax made by seal-rings. **229.** But Chrysippus thought that such a view was absurd. For first, he says, this will require that when our intellect has presentations at one time of a triangle and a tetragon, the same body will have to have in itself at the same time different shapes—triangular and tetragonal together, or even round—which is absurd. Next, since many presentations exist in us at the same time, the soul will also have many configurations. This is worse than the first problem. **230.** [Chrysippus] himself speculated, therefore, that 'impression' was used by Zeno to mean 'alteration'; so that the definition becomes like this: 'Presentation is an alteration of the soul'; for it is no longer absurd that the same body at one and the same time (when many presentations exist in us) should receive many alterations. **231.** For just as air when many people speak at once, receiving at one time an indefinite number of different blows, also has many alterations, so too the leading part of the soul will experience something similar when it receives varied presentations.

232. But others say that even Chrysippus' corrected definition is not right. For if a presentation exists, then it is an impression and an alteration in the soul. But if an impression in the soul exists, it is not necessarily a presentation. For if a blow to the finger or a scratch to the hand occurs, an impression and alteration are produced in the soul but not a presentation since the latter occurs not in any chance part of the soul but only in the intellect, i.e., in the leading part of the soul. **233.** In response, the Stoics say that 'impression in the soul' implies 'insofar as it is in the soul'. . . . **234.** Others, starting from the same basic position, have defended their position more subtly. For they say that 'soul' is meant in two senses: one referring to that which holds together the entire, continuous composite and the other referring particularly to the leading part. For whenever we say that a human being is composed of soul and body or that death is the separation of soul from body, we are speaking particularly of the leading part. . . . **236.** Therefore, when Zeno says that presentation is an impression in the soul, he should be understood to mean not the whole soul but only a part of it, so that what is said is 'presentation is an alteration in the leading part of the soul'. . . .

372. . . . For if presentation is an impression in the soul, either the impression is in terms of depressions and elevation, as Cleanthes and his followers think, or it is in terms of simple alteration, as Chrysippus and his followers thought. **373.** And if on the one hand these exist in terms of depression and elevation, then the absurdities alleged by the Chrysippeans will follow. For if the soul in experiencing a presentation is stamped like wax, the most recent change will always obscure the previous presentation, just as the outline of the second seal wipes out the former one. But if this is the case then memory, which is a storehouse of presentations, is destroyed, and so is every craft. For

craft was defined as a complex and a collection of grasps, and it is impossible
for several different presentations to exist in the leading part [of the soul] since
different impressions are conceived in it at different times. Therefore, an
impression, strictly conceived, is not a presentation. . . .

440. But in reply the dogmatists are accustomed to ask how the skeptic can
ever show that there is no criterion. For he says this either without a criterion
or with one. If without a criterion, he will be untrustworthy; and if with a criterion, he will be turned upside down; while saying that there is no criterion,
he will concede that he accepts a criterion to establish this.

441. And we in turn ask, "If there is a criterion, has it been judged [by a
criterion] or not?" And we conclude one of two things: either that there is an
infinite regress or that, absurdly, something is said to be its own criterion.
Then they say in reply that it is not absurd to allow that something is its own
criterion. **442.** For the straight is the standard for itself and other things and a
set of scales establishes the equality of other things and of itself and light seems
to reveal not just other things but also itself. Therefore, the criterion can be
the criterion both of other things and of itself.

TEXT 13: Plutarch *On Stoic Self-Contradictions* 1035f–1036a, 1037b

(1035f) . . . He [Chrysippus] says that he does not absolutely reject arguments to opposite conclusions, but he does advise that this technique be used
with caution, as in the law courts—**(1036a)** not with a sense of advocacy but
to dissolve the plausibility of these arguments. "It is appropriate," he says, "for
those who urge suspension of judgment on all things to do this, and it is helpful for their aim. But for those who work to produce knowledge according to
which we may live consistently, the opposite is appropriate, to give instruction
in basic principles to beginners, from the starting point to the conclusion. In
this context it is appropriate to mention the opposite arguments too, dissolv-
ing their plausibility just as in the law courts." . . . **(1037b)** Having said in his
book *On the Use of Argument* that one must not use the power of argument for
inappropriate ends, just as is the case with weapons, he [Chrysippus] said this
in addition, "One must use it for the discovery of truths and for coordinated
training in them but not for the opposite purposes, although many do this."
By "many" he presumably means those who suspend judgment [i.e., skeptics].

TEXT 14: Plutarch *Against Colotes* 1122a–f

(1122a) . . . Not even those who concerned themselves a great deal with
this matter and wrote exhaustive books and tracts were able to shake the doctrine of suspension of judgment on all questions. But at last the Stoics brought
against it like a Gorgon's head **(1122b)** the "argument from inaction" and then
gave up. For despite all their poking and twisting, impulse refused to become

assent and did not accept sense-perception as the basic principle that tipped the scales [i.e., determined what one would do], but it [i.e., impulse] turned out to lead to action all on its own, not needing the assent [of the agent]. For debates with those philosophers [i.e., skeptics] are carried out by the rules of dialectic and "Such a word as you spoke, that you will hear as an answer."[21]

But the discussion about impulse and assent, I think, gets no better hearing from [the Epicurean] Colotes than lyre music gets from an ass. The argument [of the skeptics] runs like this—for those who listen to it and are capable of following it: there are three movements in the soul: that of presentation, that of impulse, and that of assent. Presentation cannot be removed even by those who want to, (1122c) but it is necessary that those who meet with objects be impressed and affected by them; and impulse is awoken by presentation and moves a person to act with respect to what is appropriate for him, as though a tipping of the scales and an inclination occurred in the leading part [of the soul]. Now, those who suspend judgment on all matters do not abolish this second motion either, but they use impulse, which naturally leads a person toward what is presented as having an affinity to him.

What, then, is the only thing that the skeptics avoid? Only that by which falsehood and deception are implanted, i.e., opining and premature assent, which is a yielding to what is presented caused by weakness and is quite useless. For action requires two things: a presentation of something to which one has an affinity and an impulse toward what is presented as an object of affinity. (1122d) Neither of these is incompatible with suspension of judgment. For the skeptical argument rejects opinion, not impulse or presentation. So, when the pleasant is presented as an object of affinity, one needs no opinion in order to move and progress toward it; but the impulse, which is a motion and progress of the soul, immediately comes along. Indeed, it is their own claim [i.e., the Epicureans] that one need only have sense-perception and be made of flesh for pleasure to appear to be good. Therefore it will appear good even to someone who suspends judgment. For he has sense-perception and is made of flesh, and when he receives a presentation of something good, he desires and has an impulse and does all that he can to prevent it from escaping him. As far as possible he will be in the company of that to which he has an affinity, being drawn by necessity that is natural rather than geometrical.[22] (1122e) No teacher is needed: all on their own these fine, smooth, and agreeable movements of the flesh exert an attraction (as they themselves say) even on those who firmly refuse and reject being swayed and softened by them.

'But how can it be that he who suspends judgment does not run off to the mountain rather than to the baths and does not stand up and walk into the

21. Homer *Iliad* 20.250.
22. Plutarch alludes to Plato *Republic* 458d.

wall when he wants to go to the marketplace but rather walks to the door?' Do you [the Epicurean] ask this even though you claim that the sense organs are accurate and that our presentations are true? Surely it is because it is not the mountain that appears to him to be the baths, but the baths (1122f); and it is not the wall that appears to him to be a door, but the door; and so on in each case. For the argument for suspension of judgment does not interfere with sense-perception, nor does it introduce into our irrational experiences and movements some change which disrupts our faculty of presentation. All it does is abolish opinions; the rest it makes use of in accordance with their natures.

The Stoic-Academic Debate and Cicero's Testimony

TEXT 15: Eusebius *Prep. Ev.* 14.7–8, 736d–737a, 738c–739d

[Numenius says,]

(736d) " . . . Carneades inherited leadership of the school and founded the third Academy. In arguments he used the same approach as Arcesilaus. For he himself practiced the method of arguing on both sides of a question and demolished all the claims made by others. He set himself apart from [Arcesilaus] only in his account of suspension of judgment, saying that it was impossible for a human being to suspend judgment about absolutely everything, that there was a difference between 'non-evident' and 'ungraspable', and that everything was ungraspable, but that not everything was non-evident. (737a) Carneades was acquainted with Stoic theories and by his eristic opposition to them grew in fame by aiming not at the truth but at what appeared to be plausible to the many. As a result, he provided much discomfort to the Stoics." . . .

[The testimony of Numenius continues]:

(738c) "Antipater [the Stoic], for example, who lived at the same time as he, even intended to strain himself to write something in opposition to Carneades. He never made it public, however, in the face of the stream of arguments coming daily from Carneades. He did not say anything nor even utter a sound either in the schools or in the streets; in fact, they say that no one heard even a single syllable from him. But he kept threatening replies and stayed in a corner where he wrote books which he left for posterity which are now useless and were then even more useless against a man like Carneades, who appeared to be exceedingly great and renowned among the men of his time. (738d) Nevertheless, Carneades sowed confusion in public because of his rivalry with the Stoics, but in private with his friends he would agree to things, say that things were true, and make claims just like anyone else." . . .

(739a) And again he adds, "Carneades, expressing contradictory philosophical positions, as it were, decked himself out with falsehoods and concealed the truth beneath them. So, he used falsehoods as curtains and, hiding behind these, kept the truth in the back room, hiding it like a [crooked] shop-keeper. His nature, therefore, was like that of beans, where the empty ones float on water and rise to the top and the good ones sink and disappear." This is what is said about Carneades.

Clitomachus was installed as the successor in his school and after him Philo [of Larissa], about whom Numenius remarks, (739b) "Philo, as soon as he acquired headship of the school, was filled with joy, and rendering homage, he honored and extolled the doctrines of Clitomachus, and, against the Stoics, (739c) he 'armed himself with gleaming bronze'."[23]

As time went by and their doctrine of suspension of judgment lost the impact of its novelty, Philo could not maintain his previous way of thinking, but rather the clarity and consistency of his experiences began to turn him around. Having so much clarity in his insights, he was extremely eager, you may be sure, to find someone who would refute him so that he would not appear to have turned his back and to have fled of his own accord. Antiochus [of Ascalon] became a pupil of Philo and founded another Academy. At any rate, he attended the lectures of Mnesarchus the Stoic and adopted views contrary to (739d) those of Philo his teacher, foisting on the Academy countless alien views.

TEXT 16: Sextus Empiricus *PH* 1.235

The followers of Philo [of Larissa] say that things are ungraspable as far as concerns the Stoic criterion, i.e., the graspable presentation, but graspable as far as concerns the nature of the things themselves. Further, Antiochus [of Ascalon] transferred the Stoa into the Academy, as it was said of him that in the Academy he theorizes according to Stoic doctrine; for he tried to prove that Stoic doctrines are contained in Plato. So, the difference between the skeptical approach and that of the so-called fourth and fifth Academies is evident.

TEXT 17: Cicero *Academica*, book 1 (Varro) 40–42

40. But in that third part of philosophy [i.e., logic] he [Zeno] made quite a few changes. First, he made some new claims here about the senses themselves, which he held were joined to a sort of stimulus received from the outside world (he called this a '*phantasia*', but we may call it a 'presentation'—and let us hold onto this term, for we will have to use it often in the rest of our discussion). But to these presentations which are, as it were, received by the senses he joined the assent given by our minds, which he claims is in our power and voluntary. **41.** He said that not all presentations are reliable, but only those which have a distinctive kind of clear statement to make about the objects of presentation; when this presentation is discerned all on its own, then it is

23. Homer *Iliad* 7.206.

'graspable'. . . . But when it had been received and approved then he said it was a 'grasping'—like those things gripped by one's hand. Indeed, that is how he derived the word, since no one had previously used this term in this connection; and Zeno used quite a few new terms (for he was advancing new theories). What had been grasped by sense-perception, he called this itself a 'sense-perception' and if it was grasped in such a way that it could not be shaken by argument he called it 'knowledge'; if not, he called it 'ignorance', which is also the source of opinion that is weak and a state shared with what is false and not known. **42.** But between knowledge and ignorance he placed that 'grasp' which I just mentioned and said it was neither right nor wrong but that it alone deserved to be believed. Therefore, he said the senses too were reliable because, as I said above, he thought that a grasp made by the senses was true and reliable, not because it grasped everything about the object but because it left out nothing [about it] that could be grasped and because nature had provided this grasp as a standard for knowledge and a basis for understanding nature itself. From such [perceptual grasps] conceptions of things are subsequently impressed on the soul, and these provide not just the foundations but also certain broader paths leading to the discovery of reason. Error, however, and rashness and ignorance and opinion and conjecture—in a word, all that is hostile to a solid and stable assent—all these he banned from the sphere of wisdom and virtue. On these points rests all of Zeno's departure from and disagreement with his predecessors.

TEXT 18: Cicero *Academica*, book 2 (Lucullus) 24–145 (selections)

24. . . . And, moreover, this point is obvious, that there must be a principle which wisdom follows when it begins to do something and this principle must be according to nature. For otherwise impulse (for that is the translation we use for *hormē*), by which we are driven to act and pursue what is presented, cannot be stimulated. **25.** But that which stimulates must first be presented [to the agent] and it must be believed; and this cannot happen if what is presented cannot be distinguished from what is false. For how can the mind be moved to an impulse if there is no judgment as to whether what is presented is according to nature or contrary to it? Similarly, if the mind does not realize what is appropriate to it, it will never do anything at all, will never be driven to anything, will never be stimulated. But if it is ever to be moved, what occurs to the agent must be presented as being true.

26. And what of the fact that, if the skeptics are right, all reason is abolished, which is like the light and illumination of life? Will you persist in *that* kind of perversity? For reason provides a starting point for inquiry, which perfects virtue when reason itself has been strengthened by inquiring. And inquiry is an impulse to knowledge, and discovery is the goal of inquiry. But no one discovers what is false, nor can matters that remain uncertain be discovered. But when things that were previously veiled are revealed, then they are said to be discovered; and thus both the starting point of inquiry and the conclusion of perception and understanding are obtained by the mind. A demonstration (the Greek is *apodeixis*) is defined thus: "An argument which leads from things perceived to that which previously was not perceived." . . .

28. Hence arose the demand made just now by Hortensius, that you [skeptics] should at least concede that the wise man has grasped that nothing can be grasped. But Antipater [the Stoic] demanded the very same thing and said that it was consistent for him who affirmed that nothing could be perceived to say that [at least] this one thing could be perceived, even if other things could not. Carneades argued against him with greater acuity: for he said that far from being consistent, it was in fact totally self-contradictory. For he who denies that there is anything that can be grasped makes no exceptions; therefore, it is necessary that not even [the claim that nothing can be grasped] can in any way be grasped and perceived since it has not been excepted [from the general claim]. . . .

40. But now let us look at the opposing arguments usually advanced by the other side [i.e., the Academics]. But first you can become acquainted with what are, as it were, the foundations of their entire system. So, first of all they put together a sort of craft dealing with what we call 'presentations', and they define their character and types, and in particular they [define] what sort of thing can be perceived and grasped at as great a length as the Stoics do. Then they elaborate the two propositions which, as it were, constitute this entire investigation. [1] When there are things which are so presented that other things can be presented in the same way and that there is no difference between [the two presentations], it is not possible that the one group should be perceived and the other not. [2] However, [they say that] there is no difference, not just if they are of the same quality in all respects, but even if they cannot [in fact] be distinguished [by the perceiver]. When these premises are laid down, the whole issue is contained in one argument; and the argument is put together as follows. Some presentations are true, some false. What is false cannot be perceived, but every true presentation is such that there can be a false presentation of the same quality. And with presentations which are such that there is no difference between them, it cannot happen that some can be perceived whereas others cannot; therefore, there is no presentation which can be perceived.

41. They think that of the premises they assume in order to generate the desired conclusion, two will be granted to them (and in fact no one does reject these two); these are, [first] that false presentations cannot be perceived, and the other is that with presentations between which there is no difference, it is not possible that some should be such as to be perceived whereas others are not. The other premises they defend with a complex and lengthy discussion; these other premises are also two in number: first that some presentations are true whereas others are false, and second that every presentation coming from something true is such that it could also have come from something false.

42. They do not just fly past these two propositions; rather, they develop them with extraordinary care and diligence. For they first subdivide [the argument] into major parts: [1] first the senses, [2] then the inferences which we draw from the senses and ordinary experience (which they want to claim is obscure), and [3] finally they come to the part in which they claim that even with reason and inference it is not possible for anything to be perceived. They divide these general arguments even more finely. The method you saw them using on the senses yesterday is also used for the other parts. For in each and every case—and they subdivide very finely indeed—they want to show that true presentations are coupled with false ones which differ in no respect from the true; and since they are of this nature, they cannot be grasped. . . .

66. . . . When presentations strike my mind or senses forcefully, I accept them and sometimes I even assent to them—not that I perceive them, for I do not think that anything can be perceived. I am not wise, and so I yield to presentations and cannot resist them; but Arcesilaus agrees with Zeno [the Stoic] and holds that the wise man's chief strength is that he is careful not to be tricked and sees to it that he is not deceived; for nothing is more alien to the conception that we have of the seriousness of a wise man than error, frivolity, or rashness. What shall I say then of the wise man's steadfastness? Even you, Lucullus, concede that he never holds a [mere] opinion. And since you approve of this thesis . . . consider first the force of this argument: **67.** 'If a wise man ever assents to anything, then he will sometimes hold [mere] opinions; but he will never hold [mere] opinions; therefore he will assent to nothing'. Arcesilaus approved of this argument, for he argued in support of the first and second premises. Carneades sometimes conceded the second premise, i.e., that the wise man sometimes assents; hence it followed that the wise man holds [mere] opinions. You want to avoid this, and rightly so in my view. But the first premise, that the wise man will have [mere] opinions if he gives assent, is held to be false by the Stoics and their supporter Antiochus on the grounds that he [the wise man] can distinguish falsehoods from truths and what is not perceptible from what is perceptible. . . .

76. . . . From what follows one can understand that Arcesilaus did not fight with Zeno for the sake of quarreling but really wanted to discover the truth. **77.** None of his predecessors ever formally claimed or even merely mentioned that it was possible for a human being to hold no opinions, whereas it was not only possible but even necessary for a wise man to do so. Arcesilaus thought that this view was true, and respectable and worthy of a wise man. Perhaps he asked Zeno what would happen if [a] the wise man could not perceive anything, and [b] it was not fitting for the wise man to hold a [mere] opinion. I think that Zeno would have said that the wise man would indeed avoid forming an opinion because there was something which could be perceived. So, what would this be? A presentation, I believe. So, what kind of presentation? Then Zeno defined it as a presentation which came from an existing thing and which was formed, shaped, and molded exactly as that thing was. Next question: could a true presentation be of the same quality as a false one? Here Zeno was quite sharp and saw that no presentation could be perceived if, though it came from something which exists, it could be of the same quality as that which came from something which does not exist. Arcesilaus agrees that the addition to the definition was correct since what is false cannot be perceived and neither can what is true if it is just like what is false. The burden of his argument in those debates was to show that there in fact existed no presentation coming from something true which was not such that one of the same quality could have come from something false.

78. This is the one dispute which has persisted [unchanged] until our own day. For the claim that the wise man would assent to nothing was not in the least essential to this debate. For he could well perceive nothing and yet still hold an opinion—which is the view of which Carneades is said to have approved. However, I follow Clitomachus, rather than Philo or Metrodorus, and so think that this thesis was advanced as a debating point rather than as something of which he really approved. But never mind that now. If opinion and perception are eliminated, suspension of all assent certainly follows; consequently, if I show that nothing can be perceived you should concede that [the wise man] will never assent. . . .

95. . . . But I leave this point and ask the following question: if those propositions [i.e., the Liar paradox, etc.] cannot be explicated and there is no criterion for them such that you could answer that they are true or false, what is left of your [i.e., the Stoic] definition, which claims that a proposition is that which is true or false? For if one takes a group of propositions, I make the further claim that of these some are to be approved of and some rejected—i.e., the ones which are contradictory to the former. **96.** So, what do you make of how this argument works? 'If you say that it is now light and you speak the truth, then it is light; but you say that it is now light and you speak the truth; therefore it is light'. Surely you approve of the general form of argument and say that it is a completely valid argument; that is why you treat it as the first argument form in your teaching of logic. So, either you will approve of every argument which uses the same form, or the entire craft [of logic] is nullified. So see whether you are going to approve of this argument: 'if you say you are lying and you speak the truth, then you are lying; but you do say that you are lying and you speak the truth; therefore, you are lying'. How can you avoid approving of this argument when you have approved of the previous one which has the same form? These problems were put by Chrysippus, but even he did not solve them. For what would he make of this argument: 'if it is light, it is light; but it is light; therefore, it is light'. Surely he would allow it; for the very nature of the conditional is such that when you have granted the antecedent you are compelled to grant the consequent. How then does this argument differ from the following? 'If you are lying, you are lying; but you are lying; therefore, you are lying'. You say that you can neither approve of this nor disapprove of it; so how can you do any better with the other? If craft, reason, method, if rational inference itself have any force, then they are all found equally in both arguments.

97. Their final position is this: they demand that these [arguments] be excepted as inexplicable. I think they had better appeal to a tribune for their exception; they will certainly never get it from me. Further, they cannot get Epicurus, who disdains and scoffs at dialectic as a whole, to grant that statements of this form are true, 'either Hermarchus will be alive tomorrow or he will not', despite the declaration of the dialecticians that every utterance with this form, 'p or not-p' is not just true but necessary; but notice the cleverness of the man who those dialecticians think is slow witted: 'if I grant that one of the two is necessary, then it will be necessary tomorrow for Hermarchus either to live or not to live; but there is no such necessity in the nature of things'.

So let your dialecticians, i.e., Antiochus and the Stoics, quarrel with Epicurus; for he undermines all of dialectic since if a disjunction of contradictories (by 'contradictories' I mean two statements, one of which says p and the other not-p)—if such a disjunction can be false then none is true. **98.** So, what is their quarrel with me, who follow their own teaching on the matter? When this sort of problem arose, Carneades used to tease them as follows: 'if my argument is sound, then I will stick to it; but if it is unsound, then Diogenes should give me my mina back'. For he had studied dialectic with this Stoic, and that was the fee which dialecticians used to charge. So I follow the methods that I learned from Antiochus; and therein I do not find any reason to judge that 'if it is light, it is light' is true (for the reason that I learned that every doubled conditional is true) and not to judge that 'if you are lying, you are lying' is a conditional of the same form. Either, then, I will make both judgments, or if I should not make the one, then I should not make the other either.

But putting aside those cutting remarks and the entire tortuous class of argumentation, let us display our true position, for once all the views of Carneades are explicated, those of Antiochus will all collapse together. I will, however, say nothing such that anyone might suspect me of making it up. I shall take it from Clitomachus, who was with Carneades until his old age—[Clitomachus was] a sharp man, a Carthaginian, and exceedingly studious and hard working. There are four books of his on *Suspension of Assent,* and the things I am about to say are taken from book 1.

99. According to Carneades, there are two kinds of presentations: one kind is subdivided into those which can be perceived and those which cannot, the other kind is subdivided into those which are plausible and those which are not. So, the objections raised against the senses and clarity belong to the first division, whereas no objection should be made to the second. Therefore, he held that there is no presentation such that perception follows but many, however, such that plausibility does. For it is contrary to nature that nothing should be plausible; the overthrow of all life that you were referring to, Lucullus, follows [on that view]. Thus, many things are plausible to the senses, provided it is held that there is nothing about the presentations such that there could not possibly be a false one that did not differ from it. Thus, the wise man will employ whatever apparently plausible presentations he meets with, provided there is nothing which opposes its plausibility, and thus will every plan of life be governed. In fact, even he who is introduced by you as a wise man will follow many things as being plausible, but neither grasped nor perceived nor assented to, but as being like truth. And unless he approves of them, all life would be eliminated. **100.** What else? Surely when a wise man goes on board a ship, he has not grasped with his mind or perceived that he will sail away as intended. Who could? But if he were to set out from here to Puteoli, a distance of thirty stades, with a sound ship, a good captain, waters calm as they are now, it would seem plausible to him that he would arrive safely at his destination. In this manner, he takes presentations as guides for acting and not acting, and he will be readier to approve of the claim that snow is white than was Anaxagoras (who not only denied that snow was white but, because he knew that the water from which it was composed was black, even denied that it appeared white to himself), **101.** and will be moved by whatever thing strikes him as a presentation that is plausible and not impeded by any other thing. For he is not carved out of stone or hewn from wood: he has a body, a soul, he is moved with his mind and senses, so that many things *seem* true to him, although they do not have that distinctive and peculiar mark of perceptibility. And for that reason the wise man does not assent, for there can exist a false presentation indistinguishable from a true one. Nor do we speak against the senses differently from the Stoics, who say that many things are false and are very different from how they appear to the senses.

If, however, it is the case that the senses receive even one false presentation, he is right here to deny that anything can be perceived with the senses. In this way, without a word from us but with one principle from Epicurus and one from you [Lucullus], perception with the senses and grasping are eliminated. What is Epicurus' principle? If any presentation to the senses is false, nothing can be perceived. And yours? There are false presentations to the senses. What follows? Even if I should keep silent, the argument itself declares that nothing can be perceived. "I do not admit Epicurus' principle," he [Lucullus] says. Well, then, quarrel with him, who differs from you totally, not with me, who assent to your claim that there is something false in the senses. **102.** Still, nothing seems to me so strange as that those words should be spoken, especially by Antiochus, who was intimately acquainted with what I said a while ago. For anyone is allowed on the basis of his own judgment to take issue with our denial that anything can be perceived—that is certainly a less serious criticism; whereas our saying that some things are plausible seems inadequate to you. Perhaps so. In any case, we certainly ought to try to avoid the difficulties forcefully brought forward by you: "Do you discern nothing? Do you hear nothing? Is nothing clear to you?" I explained a little while ago, on the authority of Clitomachus, how Carneades would respond to these questions. Listen to what Clitomachus says along the same lines in the book he dedicated to the poet Gaius Lucilius, although he had written the same things to Lucius Censorinus when he was consul with Manius Manilius. He wrote in just about these words—I know them because the first introduction and, as it were, the program for the very matters we are discussing are contained in that book—anyway, he wrote as follows:

103. According to the Academics, things are dissimilar in a way such that some seem to be plausible and some otherwise. But that is not sufficient to allow you to say that some can be perceived and others not, for there are many false [presentations] that are plausible, whereas nothing that is false could be perceived or known. Therefore he says that those who say that the senses are taken away from us by the Academy are very much mistaken. For that school never said that color, taste, or sound were nothing, but they did argue that there was no peculiar feature in them that was a mark of certainty and truth which could not belong to something else. **104.** When he had set out these claims, he added that there are two senses in which the wise man is said to suspend judgment. In one sense, he gives assent to nothing at all; in the other sense, he suspends judgment by not responding to a query as to whether he approves of something or disapproves of it, so that he is not forced to deny or affirm anything. Since this is so, the one sense is accepted, so that he never assents to anything, and he holds to the other sense, so that, following plausibility wherever this should be present or absent, he is able to respond [to a question about acceptance] "yes" or "no" accordingly. Indeed, since we believe that he who withholds assent from everything is nevertheless moved and does something, there remain presentations of the sort that excite us to action and also those about which, when questioned, we would be able to respond either way, following only the claim that the presentation was like that, but still without assent. However, we do not give assent to every presentation of this sort but only to those which nothing impedes.

105. If we do not persuade you with these arguments, since they may well be false, still they are certainly not despicable; for we do not destroy the light, but rather we merely say that those things which you say are perceived and grasped 'appear' as long as they are plausible. . . .

108. The second point is that you deny that any action concerning anything can occur in someone who approves nothing with his assent. For first there must be a presentation, in which assent is involved; for the Stoics say that acts of sense-perception are themselves acts of assent and that because impulse follows on these [acts of assent], action also follows and that all of this is removed if presentations are removed.

On this topic there have been many arguments, written and oral, on either side, but the whole issue can be dealt with briefly. For my part, although I agree that the highest activity is to fight against presentations, to resist opinions, and to suspend assent, which is a slippery sort of thing, and although I agree with Clitomachus when he writes that a veritably Herculean labor was performed by Carneades when he drove assent—i.e., [mere] opinion and rashness—out of our souls, as though it were a wild and ravening beast; despite all of this (to set aside this line of defense), what will hinder the action of someone who follows what is plausible providing nothing hinders it? . . .

144. . . . First I shall expound those odious theories in which you [i.e., Stoics] say that all of those [ordinary people] who stand in the assembly are exiles, slaves, and madmen. Then I shall move on to the theories which pertain not to the mass of people but to you yourselves who are present now: Zeno and Antiochus deny that you know anything. "How so?" you will ask, "For we hold that even an unwise man grasps many things." **145.** But you deny that anyone except the wise man knows anything. And Zeno used to make this point by using a gesture. When he held out his hand with open fingers, he would say, "This is what a presentation is like." Then when he had closed his fingers a bit, he said, "Assent is like this." And when he had compressed it completely and made a fist, he said that this was grasping (and on the basis of this comparison he even gave it the name '*katalēpsis*' [grasp], which had not previously existed). But when he put his left hand over it and compressed it tightly and powerfully, he said that knowledge was this sort of thing and that no one except the wise man possessed it. But they themselves are not in the habit of saying who is or has been wise.

Conceptions and Rationality

Text 19: Augustine *City of God* 8.7

[The Platonists] are not to be compared with those who placed the criterion of truth in the bodily senses and thought that every object of learning should be measured by their standards, like the Epicureans and all others of the sort, including even the Stoics. For although they passionately loved the skill of debating, which they call dialectic, they thought it should be derived from the bodily senses, asserting that it was from this source that the soul acquired conceptions, which they call *ennoiai,* i.e., those things which are clarified by definition; from this source (they said) the entire system of teaching and learning is generated and the links within it are forged.

TEXT 20: Origen *Against Celsus* 7.37

. . . [Celsus] dogmatically asserts, like the Stoics, who abolish intelligible substances, that everything which is grasped is grasped by the senses and every act of grasping is dependent on the senses. . . .

TEXT 21: Aëtius 4.11.1–5 (Pseudo-Plutarch *On the Doctrines of the Philosophers* 900a–d = *Dox. Gr.* pp. 400–01) The origin of sense-perception, conceptions, and internal reason

1. The Stoics say when a human being is born, the leading part of his soul is like a sheet of paper in good condition for being written on. On this he inscribes each and every one of his conceptions.

2. The first manner of writing on it is through the senses. For when one perceives something, white, for example, one retains a memory after it goes away. When there are many memories similar in kind, then we say one has experience. For experience is the plurality of presentations similar in kind.

3. Of conceptions, some come into being naturally in the stated ways and without technical elaboration, but others, already, come into being through our teaching and efforts. The latter are called 'just conceptions', whereas the former are also called 'basic grasps'.

4. But reason, according to which we are termed 'rational', is said to be completely filled out with basic grasps at the age of seven years. And a concept is a phantasm of the intellect of a rational animal. For when a phantasm occurs in a rational soul, then it is called a 'concept', taking its name from 'mind' [*ennoēma*, from *nous*].

5. Therefore, all the phantasms which strike irrational animals are only phantasms, and those which occur in us and in the gods are phantasms in general and specifically concepts. (Just as denarii and staters, on their own, are denarii and staters, but when they are given to pay for a ship passage, then they are called 'ship money' in addition to being denarii [and staters].)

TEXT 22: Aëtius 4.12.1–6 (Pseudo-Plutarch *On the Doctrines of the Philosophers* 900d–901a = *Dox. Gr.* pp. 401–02) What the difference is between the presentation, the presented object, the phantastic, and the phantasm

1. Chrysippus says that these four things differ from each other. Presentation, then, is an experience which occurs in the soul and which, in [the experience] itself, also indicates that which caused it. For example, when we observe something white by means of vision, there is an experience which has occurred in the soul by means of vision; and <in virtue of> this experience we are able to say that there exists something white which stimulates us. And similarly for touch and smell.

2. 'Presentation' [*phantasia*] gets its name from 'light' [*phōs*]; for just as light reveals itself and the other things which are encompassed in it, so too presentation reveals itself and that which caused it.

3. The presented object is that which causes the presentation. For example, the presented object is the white and the cold and everything which is able to stimulate the soul.

4. The phantastic is a groundless attraction, an experience in the soul which occurs as the result of no presented object, as in the case of people who fight with shadows and punch at thin air. For a presented object underlies the presentation, but no presented object [underlies] the phantastic.

5. A phantasm is that to which we are attracted in the phantastic ground-less attraction. This occurs in the melancholic[24] and in madmen; at any rate when Orestes in the tragedy says,[25]

> Mother! I beg you, do not shake at me those bloody, snakelike maidens!
> They, they are leaping at me!

he says this like a madman, and sees nothing, but only thinks that he does. **6.** That is why Electra says to him,

> Stay, poor wretch, peacefully in your bed;
> for you see none of those things which you think you clearly know.

Similarly, there is Theoclymenus in Homer.[26]

TEXT 23: Pseudo-Galen *Medical Definitions* 126

A conception is a stored up thought, and a thought is a rational presentation.

TEXT 24: Sextus Empiricus *M* 8.56–58[27]

56. . . . For every thought comes from sense-perception or not without sense-perception and either from direct experience or not without direct experience. **57.** Hence, we shall find that not even the so-called false presentations

24. Those affected by an excess of black bile, not the melancholic in our sense.
25. Euripides *Orestes* 255–59.
26. *Odyssey* 20.350 ff.
27. Cf. TEXT 7.53 and TEXT 135.

(for example, those occurring in sleep or madness) are independent of things known to us through sense-perception by direct experience. . . . **58.** And in general one can find nothing in our conceptions is not known to oneself in direct experience. For it is grasped either by similarity to what is revealed in direct experience or by expansion or reduction or compounding.

Physics

132. They divide the account of physics into topics on bodies and on principles and elements and gods and limits and place and void. And this is the detailed division; the general division is into three topics, concerning the cosmos, concerning the elements, and the third on causal explanation. They say that the topic concerning the cosmos is divided into two parts; for the mathematicians share in one branch of its investigations, the one in which they investigate the fixed stars and the planets, for example, [to ascertain] whether the sun is as big as it appears to be and similarly if the moon is and concerning the revolution [of the cosmos] and similar inquiries.

133. The other branch of the investigation of the cosmos is the one which pertains only to natural scientists, the one in which the substance [of the cosmos] is investigated and whether it is generated or ungenerated and whether it is alive or lifeless and whether it is destructible or indestructible and whether it is administered by providence, and so forth. The topic concerning causal explanations is itself also bipartite. For medical investigation shares in one branch of its investigations, the one in which they investigate the leading part of the soul, what happens in the soul, the [generative] seeds, and questions like these. The mathematicians also lay claim on the other, for example, [investigation into] how we see, into the cause of how things appear in a mirror, how clouds are formed, and thunder and rainbows and the halo and comets and similar topics.

134. They believe that there are two principles of the universe, the active and the passive. The passive, then, is unqualified substance, i.e., matter, whereas the active is the rational principle [*logos*] in it, i.e., god. For he, being eternal and [penetrating] all of matter, is the craftsman of all things. Zeno of Citium propounds this doctrine in his *On Substance*, Cleanthes in his *On Atoms*, Chrysippus toward the end of book 1 of his *Physics*, Archedemus in his *On Elements*, and Posidonius in book 2 of his *Account of Physics*. They say that there is a difference between principles and elements. For the former are ungenerated and indestructible, whereas the elements are destroyed in the [universal] conflagration.

And the principles are bodies[1] and without form, whereas the elements are endowed with form.

---

1. So the mss; some editors prefer the emendation "incorporeal."

135. According to Apollodorus in his *Physics,* body is that which is extended in three [dimensions], length, breadth, and depth; this is also called solid body. Surface is the limit of a body or that which has only length and breadth but no depth. Posidonius, in book 5 of his *On Meteorological Phenomena,* says that it exists both in conception and in reality. A line is the limit of a surface or a length with no breadth, or that which has only length. A point is the limit of a line, and it is the smallest [possible] mark.

God and mind and fate and Zeus are one thing, but called by many different names. **136.** In the beginning, then, he was by himself and turned all substance into water via air; and just as the seed is contained in the seminal fluid, so this, being the spermatic principle of the cosmos, remains like this in the fluid and makes the matter easy for itself to work with in the generation of subsequent things. Then, it produces first the four elements, fire, water, air, earth. And Zeno discusses this in his *On the Universe* and Chrysippus [does so] in book 1 of his *Physics,* and Archedemus in some work entitled *On Elements.*

An element is that from which generated things are first generated and that into which they are dissolved in the end. **137.** The four elements together are unqualified substance, i.e., matter; and fire is the hot, water the wet, air the cold, and earth the dry. Nevertheless, there is still in the air the same part. Anyway, fire is the highest, and this is called 'aither'; in this is produced first the sphere of the fixed stars and then the sphere of the planets. Next comes the air, then the water, and, as the foundation for everything, the earth, which is in the middle of absolutely everything. They use the term 'cosmos' in three senses: [1] the god himself who is the individual quality consisting of the totality of substance, who is indestructible and ungenerated, being the craftsman of the organization, taking substance as a totality back into himself in certain [fixed] temporal cycles, and again generating it out of himself; **138.** [2] they also call the organization itself of the stars 'cosmos'; and [3] third, that which is composed of both.

And the cosmos in the sense of the individual quality of the substance of the universe is either, as Posidonius says in his *Elements of the Study of Meteorological Phenomena,* a complex of heaven and earth and the natures in them or a complex of gods and humans and the things that come to be for their sake. Heaven is the outermost periphery in which everything divine is located.

The cosmos is administered by mind and providence (as Chrysippus says in book 5 of his *On Providence* and Posidonius in book 13 of his *On Gods*) since mind penetrates every part of it just as soul does us. But it penetrates some things more than others. **139.** For it penetrates some as a condition [*hexis*], for example, bones and sinews, and others as mind, for example, the leading part of the soul. In this way the entire cosmos too, being an animal and alive and rational, has aither as its leading part, as Antipater of Tyre [says] in book 8 of his *On the Cosmos.* Chrysippus in book 1 of his *On Providence* and Posidonius in his *On Gods* say that the heaven is the leading part of the cosmos, whereas Cleanthes says it is the sun. Chrysippus, however, in the same work, again somewhat differently, says it is the purest part of the aither, which they also call the first god in a perceptible sense, [saying also] that it, as it were, penetrates the things in the air and all the animals and plants; and [it penetrates] even the earth in the form of a condition.

140. [They say] that the cosmos is one and limited at that, having a spherical shape; for that sort of thing is most fit for movement, as Posidonius, in book 5 of his *Account of Physics,* and the followers of Antipater, in their treatises on the cosmos, say.

Spread around the outside of it is the unlimited void, which is incorporeal. And the void[2] is what can be occupied by bodies but is not occupied. Inside the cosmos there is no void, but it is [fully] unified. For this is necessitated by the sympathy and common tension of heavenly things in relation to earthly things. Chrysippus speaks about the void in his *On Void* and in the first of his *Arts of Physics* and [so do] Apollophanes in his *Physics* and Posidonius in book 2 of his *Account of Physics.*

Things said [*lekta*][3] are incorporeal in the same way. **141.** Again, so too is time an incorporeal, being the interval of the movement of the cosmos. Of time, the past and future are unlimited, whereas the present is limited. They believe too that the cosmos is destructible, on the grounds that it is generated, <and>[4] on the basis of <this> argument: in the case of things conceived of by sense-perception, that whose parts are destructible is also destructible as a whole; but the parts of the cosmos are destructible since they change into each other; therefore, the cosmos is destructible. And if something is capable of change for the worse, it is destructible; and the cosmos is [capable of such change] since it is dried out and flooded.

142. The cosmos comes into being when substance turns from fire through air to moisture, and then the thick part of it is formed into earth and the thin part is rarefied and this when made even thinner produces fire. Then by a mixing from these are made plants and animals and the rest of the [natural] kinds. Zeno, then, speaks about the generation and destruction in his *On the Universe,* Chrysippus in book 1 of the *Physics,* Posidonius in book 1 of his *On the*

---

2. An emendation by von Arnim for the repeated "incorporeal." Some editors prefer to retain the text of the manuscripts. For the Stoic definition of void see Sextus *PH* 3.124 and *M* 10.3; see also TEXTS 45–47.

3. Von Arnim's emendation for "These things." Some editors prefer to retain the manuscript reading.

4. The supplements were proposed by Michael Frede. Most editors think that some version of the manuscript text can be retained. We are not convinced, but if it is possible the best version would be "by analogy with things conceived of by sense-perception; for that whose parts are destructible is destructible as a whole."

Cosmos, and [so does] Cleanthes and [also] Antipater in book 10 of his *On the Cosmos.* Panaetius, though, claims that the cosmos is indestructible.

Chrysippus in book 1 of *On Providence,* Apollodorus in his *Physics,* and Posidonius say that the cosmos is also an animal, rational and alive and intelligent; **143.** an animal in the sense that it is a substance that is alive and capable of sense-perception. For an animal is better than a non-animal; and nothing is better than the cosmos; therefore, the cosmos is an animal. And [it is] alive, as is clear from the fact that the soul of [each of] us is a fragment derived from it. Boethus says that the cosmos is not an animal. And Zeno says that it is one in his *On the Universe* and so do Chrysippus and Apollodorus in his *Physics* and Posidonius in book 1 of his *Account of Physics.* According to Apollodorus, the totality is said to be the cosmos, and in another sense it is said to be the composite system of the cosmos and the void outside it. Anyway, the cosmos is limited and the void is unlimited.

144. The fixed stars are carried around with the entire heaven, and the planets move with their own unique motions. The sun makes its elliptical journey through the circle of the zodiac; similarly, the moon makes its journey in a spiral. And the sun is pure fire, as Posidonius says in book 7 of *On Meteorological Phenomena;* and it is bigger than the earth, as the same [philosopher] says in book 6 of his *Account of Physics;* and it is also spherical, as the followers of this same man say, just like the cosmos. So [they say] it is fire, because it does everything that fire does; and that it is bigger than the earth, because the entire earth is illuminated by it—but so is the heaven. And the fact that the earth produces a conical shadow also shows that [the sun] is bigger; and because of its size it is seen from all over [the earth].

145. The moon is more like the earth since it is closer to the earth. And these fiery [phenomena] and the other stars are nourished, the sun [being nourished] by the great sea, as it is an intelligent kindling [of its exhalations]; and the moon [is nourished] by bodies of potable water since it is mixed with air and is closer to the earth, as Posidonius says in book 6 of his *Account of Physics;* the others [are nourished] by the earth. [The Stoics] believe that both the stars and the immovable earth are spherical. The moon does not have its own light but receives its light from the sun by being shone upon.

The sun is eclipsed when the moon covers it on the side that is toward us, as Zeno writes in his *On the Universe.* **146.** For at the conjunctions it [the moon] is seen gradually to approach [the sun] and to occlude it and then to pass by. This is observed in a pan of water. And the moon [is eclipsed] when it falls into the earth's shadow; and that is why there is only an eclipse at the full moon. Although [the moon] is diametrically opposite to the sun once a month, because it moves in [an orbit which is] oblique with relation to the sun's, it [usually] diverges in latitude [and so is not eclipsed every month], being either too far to the north or too far to the south. But it is eclipsed whenever its latitude lines up with that of the sun and the ecliptic and is then diametrically opposite to the sun. And its latitude lines up with that of the ecliptic in Cancer, Scorpio, Aries, and Taurus, as the followers of Posidonius say.

147. God is an animal, immortal, rational, perfect[5] in happiness, immune to everything bad, providentially [looking after] the cosmos and the things in the cosmos; but he is not anthropomorphic. [God] is the craftsman of the universe and as it were a father of all things, both in general and also that part of him which extends through everything; he is called by many names in accordance with his powers.[6] They say that *Dia* [a grammatical form of the name Zeus] is the one 'because of whom' all things are; they call [god] *Zēna* [a grammatical form of the name Zeus] insofar as he is cause of life or because he penetrates life; and Athena by reference to the fact that his leading part extends into the aither; Hera because he extends into the air; Hephaestus because he extends into craftsmanlike fire; Poseidon because he extends into the fluid; and Demeter because he extends into the earth. Similarly they also assign the other titles [to god] by fastening onto one [of his] peculiarities.

148. Zeno says that the entire cosmos and the heaven are the substance of god, and so does Chrysippus in book 1 of his *On Gods* and Posidonius in book 1 of *On Gods*. And Antipater, in book 7 of *On the Cosmos,* says that his substance is airy. Boethus [says] in his *On Nature* that the sphere of the fixed stars is the substance of god.

Sometimes they explain nature as that which holds the cosmos together, and other times as that which makes things on earth grow. And nature is a condition which moves from itself, producing and holding together the things it produces at definite times, according to spermatic principles, and making things that are of the same sort as that from which they were separated. **149.** They say that this [i.e., nature] aims at both the advantageous and at pleasure, as is clear from the craftsmanlike [structure or activity] of human beings.

Chrysippus says, in his *On Fate,* that everything happens by fate, and so does Posidonius in book 2 of *On Fate,* and Zeno, and Boethus in book 1 of *On Fate.* Fate is a continuous string of causes of things which exist or a rational principle according to which the cosmos is managed. Moreover, they say that all of prophecy is real, if providence too exists; and they even declare that it is a craft, on the grounds that sometimes it turns out [true], as Zeno says, and Chrysippus in book 2 of his *On Prophecy* and Athenodorus and Posidonius in book 12 of his *Account of Physics* and in book 5 of his *On Prophecy.* Panaetius, though, denies the reality of prophecy.

5. We excise the words "or intelligent" as a gloss. Some editors prefer to retain it.

6. These etymologies involve wordplay that needs some explanation: *dia* is the phrase "because of"; *zēn* means "to live"; the assonance of "Athena" with "aither" and of "Hera" with "air" are not much closer in Greek than in English. Hephaestus is the god of fire and metalworking, and Poseidon is god of the oceans. Demeter's name means "Earth Mother."

150. They say that primary matter is the substance of all things which exist, as Chrysippus says in book 1 of his *Physics* and [so too does] Zeno. Matter is that from which anything at all can come into being. And it has two names, 'substance' and 'matter', both as the matter of all things [as a whole] and as the matter of individual things. The matter of all things [as a whole] does not become greater or smaller, but the matter of the individual things does. Substance is, according to the Stoics, body, and it is limited, according to Antipater in book 2 of *On Substance* and Apollodorus in his *Physics*. And it is capable of being affected, as the same man says; for if it were immune to change, the things generated from it would not be generated. From this it follows that [matter] can be divided to infinity. Chrysippus says that this division is infinite, <but not to infinity>; for there is no infinity for the division to reach; rather, the division is unceasing.

151. As Chrysippus says in book 3 of the *Physics,* mixtures are total and not a matter of being surrounded or being juxtaposed. For a bit of wine thrown into the sea is for a certain time extended through it reciprocally; but then it is destroyed into it.

And they say that there also exist daimons who have a sympathy with human beings and are overseers of human affairs; and the surviving souls of virtuous men are heroes.

Of things that occur in the [region of the] air, they say that winter is the air above the earth cooled by the withdrawal of the sun; and spring is the temperate blend of the air which is a result of the [sun's] journey toward us; **152.** summer is the air above the earth warmed by the journey of the sun toward the north; and fall is caused by the return journey of the sun away from us. <The winds are flows of the air; they have different names> in accordance with the regions from which they flow. The cause of the generation of [the winds] is the sun's evaporation of the clouds. The rainbow is a refraction of the rays [of light] from moist clouds, or as Posidonius says in his *Meteorological Phenomena*, a reflection (which appears rounded in a circle) of a portion of the sun or moon in a moist and hollow cloud, continuous in its presentation. Comets and 'bearded' stars and 'torch' stars are fires that come into existence when thick air is borne up to the region of aither. **153.** A meteor is a kindled mass of fire moving quickly in the air, creating the presentation [i.e., appearance] of length. Rain is a change from cloud to water, when moisture is borne up from earth or sea and is not consumed by the sun. When it is cooled, it is called frost. Hail is a frozen cloud broken up by the wind. Snow is moisture from a frozen cloud, as Posidonius says in book 8 of his *Account of Physics*. Lightning is a kindling of clouds that are rubbed together or broken by the wind, as Zeno says in his *On the Universe*. Thunder is the noise produced by these [clouds] when they are rubbed together or broken. **154.** A thunderbolt is a vigorous kindling of clouds that falls on the earth with great violence when clouds are rubbed together or broken by the wind. Others say it is a compacted mass of fiery air that descends violently. A typhoon is a great thunderbolt, violent and windlike, or a windlike smoke from a broken cloud. A tornado is a cloud split by fire together with wind. <Earthquakes occur when wind flows> into the hollows of the earth or when wind is closed up in the earth, as Posidonius says in book 8. Some of them are 'shaking' [earthquakes], some 'openings', some 'slippings', and others are 'bubblings'.

155. They believe that the organization is like this: in the middle is earth, playing the role of center, after which is water spherically arranged with the same center as the earth so that the earth is inside the water. After water is a sphere of air. There are five circles in the heaven; of these the first, the arctic, is always apparent; the second is the summer tropic; the third is the equinoctial circle; the fourth the winter tropic; the fifth is the antarctic, which is invisible. They are called parallels in that they do not converge; still, they are inscribed about a common center. The zodiacal [circle] is oblique since it crosses the parallel circles. There are five zones on the earth: **156.** the first is the northern zone, beyond the arctic circle, uninhabited because of the cold; the second is temperate; the third is uninhabited because of scorching heat and is called the torrid zone; the fourth is the countertemperate; the fifth is the southern, uninhabited because of cold.

They believe that nature is a craftsmanlike fire, proceeding methodically to generation, i.e., a fiery and craftsmanly *pneuma*. And soul is a <nature> capable of sense-perception. And this [soul] is the inborn *pneuma* in us. Therefore, it is a body and lasts after death. It is destructible, but the soul of the universe, of which the souls in animals are parts, is indestructible. **157.** Zeno of Citium and Antipater in their treatises *On the Soul* and Posidonius [say] that the soul is a warm *pneuma*. For by means of this we live and breathe and by this we are moved. So Cleanthes says that all [souls] last until <the> conflagration, but Chrysippus says that only those of the wise do so.

They say that there are eight parts of the soul, the five senses, the spermatic principles in us, the vocal part, and the reasoning part. We see when the light which is the medium between the [power of] vision and the external object is tensed in a conical fashion, as Chrysippus, in book 2 of his *Physics,* and Apollodorus say. The conical part of the [tensed] air meets our visual organ, and its base meets the object seen. So the observed object is 'announced' [to us] by the tensed air, just as [the ground is revealed to a blind person] by his walking stick. **158.** We hear when the air which is the medium between the speaker and the hearer is struck in spherical fashion and then forms waves and strikes our auditory organs, just as the water in a cistern forms circular waves when a stone is thrown into it. Sleep occurs when the perceptual tension is relaxed in the region of the leading part of the soul. They say that alterations of the *pneuma* are the causes of the passions. They say that a seed is that which is able to generate other things that are of the same sort as that from which it itself [the seed] was separated. Human seed, which a human emits together with a moist [carrier], is blended with the parts of the soul in a mixture of the [spermatic or rational] principles of his ancestors. **159.** In book 2 of his *Physics,* Chrysippus says that it is *pneuma* in its substance, as is clear from seeds which are sown in the earth: when they get old they no longer germinate, obviously because their potency has evaporated. And the followers of Sphaerus say that the seed is derived from the whole body; at any rate, [the seed] is able to generate all the parts of the body. But they claim that the [seed] of the female is sterile; for it lacks tension, is limited in quantity, and is watery, as Sphaerus says. And the leading part is the most authoritative [or: dominant] part in the soul; in it occur the presentations and impulses, and from it rational discourse is emitted. It is in the heart.

160. These are their physical doctrines, as far as seems sufficient for us [to relate], keeping in view [the need for] due symmetry in [the plan of] my work. . . .

TEXT 26: Philo *On the Eternity of the Cosmos* 76–77

At any rate, Boethus of Sidon and Panaetius, although they were men strongly committed to the doctrines of the Stoics, were divinely inspired and so abandoned the doctrine of conflagrations and regenerations and came over to the more pious doctrine, that the entire cosmos in its entirety is indestructible.

TEXT 27: Stobaeus *Anthology* 1.20.1e (vol. 1, pp. 171.2–7 W-H)

The view of Zeno, Cleanthes, and Chrysippus is that substance changes into fire, as a seed,[7] and from this fire another organization just like the previous one is produced once again. Panaetius thinks that the eternity of the cosmos is more convincing and a view more acceptable to himself than the change of the universe into fire.

Theology

TEXT 28: *Hymn to Zeus* by Cleanthes (Stobaeus *Anthology*
               1.1.12, vol. 1, pp. 25.3–27.4 W-H)

> Most glorious of the immortals, called by many names, ever almighty
> Zeus, leader of nature, guiding everything with law,
> Hail! For it is right that all mortals should address you,
> since all are descended from you and imitate your voice,
> alone of all the mortals which live and creep upon the earth.

7. This seems to be the obvious sense whether *eis* is supplied before *to,* as Heeren suggested, or some other correction to the text is adopted.

So I will sing your praises and hymn your might always.
This entire cosmos which revolves around the earth obeys you,
wherever you might lead it, and is willingly ruled by you;
such is [the might of] your thunderbolt, a two-edged helper
in your invincible hands, fiery and everliving;
for by its blows all deeds in nature are <accomplished>.
By it you straighten the common rational principle which penetrates
all things, being mixed with lights both great and small.
By it you have become such a lofty power and king forever.
Nor does any deed occur on earth without you, god,
neither in the aithereal divine heaven nor on the sea,
except for the deeds of the wicked in their folly.
But you know how to set right what is excessive,
and to put in order what is disorderly; for you, even what is not dear is
    dear.
For thus you have fitted together all good things with the bad,
so that there is one eternal rational principle for them all—
and it is this which the wicked flee from and neglect,
ill-fated, since they always long for the possession of good things
and do not see the common law of god, nor do they hear it;
and if they obeyed it sensibly they would have a good life.
But foolishly they rush off, each to his own evil,
some with a strife-torn zeal for glory,
others devoted to gain in undue measure,
others devoted to release and the pleasures of the body.
. . . they are swept off in pursuit of different things at different times
while rushing to acquire the exact opposites of these things above all.
But Zeus, giver of all, you of the dark clouds, of the blazing thunderbolt
save people from their baneful inexperience
and disperse it, father, far from their souls; grant that they may achieve
the wisdom with which you confidently guide all with justice
so that we may requite you with honor for the honor you give us
praising your works continually, as is fitting
for mortals; for there is no greater prize, neither for mortals
nor for gods, than to praise with justice the common law for ever.

TEXT 29: From another *Hymn* by Cleanthes: Epictetus *Enchiridion* 53

Lead me, O Zeus, and you O Fate,
to whatever place you have assigned me;
I shall follow without reluctance, and if I am not willing to
because I have become a bad man, nevertheless I will follow.

TEXT 30: Cicero *On the Nature of the Gods* 2.3–164 (selections)

3. Then Balbus [the Stoic] said, "I shall indulge you, and deal with things as briefly as I can; indeed, once one has exposed the errors of Epicurus my speech is stripped of all [excuse for] length. Our school exhaustively divides this whole question about the immortal gods into four parts: first they teach that there are gods, then what they are like, then that the cosmos is governed by them, and finally that they take thought for the affairs of human beings." . . .

4. Then Lucilius [Balbus] said, "The first part hardly even seems to require discussion. For what is so obvious or clear, when we have gazed up at the heaven and contemplated the heavenly bodies, as that there exists some divine power of most exceptional intelligence by which these phenomena are governed? . . . If someone were to doubt this, I do not at all understand why the same fellow could not also doubt whether there is a sun or not; **5.** for how is this any more evident than that? And unless [such a conception] were known and grasped in our minds, our opinion would not persist in such a stable fashion, nor would it be confirmed by the passage of time, nor could it have become fixed as the centuries and generations of humankind passed. We notice that other opinions, which are ungrounded and empty, have faded away with the passage of time." . . .

12. Augurs have great authority. Is the craft of the soothsayers not divine? Is not someone who witnesses these things [cases of successful prediction] and countless others of the same sort not compelled to admit that there are gods? For it is certainly necessary, if there are spokesmen for certain beings, that those beings themselves exist; but there are spokesmen for the gods. Let us, therefore, admit that there are gods. But perhaps not all predictions are fulfilled. Well, just because not all sick people recover, it does not follow that there is no craft of medicine. Signs of future events are shown by the gods; if some people make mistakes in [interpreting] them, it is not the nature of the gods that erred but human inference.

And so the general issue is agreed upon by all people of all nations; for in the minds of all there is an inborn and, as it were, engraved [conviction] that there are gods. **13.** There is disagreement about what they are like, but no one denies that they exist. Cleanthes, [a leader of] our [school], said that four causes accounted for the formation of conceptions of the gods in the minds of human beings. First, he cited the cause I was just mentioning, which is derived from the premonition of future events; second, one we have derived from the magnitude of the benefits we receive from our temperate climate, the fertility of the land and the bounty of many other benefits; **14.** third, one that strikes fear into our minds because of thunderbolts, storms, cloudbursts, snowstorms, hail, natural devastation, plagues, earthquakes and underground rumblings, showers of stones and blood-colored raindrops, and monstrosities which violate nature, whether human or animal, and flashes of light seen in the sky, and the stars that the Greeks call 'comets' and we [Romans] call 'curly-haired' [stars] . . . when frightened by these, humans came to believe that there is a certain divine power in the heavens; **15.** the fourth cause, and also the most effective, is the regularity of the motions and revolutions of the heaven and the distinctive and varied, yet orderly beauty of the sun, moon, and all the stars; just looking at them indicates clearly enough that these things are not the result of chance. When someone goes into a house or gymnasium or public forum and sees the orderliness of everything and its regularity and systematic character, he cannot judge that these things happen with no cause, but he understands that there is someone who is in charge and runs things; in the same way, but much more so, in the midst of so many motions and changes and the orderly patterns of so many things of such great size which since the beginning of time have never belied themselves, one must decide that natural motions on such a scale are governed by some intelligence.

16. For all his intellectual acuity, Chrysippus nevertheless puts these points in such a way that they seem to be the teachings of nature and not his own discoveries. "If," he says, "there is something in nature which the human mind, reason, strength, and power cannot accomplish, then certainly that which does accomplish it is better than a human being; but the heavenly bodies and everything which is part of the eternal natural order cannot be created by a human being; therefore, that by which they are created is better than a human being; but what would you call this thing if not god? Indeed, if there are no gods, what can there be in nature that is better than humans? For reason exists in humans alone, and there is nothing more splendid than that; but it is arrogant lunacy for there to be a human being who supposes that there is nothing in the whole cosmos better than he; therefore, there is something better; therefore, obviously, there is a god."

17. If you see a large and beautiful house, you could not be induced to think that it was built by mice and weasels, even if you do not see the master of the house. If, then, you were to think that the great ornament of the cosmos, the great variety and beauty of the heavenly bodies, the great power and vastness of the sea and land were your own house and not that of the immortal gods, would you not seem to be downright crazy? Or do we not understand even this, that everything above is better and that the earth is in the lowest position and is surrounded by the densest form of air? As a result, for the same reason that applies when we observe that some regions and cities have duller witted inhabitants because of the more congested nature of their climatic conditions, the human race too is afflicted by this because they are located on the earth, i.e., in the densest part of the universe. **18.** And yet, we ought to infer from the very cleverness of humans that there is some intelligence [in the universe as a whole], indeed one which is more acute and divine. For where did humans 'snatch' this intelligence from (as Socrates puts it in Xenophon)?[8] Indeed, if someone were to inquire about the source of the moisture and heat that is distributed throughout our bodies and of the earthy solidity of our organs and finally about [the source of] the airlike spirit [i.e., *pneuma*] which we have, it appears that we derived one from the earth, another from the moisture, another from fire, and another from the air which we inhale as we breathe. But the most important of these, I mean reason and (if it is all right to use a number of words) intelligence, planning, thought, and prudence, where did we find this? Where did we derive it from? Or does earth have all the rest and not have this one thing that is of the highest value? And yet, it is certain that nothing at all is superior to or more beautiful than the cosmos; and not only is there nothing better, but nothing can even be conceived of that is better. And if nothing is better than reason and wisdom, it is necessary that these be present in that which we have granted to be the best.

19. What? Who is not compelled to accept what I say by [consideration of] the tremendous sympathy, agreement, and interconnected relationships [of the cosmos]? Could the earth bloom at one time and be barren at another in turn? Could the approach and retreat of the sun at the summer and winter solstices be known by the manifold changes of things? Could the sea tides in channels and straits be moved by the risings and settings of the moon? Or could the variable orbits of the heavenly bodies be maintained despite the uniform revolution of the entire heavens? These things, and the mutual harmony of the parts of the cosmos, certainly could not happen as they do unless they were bound together by one divine and continuously connected *pneuma*.[9]

20. When these doctrines are expounded in a fuller and more flowing fashion, as I intend to do, they more easily escape the captious criticisms of the Academy; but when they are demonstrated in the manner of Zeno, in shorter and more cramped syllogisms, then they are more open to attack. For just as a flowing river is virtually free of the risk of pollution, whereas a confined body of water is polluted quite readily, in the same way the reproaches of a critic are diluted by a flowing oration, whereas a cramped syllogistic demonstration cannot easily protect itself.

Zeno used to compress the arguments which we expand upon, in the following manner. **21.** "That which is rational is better than that which is not rational; but nothing is better than the cosmos; therefore, the cosmos is rational." It can be proven in a similar manner that the cosmos is wise, happy, and eternal, since all of these are better than things which lack them, and nothing

---

8. *Memorabilia* 1.4.8.

9. Cicero uses the term *spiritus,* but the Greek term he has in mind is obviously *pneuma,* which has been transliterated where it occurs in Greek sources. Similarly, Cicero's *mundus* has been rendered "cosmos" for the sake of uniformity with the Greek sources.

is better than the world. From all of this it will be proven that the cosmos is a god. Zeno also used this argument: **22.** "If something lacks the ability to perceive, no part of it can have the ability to perceive; but some parts of the cosmos have the ability to perceive; therefore, the cosmos does not lack the ability to perceive." He goes on and presses his point even more compactly. He says, "Nothing which lacks life and reason can produce from itself something which is alive and rational; but the cosmos produces from itself things which are alive and rational; therefore, the cosmos is alive and rational." He also argues by means of a comparison, as he often does, as follows: "If flutes playing tunefully grew on olive trees, surely you would not doubt that the olive tree possessed some knowledge of flute playing? What if plane trees bore lyres playing melodiously? Surely you would also decide that there was musical ability in plane trees. Why, then, is the cosmos not judged to be alive and wise, when it produces from itself creatures that are alive and wise?"

23. But since I have already begun to digress from the mode of discussion which I announced at the beginning—for I said that this first part of [our theme] did not require discussion since it was obvious to everyone that there are gods—well, despite this I want to support the same point by proofs drawn from physics, i.e., from the study of nature. For the fact is that everything which is nourished and grows contains within itself a large measure of heat, without which these things could neither be nourished nor grow. For everything which is warm and fiery is set going and kept in motion by its own characteristic motion; but that which is nourished and grows makes use of a certain definite and regular motion. As long as this remains in us our power of sense-perception and life remains, but when this heat is cooled and extinguished, then we ourselves die and are extinguished. **24.** On this point, Cleanthes also uses these arguments to show how great is the power of heat in every body. He says that there is no food that is so heavy that it cannot be digested[10] within a night and a day, and even the residues of the food, which are naturally eliminated, contain heat. Moreover, the veins and arteries do not cease to pulsate with a certain flamelike motion; and it has often been observed that when some animal's heart is removed, it continues to beat as rapidly as a flickering flame. Therefore, everything that lives, whether an animal or a vegetable, lives because of the heat contained within it. From this one should understand that the nature of heat has within itself the power of life which penetrates the entire cosmos.

25. This will be easier to see if we give a more detailed account of this all-pervasive fiery stuff as a whole. All parts of the cosmos (though I will only deal with the most important parts) are supported and sustained by heat. This can be seen first in the nature of earth. For we see that fire is produced when

---

10. The word literally means "cooked"; hence the point about heat.

stones are struck or rubbed together, and when a hole has just been dug we see 'the warm earth steaming'. And warm water is drawn even from spring-fed wells, especially in winter, because the hollow parts of the earth contain a great deal of heat and in winter [the earth] is denser and so confines the heat which is native to it more tightly. **26.** It could be shown, by a long discourse and many arguments, that all the seeds which the earth receives and all the plants which are generated from her and which she holds rooted in her are born and grow because of her temperate heat.

And that heat is also blended with water is shown first of all by the fluidity of water, which would neither be frozen by the cold nor solidified into snow and frost if it did not also dissolve and liquefy itself when heat is added. Thus moisture hardens when it is affected by the blasts of the north wind and other sources of cold and, in turn, is softened when warmed and is [even] dried up by heat. Even the seas, when tossed by the winds, warm up to such an extent that one can easily see that heat is enclosed in these vast bodies of water. And one must not suppose that the warmth in question comes from some external and extraneous source, but rather that it is stirred up by the [wind-induced] motion from the deepest parts of the sea. This also happens to our own bodies when they warm up with motion and exercise.

Air itself, which is by nature the coldest [element], is hardly devoid of heat. **27.** Indeed, it is mixed with a very great deal of heat, since it arises from the evaporation of bodies of water, and air should be held to be a kind of vapor arising from them; anyway, air comes to be as a result of the motion of the heat contained in bodies of water. We can see something like this when water is brought to a boil by putting a fire beneath it.

What now remains is the fourth part of the cosmos; it itself is in its entirety a hot nature and it communicates its salutary and life-giving heat to all other natures. **28.** From this it is argued that, since all the parts of the cosmos are sustained by heat the cosmos itself is preserved for an immense time by an exactly similar nature, all the more so since one ought to understand that this hot and fiery nature is blended throughout all of nature in such a way that it contains in itself the procreative power and cause of generation; all animals and everything which is rooted in the earth must be born from and nourished by this [principle of heat].

29. There is, therefore, a nature which holds the entire cosmos together and preserves it and which is endowed with sense-perception and reason. For every nature which is not isolated and simple but rather is joined and connected with something else must have in itself some leading part, like the mind in a human being and in a brute beast something analogous to mind which is the source of its desires for things; in trees and plants that grow in the earth the leading part is thought to reside in their roots. By 'leading part' I mean that which the Greeks call *hēgemonikon;* in each type of thing there cannot and should not be anything more excellent than this. Necessarily, then, that in which the leading part of nature as a whole resides must be the best of all and the most worthy of power and authority over all things. **30.** We see, moreover, that the parts of the cosmos (and there is nothing in the whole cosmos that is not a part of the whole) contain the powers of sense-perception and reason. These powers must, then, be present in that part of the cosmos which contains its leading part—and in a more acute and powerful form. That is why the cosmos must be wise and why the nature which contains in its grasp all things must surpass them in the perfection of its reason; so the cosmos is a god, and all the powers of the cosmos are held together by the divine nature. . . .

32. . . . One can also see that the cosmos contains intelligence from the fact that it is without doubt better than any other nature. Just as there is no part of our body which is not of less value than we ourselves are, so the cosmos as a whole must be of more value than any part of it. But if this is so, the cosmos must necessarily be wise, for if it were not, then human beings, who are part of the cosmos, would have to be of more value than the entire cosmos in virtue of participation in reason.

33. And if we want to proceed from primary and rudimentary natures to those which are highest and perfect, it is necessary that we arrive at the nature of the gods. We notice first that nature sustains things produced from the earth, to whom she gave nothing more than the ability to nourish themselves and to grow. **34.** But she gave to beasts the powers of sense-perception and motion and the ability to use a kind of impulse to acquire beneficial things and avoid dangerous things. Her gifts to humans were greater in that she added reason, by which the soul's impulses could be governed by being alternately set loose and restrained. The fourth and highest level belongs to those who are by nature born good and wise, those in whom right and consistent reason is inborn from the very beginning. This kind of reason must be thought of as beyond human capacity and should be assigned to a god, i.e., the cosmos, which must necessarily contain that perfected and completed form of reason.

35. Nor can one say that in any complex system ultimate perfection does not occur. In the case of vines or cattle we see that, unless some [external] force interferes, nature follows its own path to its final goal. In painting, building, and the other crafts we can point to the completion of a perfect piece of workmanship; similarly (but much more so), it is necessary that something be completed and perfected in nature as a whole. Indeed, other natures can be prevented by many external factors from achieving perfection; but nature as a whole cannot be hindered by anything, for the very reason that it itself embraces and contains all [other] natures. That is why it is necessary that there be this fourth and highest level which is immune to all outside force. **36.** It is on this level that we find the nature of the universe; and since this nature is superior to all things and is immune to hindrance by anything, it is necessary that the cosmos be intelligent and even wise.

And what is more foolish than to deny that the nature which contains all things is best or to say that, although it is best, it is not in the first place alive, secondly, equipped with reason and deliberative ability, and finally, wise? How else could it be best? For if it resembles plants or even the lower animals, it must be thought of not as the best but as the worst. And if it is rational but not wise from the very beginning, the condition of the cosmos is worse than that of human beings; for a human can become wise, but if the cosmos has been foolish throughout the eternity of preceding time, surely it will never achieve wisdom—and so it will be worse than a human being. And since this is absurd, one must hold that the cosmos is both wise from the very beginning and a god.

37. Nor does anything else exist which lacks nothing and is completely equipped, perfect, and fulfilled in all aspects and parts of itself, except the cosmos. Chrysippus put the point well when he said that just as the cover was made for the sake of the shield and the sheath for the sword, in the same way everything else except the cosmos was made for the sake of other things. For example, the crops and fruits which the earth bears exist for the sake of animals, but animals for the sake of humans; the horse exists for riding, the ox for plowing, and the dog for hunting and guarding, but a human being himself was born for the sake of contemplating and imitating the cosmos—he is not at all perfect, but he is a certain small portion of what is perfect. **38.** But since the cosmos embraces everything and since there is nothing which is not in it, it is perfect in all respects. How, then, can it lack what is best? But nothing is better than mind and reason. Therefore, the cosmos cannot lack these things. Chrysippus also uses comparisons to show effectively that everything is better in perfected and full-grown [specimens], for example, better in a horse than in a colt, in a dog than in a puppy, in a grown man than in a boy. Similarly, what is best in the cosmos as a whole ought to exist in something which is perfected and completed; **39.** but nothing is more perfect than the cosmos, nothing better than virtue. Therefore, virtue is a property of the cosmos. Indeed, human nature is not perfect, and nevertheless virtue is produced in humans. How much more easily, then, could it be produced in the cosmos. Therefore, it contains virtue. Therefore, it is wise and consequently a god.

Now that we have seen that the cosmos is divine, we should assign the same sort of divinity to the stars, which are formed from the most mobile and pure part of the aither and have no additional elements mixed into their nature; they are totally hot and bright, so that they too are also said quite correctly to be animals and to perceive and to have intelligence. **40.** And Cleanthes thinks that the evidence of two senses, touch and sight, shows that they are totally fiery. For the sun's light is brighter than that of any fire, seeing that it shines so far and wide across the boundless cosmos, and the effect of its contact is such that it not only warms but also often burns things; it could not do either of these things unless it were fiery. "Therefore," he says, "since the sun is fiery and is nourished by the moisture from the ocean (since no fire can persist without fuel), it is necessary either that it be similar to the fire that we use for our daily purposes or to the fire that is contained in the bodies of animals. **41.** But the fire that we are familiar with and that we need for the purposes of daily life consumes and destroys everything, and wherever it penetrates it upsets and scatters everything. By contrast, the fire found in bodies is life-giving and beneficial, and in everything it preserves, nourishes, promotes growth, sustains, and provides the power of sense-perception."

Consequently, he says that there is no doubt about which sort of fire the sun is like since it too causes everything to flourish and mature according to its kind. Therefore, since the sun's fire is like those fires which are in the bodies of animals, the sun too should be alive, and indeed so too should the rest of the heavenly bodies which take their origin from the celestial heat, which is called aither or heaven [sky].

42. So, since some animals are born on earth, some in the water, some in the air, it seems absurd to Aristotle[11] to suppose that no animals are born in that part [of the cosmos] which is most suited for the production of animal life. But the stars reside in the aither, and since this is the rarest element and is always alive and moving, it is necessary that an animal born there should also have the most acute senses and the most rapid motion. And since the heavenly bodies are born in the aither, it is reasonable that they should possess the powers of sense-perception and intelligence; from which it follows that the heavenly bodies should be counted among the gods.

Indeed, one may observe that people who live in lands blessed with pure and thin air have keener intellects and greater powers of understanding than people who live in dense and oppressive climatic conditions. **43.** Moreover, they also think that the food one eats makes a difference to one's mental acuity. So, it is plausible that the stars should have exceptional intelligence since they inhabit the aitherial part of the cosmos and are nourished by moisture from the land and sea which is rarefied by the great distance it has traveled. The orderliness and regularity of the heavenly bodies is the clearest indication of their powers of sense-perception and intelligence. For nothing can move rationally and with measure except by the use of intelligence, which contains nothing haphazard or random or accidental. But the orderliness and perpetual consistency of the heavenly bodies does not indicate a merely natural process (for it is full of rationality) nor one produced by chance, which tends to

11. In the lost work *On Philosophy.*

produce haphazard change and is hostile to consistency. It follows, therefore, that they move on their own, by their own wills, perceptions, and divinity.

44. And Aristotle is to be praised for his opinion that everything which moves does so either by nature or force or will. Now the sun and moon and all the heavenly bodies move. Things which move by nature either move straight down because of weight or straight up because of lightness; but neither of these applies to the heavenly bodies, since their motion is circular revolution. Nor can it be said that the heavenly bodies are compelled by some greater force to move contrary to their nature—for what force could be greater? The only remaining possibility is that the motion of the heavenly bodies is voluntary.

Anyone who [so much as] sees them would be not only ignorant but even impious to deny that there are gods. Nor does it really make much difference whether he denies that or merely deprives them of all providential concern and activity; for in my view [a god] who does nothing might as well not exist. Therefore, it is so obvious that there are gods that I can hardly consider anyone who denies it to be in his right mind. . . .

57. So I hardly think that I will go wrong to take my lead in discussing this subject from a leading investigator of truth. Zeno, then, defines nature thus: he says that it is a craftsmanlike fire which proceeds methodically to the task of creation. For he thinks that creating and producing are most characteristic of a craft and that nature (i.e., the craftsmanlike fire, as I said, which is the instructor of all the other crafts) accomplishes the same sort of thing as our hands do when they are used in human crafts, but much more skillfully. And on this theory nature as a whole is craftsmanlike because it has a kind of method and path to follow; **58.** but the nature of the cosmos itself, which constrains and contains all things in its embrace, is said by the same Zeno not only to be craftsmanlike but, to put it directly, a craftsman, since it looks out for and is provident about all kinds of usefulness and convenience. And just as all other natural entities are produced, grow, and are held together each by its own seeds, so too the nature of the cosmos has all the voluntary motions, endeavors, and impulses (which the Greeks call *hormai*) and carries out the actions consequent on them, just as we ourselves do who are set in motion by our minds and senses. For since the mind of the cosmos is like this and can for this reason properly be called prudence or providence (in Greek the term is *pronoia*), the principal concern of this providence and its greatest preoccupation is, first, that the cosmos be as well suited as possible for remaining in existence, second, that it be in need of nothing, but most of all that it should possess surpassing beauty and every adornment.

59. The cosmos as a whole has been discussed; so have the heavenly bodies. We now have a pretty clear picture of a large number of gods who are not idle, but who do not have to carry out the tasks they perform with laborious and unpleasant effort. For they are not held together by veins and nerves and bones; nor do they consume the sort of food and drink that would make their humors either too sharp or too dense; nor do they have the sorts of bodies that would lead them to dread falls or blows or fear diseases produced by physical exhaustion. It was for fear of this sort of thing that Epicurus invented his insubstantial and idle gods. **60.** Endowed with that most beautiful of shapes, located in the purest region of the heaven, they move and steer their courses in such a way that they seem to have come to an agreement to preserve and protect everything. . . .

73. The next thing is for me to explain that the world is governed by the providence of the gods. This is a large topic indeed, and one on which we are challenged by your school [i.e., the Academics], Cotta; to be sure the whole debate is with you. . . . **75.** So, I say that the cosmos and all its parts were in the beginning constituted by the providence of the gods and are governed by it for all time. Our school usually divides the discussion of this topic into three parts. The first is derived from the argument used to show that the gods exist; when that is granted one must admit that the cosmos is governed by their rational planning. The next shows that all things are subordinate to a perceptive nature and are managed by it most beautifully; when that point is settled it follows that they were produced by first principles endowed with life. The third topic is derived from our feelings of admiration for celestial and terrestrial phenomena.

76. First of all, then, either one must deny that there are gods, as Democritus does in a way, by bringing in his 'effluences', and Epicurus with his 'images', or those who admit that there are gods must concede that they do something impressive. But nothing is more impressive than the governance of the cosmos; therefore, it is governed by the rational planning of the gods. But if this is not so, certainly there must be something which is better and endowed with greater power than a god—whatever it is, a lifeless nature or necessity set in motion with great force—which produces all these most beautiful works which we see; **77.** it follows then that the nature of the gods is not preeminently powerful or excellent, since it is subordinated to that other power, whether it be necessity or nature, by which the heaven, seas, and earth are ruled. But nothing is superior to god; therefore, it is necessary that the world be ruled by god. Therefore, god is not obedient to nature and is not subjected to it; and so god himself rules all of nature.

Indeed, if we grant that the gods are intelligent, we grant also that they are provident, especially about the most important things. Are the gods, then, ignorant about which things are the most important and about how they are to be handled and preserved? Or do they lack the power to sustain and carry out such great tasks? But ignorance of things is foreign to the nature of the gods, and it is inconsistent with the gods' majesty to have difficulty carrying out their duties because of some weakness. From these premises our desired conclusion follows: that the cosmos is governed by the providence of the gods.

78. And yet, since there are gods (if they really exist, as they certainly do), it is necessary that they be alive, and not only alive but also rational and bound to each other by a kind of political affinity[12] and society, governing this single cosmos like some shared republic or city. **79.** It follows that they possess the same kind of reason as is present in humankind, that the same truth is found in both [gods and human beings] and the same law, which consists in injunctions to do what is right and avoid what is wrong. From this one can see that the gods are the source of human prudence and intelligence; and that is why our ancestors consecrated and publicly dedicated temples to [gods such as] Intelligence, Faith, Virtue, and Concord. How can we deny that [such things] exist among the gods when we worship their revered and sacred images? But if humankind possesses intelligence, faith, virtue, and concord, from where could they have come down [to us] here on earth if not from the [gods] above? And since we have deliberative ability and reason, it is necessary that the gods have them in even greater abundance, and not just have them but also use them in matters of the greatest value and import. **80.** But nothing is of greater value or import than the cosmos; therefore, it is necessary that it be administered by the deliberation and providence of the gods. Finally, since we have shown clearly enough that those whom we see to possess remarkable power and extraordinary beauty are gods (I mean the sun and moon and the planets and the fixed stars and the heaven and the cosmos itself, and the multitude of things which are present throughout the cosmos and are of great utility and convenience for humankind), it follows that everything is ruled by the intelligence and providence of the gods. But enough has been said about the first topic.

81. Next I must show that everything is subordinate to nature and is ruled by it in the finest possible manner. But first, I must give a brief explanation of what nature is to facilitate the understanding of what I want to show. For some think that nature is a type of non-rational force which induces necessary motions in bodies; others that it is a force endowed with reason and orderliness, proceeding methodically, as it were, and showing what the cause of each thing brings about and what follows upon it, [a force] whose cleverness could not be emulated by any craft, skill, or craftsman. [They say] that the power of a seed is such that, despite its minute size, if it meets with a receptive and favorable nature and gets hold of the sort of matter which can nourish it and foster its growth, the seed can produce each sort of thing, according to its kind—some things which are nourished only via their roots, others which can set themselves in motion and perceive and desire and produce others like

12. The Latin is *conciliatio,* usually Cicero's translation for the Greek *oikeiōsis.*

themselves. **82.** And there are also those who use the term 'nature' to refer to everything, like Epicurus, who makes the following division: the nature of all things which exist is bodies and void and their attributes. But since we say that the cosmos is constituted and governed by nature, we do not mean that it is like some lump of mud, piece of stone, or anything else with only a natural power of cohesion, but rather that it is like a tree or animal. For nothing is random in them; rather, it is evident that they possess a certain orderliness and craftsmanlike quality.

83. But if nature's craft is responsible for the life and vigor of plants which are held together by being rooted in the earth, certainly the earth itself is held together by the same force, since when the earth is impregnated by seeds she gives birth to and brings forth all things, embraces their roots, nourishes them, fosters their growth, and is herself nourished in turn by external and superior natural elements. And the air and the aither and all superior entities are nourished by vapors produced from the earth. So, if the earth is held together by nature and owes its vigor to nature, then the same rational force is present in the rest of the cosmos. For the roots [of plants] are bound to the earth, whereas animals are sustained by inhalation of air and the air itself helps us to do our seeing, helps us to do our hearing and speaking; for none of these functions can be carried out without air. Indeed, it even helps us to move, since wherever we go or we move to, it seems to give way and yield to us.

84. And the motion of things to the central, i.e., lowest, region of the cosmos and the motion of other things from the middle to the upper regions and the circular orbit of others around this midpoint all combine to make the nature of the cosmos a single and continuous whole. And since there are four kinds of bodies, nature is rendered continuous by their mutual interchange. For water comes from earth, air from water, and aither from air; then in reverse air comes from aither, then water, and from water comes earth, the lowest element. Thus the union of the parts of the cosmos is held together because the elements from which everything is composed move up and down and back and forth. **85.** And this union must either be everlasting, exhibiting the very order which we now see, or at the very least very stable, enduring for a long, nearly boundless expanse of time. And either way it follows that the cosmos is governed by nature.

Consider the sailing of a fleet of ships, the formation of an army, or (to return to examples drawn from the works of nature) the reproduction of vines or trees, or furthermore the shape and organization of the limbs of an animal: which of these points to as great a degree of cleverness as the cosmos itself does? Either, therefore, there is nothing ruled by a nature capable of perception or one must admit that the cosmos is so ruled. **86.** Moreover, how can that which contains all natures and the seeds which produce them fail to be itself governed by nature? So, if someone were to say that the teeth and body hair exist by nature but that the human being to whom they belong was not constituted by nature, he would simply be failing to understand that those things which produce something from themselves have natures more perfect than the things produced from themselves. But the cosmos is the sower and planter and (if I may so put it) the parent and nurse and nourisher of all things governed by nature. The cosmos nourishes and holds together everything as though those things were its limbs and parts of itself. But if the parts of the cosmos are governed by nature, it is necessary that the cosmos itself be governed by nature. And the governance of the cosmos contains nothing which is subject to criticism; the best possible result that could be produced from those natures which existed was indeed produced. **87.** Let someone, then, show that something better could have been produced! But no one will ever show this. And if someone wants to improve on something [in the cosmos], either he will make it worse or he will be longing for something which simply could not have happened.

But if all parts of the cosmos are so constituted that they could neither have been more useful nor more beautiful, let us see whether they are the products of chance or of such a character that they could never even have held together if not for the control exerted by a perceptive and divine providence. If, therefore, the products of nature are better than those of the crafts and if the crafts do nothing without the use of reason, then nature too cannot be held to be devoid of reason. When you look at a statue or a painting, you know that craftsmanship was applied; and when you see from afar the course steered by a ship, you do not doubt that it is moved by rational craftsmanship. When you gaze on a sundial or waterclock, you understand that the time is told as a result of craft and not as a result of chance. So, what sense does it make to think that the cosmos, which contains these very crafts and their craftsmen and all else besides, is devoid of deliberative ability and reason? . . .

94. . . . So Aristotle puts it splendidly:[13] **95.** "If," he says, "there were people who lived under the earth in fine and splendid houses adorned with statues and paintings and outfitted with all those things which those who are considered happy have in great abundance, but who had never come out onto the surface of the earth though they had heard by rumor and hearsay that some divine force and godly power existed; and then one day the earth opened its maw and they could emerge from those hidden places and come out into the regions that we inhabit, and they then became aware of the huge clouds and the force of the winds and saw the sun in all its great size and beauty and also became aware of its creative power (for it created the day by spreading its light throughout the entire heaven); and then when night darkened the earth they could see the whole heaven adorned and ornamented with stars, and the

---

13. In the lost work *On Philosophy*.

changes in the illumination of the moon as it waxed and waned, and the risings and settings of all those heavenly bodies moving in courses immutably
fixed for all of eternity—when they saw all of this, certainly they would think
both that there are gods and that these things are their handiwork." . . .

115. . . . And not only are these things amazing, but there is nothing more
so than the fact that the cosmos is so stable and so internally coherent that
nothing can even be conceived of which is more suited to permanent existence. For all of its parts from every direction exert an equal effort to reach the
center. Moreover, compound bodies maintain their existence most effectively
when they are surrounded by a kind of bond which ties them together; and
this is done by that nature which penetrates the entire cosmos and causes
everything with its intelligence and rationality, rapidly drawing the outermost
parts [of the cosmos] back toward the center. **116.** So, if the cosmos is spherical, and as a result all its parts from every direction are held together in an
equal balance by each other and with each other, then it is necessary that the
same thing must apply to the earth too; consequently, since all the parts of the
earth tend toward the center (and the center is the lowest point in a sphere),
there is no break in its continuity which might cause such a large and coordinated system of weight and gravity to crumble. And similarly the sea, which
lies above the earth and yet strives to reach the center of the earth, is evenly
balanced on all sides and so forms a sphere; it never overflows or exceeds its
bounds. **117.** Air is continuous with the sea and is borne aloft by its lightness;
but still it distributes itself in all directions. And so it is both continuous with
the sea and joined to it, and by nature it moves upward to the heavens, whose
rareness and heat blend with it and so enable the air to provide to animals life-
giving and beneficial *pneuma*. The highest part of the heaven, which is termed
'aitherial', embraces the air and also retains its own rarefied heat, being compounded with nothing else; and [yet] it is conjoined with the boundaries of
the air. And the heavenly bodies revolve in the aither; by their own effort they
hold themselves together in their spherical shape, and in virtue of their shape
and form they sustain their movements—for they are round and, as I think I
said before, things that have this shape are least susceptible to harm. **118.** The
stars, moreover, are by nature fiery and so are nourished by vapors that rise
from the earth, sea, and bodies of water, having been produced by the sun's
warming of the fields and waters. The stars, and the entire aitherial region, are
nourished and renewed by these vapors; and then they pour them forth again
and in turn draw them back from the same source, with virtually no loss [to
the vapors] except for a very little bit which is consumed by the fire of the
heavenly bodies and the flames of the aither. And for this reason our school
[the Stoics] thinks that there will someday occur the event which they say
Panaetius had his doubts about, i.e., the final conflagration of the entire cosmos. This will happen when all the moisture is used up and the earth cannot

be nourished [any longer] and the air cannot return—for air cannot arise if all the water is consumed; so there will be nothing left except fire. This, though, is an animal and a god, and so in turn it produces the renewal of the cosmos and the emergence of the same beautiful order. . . .

127. . . . A great deal of care was taken by divine providence to assure the eternity of the adornment of the cosmos by working to assure the constant existence of the races of beasts, of trees, and of all the plants whose roots are bound in the earth. All of these possess a seminal power which enables one [living thing] to produce many offspring, and this seed is closed up in the inmost core of the fruits produced by each kind of plant. These same seeds give a good supply of food to human beings as well as filling the earth with new stock of the same type. **128.** Why should I even mention the high degree of reason displayed in the efforts of beasts to assure the perpetual preservation of their species? First, some are male and others female—a plan devised by nature to promote their perpetuity—and their organs are very well suited for the tasks of procreation and conception; and then there is the astounding desire that both, male and female, feel for copulation. When the seed [i.e., the semen] has settled in place, it draws virtually all the [mother's] nutrition to itself and protected within it, it produces a [new] animal. And when the off-spring is born, then in mammalian species virtually all of the mother's food begins to turn to milk and the offspring which are newly born seek [their mother's] breasts under the sole guidance of nature, being taught by no one, and are satisfied by their rich abundance. And to prove that none of this is a matter of chance but rather that all of these arrangements are the work of provident and intelligent nature, [note that] those animals who bear many offspring at once (such as pigs and dogs) have been given a large number of teats; those animals who bear fewer offspring have fewer teats. **129.** What should I say about the love there is in beasts for rearing and caring for the young they have produced until such time as the young can defend them-selves? Although fish are said to abandon their eggs once they have laid them, it is easy for them to be supported by the water and to hatch in it. Turtles, though, and crocodiles are said to bear their young on land, then bury the eggs and go away, leaving them to be born and raised all by themselves. But hens and other birds seek a peaceful place for bearing their young and there build dwellings and nests, making them as soft as possible a support for the eggs in order to promote their survival. And when the chicks hatch, [the adults] protect them and cuddle them with their wings so that the cold will not hurt the young; or if it is hot, they shade them from the sun. But when the chicks can first make use of their wings, then their mothers accompany them on their flights but otherwise need care for them no further. **130.** Human care and intelligence is also a factor contributing to the preservation and well-being of several species of animals and of plants born from the earth;

for there are many kinds of domesticated animals and plants which could not survive without the care of human beings. The agricultural activities of human beings and their success are made easier by a variety of different factors in different regions. The Nile irrigates Egypt, keeping the land flooded all summer until it recedes and leaves the fields softened and muddy for the planting season. The Euphrates makes Mesopotamia fertile by bringing new soil to the fields every year. And the Indus River, the largest of all, not only fertilizes the fields and softens them but even sows them; for it is said to bring with its waters a great quantity of seeds which resemble those of grain. **131.** I could mention many other noteworthy things from a variety of areas and many regions all of which are fertile for different kinds of crops. But how great is nature's generosity! She produces so many different kinds of appetizing food, at all different times of the year, that we are always delighted by both its abundance and its novelty. She has given us the Etesian winds; how fitting to their season and how salutary not just for humankind but also for the animal species and even for plants which grow from the earth. Excessive heat is moderated by their [gentle] breath, and they also help our ships to steer a swift and certain course at sea. I must pass over many points. **132.** For the blessings provided by rivers are beyond counting, as are those of the tides which ebb and flow, of the mountains clad in forests, of salt pools found far from the sea shore, regions where the very soil teems with medicinal substances, and finally, [so are the blessings] of numberless crafts which are essential for our life and well-being. Even the alternation of day and night helps to preserve animal life by setting aside different times for action and for rest. Thus from every angle and by every line of reasoning, our minds prove that everything in this cosmos is wonderfully governed by the intelligence and deliberative ability of the gods for the purpose of the well-being and preservation of all.

133. Here someone will ask, "For whose benefit was such a complex system created?" For the sake of trees and plants, which despite their lack of sense-perception are nevertheless sustained by nature? But surely that is absurd. For the beasts then? It is no more likely that the gods should have worked so hard for mute animals which understand nothing. So, for whose sake will we say that the cosmos was made? Surely for the sake of those animals which use reason, and those are gods and humans. Surely nothing is better than they are since reason is superior to all other things. So, it turns out to be plausible that the cosmos and everything in it were created for the sake of gods and humans. It will be easier to see that human beings have been well provided for by the immortal gods if the entire structure of a human being is considered along with the entire form and perfection of human nature. . . .

140. This catalog of nature's painstaking and intelligent providence could be greatly enriched by a consideration of how many rich and splendid gifts have been bestowed on human beings by the gods. First of all, she raised them up from the earth and gave them a lofty and erect posture, in order that they might gaze upon the heavens and so acquire knowledge of the gods. For human beings come from the earth, not to be its inhabitants and tenants but to be, as it were, spectators of higher, indeed celestial, things, the contemplation of which belongs to no other race of animals. . . .

145. . . . All human senses are far better than those of the lower animals. First, in those crafts in which the eyes make the crucial distinctions, painting, sculpture, and engraving, and also in distinguishing bodily motion and gestures, the [human] eye makes many distinctions more subtly; for the eyes judge the beauty and order and, I may say, the propriety of colors and figures. And there are other, even more important distinctions which it makes since it recognizes the virtues and the vices and an angry or friendly person, a happy or sad one, a brave or cowardly one, a bold or timid one. **146.** The ears too possess a remarkably craftsmanlike sense of judgment by which we can distinguish, in vocal music and in wind or string instruments, timbre, pitch, and key and a great many vocal qualities as well: a melodious or 'dark' voice, a smooth or rough one, a flexible or inflexible one. These distinctions are made only by the human ear. Smell, taste, and touch also possess <to some extent> great powers of judgment. . . .

147. Moreover, he who does not see the divine effort which was put into the perfection of human mind, intelligence, reason, deliberative ability, and prudence, seems to me to lack these same qualities. And in discussing this topic, I wish, Cotta, that I had your eloquence. How [wonderfully] you could describe, first of all, human understanding and then our ability to link conclusions with premises and grasp the result, i.e., the ability by which we judge what follows from what and prove it in the form of a syllogism and define in a compact description each kind of thing. And from this we can grasp the power and characteristics of knowledge, a thing whose excellence even the gods cannot surpass. How extraordinary, indeed, are those powers which you Academics try to undermine and even to destroy: the ability to perceive and grasp external objects with our senses and mind. **148.** It is by comparing and contrasting these with each other that we can produce the crafts, some of which are necessary for the practicalities of life and some for the sake of pleasure.

Indeed, the mistress of all, as you call it, is the power of eloquence—how wonderful and divine it is! First, it enables us to learn what we do not know and to teach others what we do know; next, we use it to exhort and persuade, to comfort the unfortunate and to distract the timid from their fears, to calm those who are passionate and dampen their desires and anger. It is the bond that unites us in law, legislation, and civil society. It is eloquence which has raised us from a state of uncouth savagery. . . .

153. What then? Does human reason not penetrate even to the heavens? For we are the only animals who know the risings, settings, and courses of the heavenly bodies; it is the human race which has defined the day, the month, and the year, has learned about solar and lunar eclipses and predicted their dates of occurrence and degree for all time to come. By contemplating these things, our mind attains to knowledge of the gods; and that is the origin of piety, which is closely linked with justice and the other virtues, which are in turn the source of a life which is happy and similar, even equivalent, to that of the gods—yielding to the heavenly beings only in respect to immortality, which is quite irrelevant to the good life. After explaining this, I think that I have shown clearly enough by how much human nature is superior to the [other] animals. And from that one ought to see that chance could never have created the form and arrangement of our limbs or the power of our mind and intelligence.

154. It remains for me to come to my conclusion at last by showing that everything in this cosmos which is of use to human beings was in fact made and provided for their sake. First of all, the cosmos itself was made for the sake of gods and humans, and the things in it were provided and discovered for the use of human beings. For the cosmos is like a common home for gods and humans or a city which both [gods and human beings] inhabit. For only creatures who use reason live by law and justice. So, just as one must hold that Athens and Sparta were founded for the sake of the Athenians and Spartans and everything in these cities is properly said to belong to those peoples, in the same way one must hold that everything in the entire cosmos belongs to gods and humans. **155.** Moreover, although the orbits of the sun and moon and the other stars help the cosmos hold together, they also serve as a [wonderful] spectacle for human beings. For no sight is less likely to become boring, none is more beautiful, and none is more outstanding with respect to rationality and cleverness. For by measuring out their courses, we learn when the various seasons change and reach their peaks. And if human beings alone know these things, one must judge that they were created for the sake of human beings.

156. The earth is rich with grain and other kinds of vegetables and pours them forth with the greatest generosity; do you think that it was made for the sake of beasts or of humans? What should I say about vines and olive trees? Their most rich and fertile fruits are of no use at all to beasts. Beasts have no knowledge of sowing, cultivating, reaping, and bringing in the harvest at the proper time, nor of putting it up and storing it; only humans can use and care for these things. **157.** Just as we should say that lyres and flutes are made for the sake of those who can use them, so one must admit that the things I have been talking about are provided only for the sake of those who use them. And if some animals steal or snatch some of it from them, we shall still not say that those things were made for their sake. For human beings do not store grain for the sake of mice or ants, but rather for the sake of their wives, children, and households. So, animals use such things by stealth, as I said, but their masters do so openly and freely. **158.** So, one must concede that this generous supply of goods was provided for the sake of human beings, unless the great richness and variety of fruits and their pleasant taste, odor, and appearance leave any doubt about whether nature presented them to humans alone.

So far is it from being true that these things were provided for the sake of the beasts, that we can see that even the beasts themselves were created for the sake of human beings. What are sheep for except to provide wool which can be worked and woven into clothes for humans? And without human cultivation and care, they could not have been nourished or maintained nor produced anything of use to others. What can be the meaning of the faithful guard service of dogs, their loving admiration of their masters, their hatred of outsiders, and their remarkable skill in tracking and speed in the hunt? Only that they were created to serve human needs.

159. . . . It would take too long to recount the useful services provided by mules and asses, which were certainly provided for human use. **160.** What is there in pigs, except food? Chrysippus says that the pig was given a soul in place of salt, to keep the meat from spoiling. Because it is well suited for feeding humans, no other type of animal is more prolific of offspring. . . . **161.** . . . You can scan the land and all the seas with your mind, as though with your eyes, and you will immediately see huge expanses of land which bear fruit and densely forested mountains, pastureland for cattle, and also sea-lanes for ships to sail in with remarkable speed. **162.** It is not just on the earth's surface either, but even in the deepest, darkest bowels of the earth there lies hidden a great store of useful materials which were made for human beings and are only discovered by them.

There is another point, too, which both of you will perhaps seize on for criticism—you, Cotta, because Carneades loved to attack the Stoics, Velleius because Epicurus ridiculed nothing so much as the prediction of future events. But I think that it proves better than anything else that divine providence takes thought for human affairs. For divination certainly does exist since it shows up in many different places and at many different times in both private and public affairs. **163.** . . . This power, or art, or natural ability of knowing future events was certainly given to humans and to no other animal by the immortal gods. . . . **164.** And the immortal gods do not limit themselves to taking thought for humankind as a whole, but they even concern themselves with individual human beings. For one may gradually reduce the scope of universality, from humankind to smaller and smaller numbers of people, and finally get down to single individuals [applying the same arguments at each stage]. . . .

TEXT 31: Aëtius 1.6.1–16 (Pseudo-Plutarch *On the Doctrines of*
the Philosophers 879c–880d = *Dox. Gr.* pp. 292–97)
Where did human beings get their conception of the
gods?

1. The Stoics define the substance of god thus: it is an intelligent and fiery *pneuma*, which does not have a shape but changes into whatever it wishes and assimilates itself to all things. **2.** They acquired the conception of god first by getting it from the beauty of the things which appear to them. For nothing beautiful becomes so at random and haphazardly but rather by a craft which acts as an artisan. And the cosmos is beautiful; this is clear from its shape and its color and its size and the varied adornment of the heavenly bodies around the cosmos. **3.** For the cosmos is spherical and this is the best shape of all. For this shape alone is similar to its own parts. And since it is rounded, it contains parts that are round. For it is for this reason that Plato held that the most sacred [part], the mind, is in the head. **4.** And its color is beautiful too. For it has a bluish color, which is darker than purple but has a shining quality. And for this reason it can be observed from such great distances because it cuts through so great an expanse of air in virtue of the intensity of its color. **5.** And it is also beautiful because of its size. For among things that are of the same type, the one that includes [or: surrounds] [the others] is beautiful, as in the case of an animal or a tree. **6.** And these phenomena, too, complete the beauty of the cosmos; for the ecliptic in the heavens is adorned with a variety of different constellations:[14]

> Cancer is there, and so is Leo, and after him Virgo and
> Libra, and Scorpio himself and Sagittarius and Capricorn too,
> and after Capricorn comes Aquarius; and Pisces with its
> shining stars is next, after which come Aries and Taurus and Gemini.

7. And [god] has produced thousands of other [constellations] by similar revolutions of the cosmos. Hence Euripides, too, says,[15]

> The starry gleam of heaven,
> the fair adornment of Time, the wise craftsman.

8. From this we have acquired the conception of god. For the sun and the moon and the rest of the heavenly bodies moving around the earth always rise, [displaying] the same colors, the same sizes, and in the same places at the

14. Aratus *Phainomena* 545–49.
15. Actually the poet Critias, fr. 1.33–34, p. 771, Nauck.

same times. **9.** Therefore, the initiators of religious observance expounded it for us in three forms: first, that based on physics; second, that based on myths; and third, that based on the testimony of customs. The philosophers teach the one that is based on physics and the poets the one based on myths, whereas the customary forms of religious observance are always established by individual cities.

10. Their entire teaching is divided into seven 'species'. The first is that based on the phenomena of the heavens; for we acquired our conception of god from the phenomena of the heavenly bodies by seeing that they are the cause of great harmony and [by seeing] the regularity of day and night, winter and summer, risings and settings, and of the birth of animals and plants on the earth. **11.** Therefore, they thought that the heaven was a father whereas earth was a mother. Of these, the one is father because the effusions of water play the role of seeds whereas the other is mother because she receives these [seeds] and bears [offspring]. And seeing that the heavenly bodies are always moving and are the cause of our ability to observe [things], they called the sun and moon gods.

12. For the second and third types, they divided the gods into the harmful and the beneficial; the beneficial ones are Zeus, Hera, Hermes, and Demeter whereas the harmful ones are the Penalties, the Furies, [and] Ares; these they abhor since they are difficult to deal with and violent.

13. They assigned a fourth and a fifth [type of god] to activities and passions, Eros, Aphrodite, and Longing being passions and Hope, Justice, and Good Order being activities.

14. As a sixth type they added the fictions of the poets. For when Hesiod wanted to make gods fathers of gods who were born, he introduced sires for them like these:[16]

> Coeus, Krios, Hyperion, and Iapetos.

15. And it is for this reason that it is called mythical. As a seventh, in addition to all these, there are [gods who were] born human but were honored because of their good deeds which benefited the life of all human beings: for example, Heracles, the Dioscuri, and Dionysus.

16. They said that they were anthropomorphic on the grounds that the divine is the most authoritative of all things and that human beings are the most beautiful of animals, being adorned in a distinctive way by virtue in accordance with the constitution of his mind. So, they thought that what is best [in the cosmos] would be similar to those who are superior [among animals].

---

16. *Theogony* 134.

TEXT 32: Plutarch *On Common Conceptions* 1076a–b

(1076a) . . . So, the third element in their conception of the gods is that the gods are superior to human beings in respect to nothing so much as their happiness and virtue. But according to Chrysippus they do not have even this superiority, for Zeus does not surpass Dion in virtue, and Zeus and Dion are benefited equally by each other when one meets with a motion of the other since they are [both] wise. For this is the only good that human beings get from the gods and the gods get from humans when they become wise. **(1076b)** They say that if a person is not deficient in virtue, he in no way falls short in happiness, but Zeus the savior is no more blessed than the unfortunate person who commits suicide because of his bodily diseases and impairments—providing that he is wise.

TEXT 33: Sextus Empiricus *M* 9.13–137 (selections)

13. The reasoning about gods seems to be most necessary to those who philosophize dogmatically. Therefore, they say that philosophy is the cultivation of wisdom and wisdom is the knowledge of divine and human matters. For this reason, if we show the doubtful nature of the investigation concerning gods, we will have implicitly established that wisdom is not the knowledge of divine and human matters and that philosophy is not the cultivation of wisdom. . . .

60. Those then who think it right to hold that gods exist attempt to establish their thesis by four modes: the first is the argument from the agreement among all human beings; the second is the argument from cosmic design; the third draws the absurd consequences of denying the divine; the fourth and last is the refutation of opposing arguments.

61. Now arguing on the basis of the common conception, they say that practically all human beings, Greeks and barbarians, believe that the divine exists, and because of this they agree in making sacrifices and prayers and in erecting shrines for the gods even though they do this in different ways. So, although they hold in common the belief that something divine exists, they do not have the same basic grasp of its nature. But if this basic grasp were false, they would not all have agreed thus. Therefore, gods exist.

62. Besides, false opinions and ad hoc declarations do not stay around for a long time but last as long as those things for the sake of which they were maintained. For example, people honor kings with sacrifices and with all the other religious observances with which they revere <them> as gods. But they retain these only while the kings are alive, and as soon as they have died they abandon them as irreligious and impious. But the conception of the gods, at any rate, has always existed and persists forever, as is likely since they are testified to by events themselves. **63.** Moreover, even if one ought to ignore the

idiosyncratic ideas and ought to have confidence in the most talented and
wise men, one can see that the poetic art produces no great or luminous
work in which god is not the one who is endowed with power and authority
over events, just as he is in the poet Homer's writings about the war between
Greeks and barbarians. **64.** One can also see that the majority of natural philosophers are in agreement with the poets. For Pythagoras, Empedocles, the
Ionians, Socrates, Plato, Aristotle, the Stoics, and perhaps the philosophers
of the Garden (as the very words of Epicurus testify) all allow [the existence
of] god. **65.** Therefore, just as if we were investigating some visible object, it
would be reasonable to put our confidence in those with the keenest sight,
and if some audible object, those with the keenest hearing. So since we are
investigating a matter perceived by reason, we ought to put our confidence
in those with the keenest minds and reasoning ability, such as were these
philosophers. . . .

    74. . . . This, then, is the argument based on the common conception and
agreement in thinking about god. **75.** Let us then examine the argument
from the organization of the surrounding cosmos. Now, they say that the
substance of things [i.e., matter], being in itself immobile and shapeless,
requires some cause by which it is moved and shaped. And therefore just as
when we see a well-shaped work of bronze we long to know the craftsman—
since it is itself constituted of immobile matter—so, seeing the material of
the universe moving and endowed with form and organization, we might
reasonably inquire into the cause that moves it and shapes it variously. **76.** It
is not plausible to suppose this to be anything other than a power that pervades in the [same] way that our soul pervades us. So, this power is either
self-moving or moved by some other power. And if it is moved by some other
power, it will be impossible for the other power to be moved unless it is
moved by another, which is absurd. There is, then, some power, self-moving
in itself, which would be divine and everlasting. For either it will move itself
everlastingly or move itself beginning at some particular time. But it will not
move itself beginning at some particular time. For there will not be a cause of
its moving itself at some particular time. Therefore, the power that moves
matter and leads it in orderly fashion to generations and changes is everlasting. So, this is god.

    77. Further, that which generates rational and prudent beings is itself cer-
tainly rational and prudent. Indeed, the above-mentioned power is of the
nature to produce human beings, and so it will be rational and prudent, and
this is just what a divine nature is. Therefore, gods exist. . . .

    88. And Cleanthes argued as follows. If one nature is better than another,
there is some nature that is best. If one soul is better than another, there is
some soul that is best. And if one animal is better than another, there is some
animal that is best. For such [comparisons] are not of a nature to fall into an

infinite regress. So, just as nature could not be infinitely increased in greatness, so too neither could soul or animal. **89.** But one kind of animal is better than another, as, for example, the horse is better than the tortoise and the bull is better than the ass, and the lion better than the bull. And the human being, in his bodily and psychic disposition, excels and is the best of all the terrestrial animals. Therefore, there is some animal that is best and most excellent.

90. Yet a human cannot be the absolutely best animal, considering just the fact that he conducts his whole life in vice—and if not exactly his whole life, then the greatest part of it, for if he ever does get ahead in virtue, he does so late and in the evening of his life. His life is subject to fate and is weak and in need of countless things to assist him in living, such as food, shelter, and other kinds of care for the body, which importune him and exact daily tribute like a cruel tyrant. And if we do not render the body homage by washing, anointing, clothing, and feeding it, it threatens us with disease and death. So, a human being is not a perfect animal, but rather imperfect and far removed from perfection. **91.** But that which is perfect and best would be better than a human being, fulfilled in every virtue and impervious to all bad things. And this will not differ from god. Therefore, god exists. . . .

101. And Zeno of Citium, taking his inspiration from Xenophon, makes this argument. The thing which emits seed of something rational is also itself rational; but the cosmos emits seed of something rational; therefore, the cosmos is something rational. With this its existence is also established. **102.** The plausibility of the argument is manifest. For in every nature and soul the starting point for motion seems to come from the leading part of it, and all the powers which are sent out from the whole to the parts are sent out from the leading part as though from a wellspring, so that every power found in the part is also found in the whole, because it is distributed to [the parts] from the leading part in it. Hence, whatever powers the part has, the whole has too, and preeminently so. **103.** And for this reason, if the cosmos emits seed of a rational animal, [it does not do so as] a human being does by emitting a frothy substance, but rather [it does so] insofar as it contains seeds of rational animals. And it includes [them] not in the way we would say that the vine contains grape pits, i.e., by including them [in a derivative way], but rather because spermatic principles of rational animals are [directly] contained in it. So the sense of the argument is this: the cosmos contains spermatic principles of rational animals. Therefore, the cosmos is rational.

104. And again Zeno says, "The rational is better than what is not rational; but nothing is better than the cosmos; therefore, the cosmos is something rational." And [he argues] in the same way for its being intelligent and animate: "For the intelligent is better than what is not intelligent, and the animate is better than what is not animate; but nothing is better than the cosmos; therefore, the cosmos is intelligent and animate." . . .

108. But Alexinus attacked Zeno thus: "What is poetic is better than what is not poetic and what is grammatical is better than what is not grammatical and what possesses theoretical knowledge in the other crafts is better than what is not like that; but no one thing is better than the cosmos; therefore, the cosmos is something poetic and grammatical." **109.** The Stoics respond to this attack by saying that Zeno was referring to what is better in an absolute sense—i.e., the rational [is better] than what is not rational and the intelligent than what is not intelligent and the animate than what is not animate—but that Alexinus was not [speaking in this sense]; **110.** for the poetic is not better than what is not poetic in the absolute sense, nor is the grammatical [better] than what is not grammatical [in this sense]. Consequently, a great difference can be observed in the arguments. Think about it: Archilochus, although he is poetic, is not better than Socrates, who is not; and Aristarchus, although he is a grammarian, is not better than Plato, who is not.

111. In addition to these arguments, the Stoics and those who agree with them try to establish the existence of the gods from the motion of the cosmos. For anyone would agree on the basis of many considerations that the entire cosmos is in motion. **112.** So, it is moved either by nature or intention or by the necessity of a vortex. But it is not reasonable that it should be moved by the necessity of a vortex. For the vortex is either orderly or disorderly. If it is disorderly, it would not be able to move something in an orderly way. And if it moves something in an orderly and harmonious way, it will be something divine and supernatural. **113.** For the universe would not have been able to move something in an orderly way that preserves it if it were not intelligent and divine. And being such, it would no longer be a vortex, for a vortex is something disorderly and lasts for a short time. So, the cosmos would not be moved according to the necessity of a vortex, as Democritus and his followers said. **114.** Nor is it moved by a nature deprived of the power of presentation since intelligent nature is better than this, and such natures are seen to be contained in the cosmos. Therefore, it necessarily has an intelligent nature by which it is moved in an orderly way, which evidently is a god. . . .

123. This, then, is the nature of these arguments. Let us then examine next the kind of absurd consequences that follow for those who reject the divine.

If the gods do not exist, there is no piety—which is one of the virtues. . . . [Here there is a corrupt phrase.] For piety is the knowledge of how to serve gods, and it is not possible for there to be service to non-existent things; hence there will be no knowledge of such service. Just as it is not possible for there to be knowledge of how to serve non-existent entities like hippocentaurs, so, if the gods do not exist, there will be no knowledge of how to serve them. So, if the gods do not exist, piety is non-existent. But piety exists. Therefore, the existence of gods ought to be declared.

124. Again, if gods do not exist, holiness is non-existent, holiness being a sort of justice in relation to gods. Indeed, holiness exists according to the common conceptions and basic grasps of all human beings, insofar as something holy exists. Therefore, the divine exists. **125.** But if gods do not exist, wisdom, the knowledge of divine and human things, is abolished. And since there is no [generic] knowledge of human and hippocentaurian things, for one exists and the other does not, so there will be no [generic] knowledge of divine and human things, if humans exist but gods do not. But it is absurd to say that wisdom does not exist. Therefore, it is absurd to hold that gods do not exist.

126. Further, if justice has been introduced for the sake of the interrelation of human beings with each other and with gods, if gods do not exist, neither will justice endure. And that is absurd. . . .

133. Zeno offered this sort of argument. One might reasonably honor the gods. <But one might not reasonably honor the non-existent.> Therefore, gods exist. Some counter this argument by saying that one might reasonably honor wise men; but one might not reasonably honor non-existent things; therefore, wise men exist. But this was not acceptable to the Stoics; for according to them, the wise man is hitherto undiscovered. **134.** Opposing this counterargument, Diogenes of Babylon says that the second premise of Zeno's argument is implicitly this: one might not reasonably honor things whose nature it is not to exist. For understanding [the premise] in this way, it is clear that the gods are of such a nature as to exist. **135.** And if so, then they thereby exist. For if once they existed, they exist now, just as, if atoms once existed, they exist now. For such things are indestructible and ungenerated, according to our conception of their bodies. Therefore, the argument will conclude with a consistent logical connection. But wise men, even though they are of such a nature as to exist, do not thereby exist. **136.** Others say that Zeno's first premise, 'one might reasonably honor the gods', is ambiguous. For in one sense it means that it may be reasonable for someone to worship gods, but in another sense it means someone may hold them in high regard. The premise is to be taken in the former sense, in which case it will be false as applied to wise men.

137. Such is the character of the arguments furnished by the Stoics and by the disciples of other systems on behalf of the existence of gods.

Bodily and Non-bodily Realities

TEXT 34: Sextus Empiricus *M* 8.263

According to them, the incorporeal can neither do anything nor have anything done to it.

TEXT 35: Aëtius 1.3.25 (Pseudo-Plutarch *On the Doctrines*
   of the Philosophers 878b = *Dox. Gr.* p. 289)

Zeno of Citium, son of Mnaseas, says the principles are god and matter, the
former being responsible for acting, the latter for being acted upon. And there
are four elements.

TEXT 36: Achilles *Introduction to Aratus* 3.1–3

Zeno of Citium says that the principle of the universe is god and matter, god
being the active and matter that which is acted upon. From these the four elements came into being.

TEXT 37: Cicero *Academica,* book 1 (Varro) 39

[Zeno] held this view about the elements [lit., natures]. First, he did not
include the fifth element, which is what his predecessors thought the senses
and mind are made of alongside the established four elements [earth, air, fire,
water]. For he claimed that fire itself is the element which generates everything, including the mind and the senses. Moreover, he disagreed with these
same predecessors in that he thought it totally impossible for anything to be
effected by what lacked body (which is the kind of thing that Xenocrates and
his predecessors had said that even the mind is) and indeed that whatever
effected something or was affected by something must be body.

TEXT 38: Aëtius 1.10.5 (Pseudo-Plutarch *On the Doctrines*
   of the Philosophers 882e = *Dox. Gr.* p. 309)

Zeno's followers, the Stoics, said that the Ideas [i.e., Platonic Forms] are our
own thoughts.

TEXT 39: Syrianus *Commentary on Aristotle's Metaphysics*
   1078b12 (*CIAG* 6.1, pp. 105.22–23)

. . . that the Forms were not introduced, as Chrysippus and Archedemus and
the majority of the Stoics thought, by these godlike men [Socrates, Plato, the
Parmenideans, and the Pythagoreans] to account for our customary use of the
names of things [i.e., common nouns] . . .

TEXT 40: Seneca *Letters on Ethics* 58.11–15 (selections)

11. Moreover, there is something higher than body; for we say that some
things are corporeal, some incorporeal. What, therefore, is that from which
these are derived? That to which we just now assigned the technical term 'that
which is'. It will be divided into species so that we say 'that which is' is either

corporeal or incorporeal. **12.** . . . That genus, 'that which is', has no genus above it; it is the first principle of things; everything is subordinate to it. **13.** But the Stoics want to set yet another genus above this one, which is a higher principle; I will speak of it now. . . . **15.** Some Stoics held that the first genus is the 'something'; I shall add an explanation of why they held this. They say that in the nature of things, some things are and some are not; and nature also includes those things which are not but which occur to our mind, such as Centaurs, Giants, and whatever, being formed by a false concept, begins to take on a certain image [in our minds] although it does not have substance.

TEXT 41: Alexander of Aphrodisias *Commentary on Arisotle's Topics* 121a10, 127a26 (*CIAG* 2.2, pp. 301.19–25, 359.12–16)

301.19 In this way you might show that the Stoics do not properly posit the something as a genus of 'that which is'; for obviously, if it is a something, it is something which is. And if it is something which is, then the definition of being would apply to it. But they made an idiosyncratic stipulation to the effect that 'that which is' applies only to bodies and so tried to evade the paradox. For thus they say that the 'something' is its highest genus and is predicated not just of bodies but also of incorporeals. . . . **359.12** In this way it will be shown that the something is not the genus of everything. For it will also be the genus of the one, which is either coextensive with it or of even wider extent, if indeed the one also applies to the concept; but the something applies only to bodies and incorporeals, whereas the concept, according to the proponents of this theory, is neither of these.

TEXT 42: Sextus Empiricus *M* 10.218

The Stoics, though, thought that time is incorporeal. For they say that of 'somethings' some are bodies and some are incorporeals, and they listed four kinds of incorporeals: *lekton* [thing said] and void and place and time. From which it is clear that in addition to supposing that time is incorporeal they also believe that it is a thing conceived of as existing on its own.

TEXT 43: Plutarch *On Common Conceptions* 1081c–1082a (selections)

(1081c) It is paradoxical for the future and past time to exist and for present time not to exist, but for the recent and more remote past to subsist and for the 'now' not to exist at all. But this result does obtain for the Stoics, who do not allow a minimal time to exist and do not want to have a partless 'now'; but they say that whatever one thinks one has grasped and conceived as present is in part future and in part past. Consequently there neither remains nor is left in the 'now' any part of present time **(1081d)** if the time which is called 'present' is divided up, some of it being future and some past. . . .

(1081f) . . . Chrysippus wishing to be subtle about the division [of time] says in his *On Void* and in some other writings that the past part of time and the future part do not exist but subsist and only the present exists. But in the third, fourth, and fifth books of *On Parts,* he posits that part of the present time is future and part is past. **(1082a)** Consequently, it turns out that he divides the existing part of time into the non-existing parts and the existing part; or rather, he leaves absolutely no part of time in existence if the present has no part that is not future or past.

TEXT 44: Stobaeus *Anthology* 1.8.42 (vol. 1, pp. 105.17–106.23 W-H)

Posidonius: Some things are infinite in every respect, such as time as a whole. Others are infinite in a particular respect, such as past time and future time. For both of these are limited only by the present. And he defines time thus: it is the interval of motion or the measure of speed and slowness, and this accords with our conception. And with respect to the 'when', part of time is past, part is future, and part is present (which is established partly of the past and partly of the future around the division itself; and the division is point-like). And the 'now' and similar expressions are time understood in a broad sense and not with precision. The 'now' and the minimal perceptible time are established around the division between future and past.

Chrysippus: Chrysippus says that time is the interval of motion according to which the measure of speed and slowness is sometimes spoken of; or, time is the interval which accompanies the motion of the cosmos. And each and every thing is said to move and to exist in accordance with time, unless of course time is spoken of in two senses, as are earth and sea and void and the universe and its parts. And just as void as a whole is infinite in every direction, so too time as a whole is infinite in both directions; for both the past and the future are infinite. He says most clearly that no time is wholly present; for since the divisibility of continuous things is infinite, time as a whole is also subject to infinite divisibility by this method of division. Consequently, no time is present in the strictest sense but only in a broad sense. He says that only the present exists, whereas the past and future subsist but do not at all exist— unless it is in the way that predicates are said to exist, though only those that actually apply; for example, walking 'exists for me' when I am walking, but when I am reclining or sitting it does not 'exist for me'. . . .

TEXT 45: Aëtius 1.18.5, 1.20.1 (Stobaeus *Anthology* 1.18.1d,
         Pseudo-Plutarch *On the Doctrines of the Philosophers*
         884a–b = *Dox. Gr.* pp. 316, 317)

1.18.5 Zeno and his followers say that there is no void within the cosmos but an indefinite void outside it. . . . **1.20.1** The Stoics and Epicurus say that void, place, and space are different. Void is the privation of body, place is what is occupied by body, and space is what is partly occupied, as in the case of wine in a jar.

TEXT 46: Aëtius 2.9.3 (Stobaeus *Anthology* 1.18.4b = *Dox. Gr.* p. 338)

Posidonius said that [the void] outside the cosmos is not infinite but as much as suffices for the dissolution [of the cosmos at conflagration].

TEXT 47: Stobaeus *Anthology* 1.18.4d (vol. 1, pp. 161.8–26 W-H)

Chrysippus proclaimed that place is that which is occupied throughout by what exists or what is such as to be occupied by what exists and is occupied throughout by some thing or things. And if what is such as to be occupied is partly occupied by what exists and partly not, the whole will be neither void nor place, but another unnamed thing. For the void is spoken of similarly to empty containers, and place similarly to full ones.

Is space what is such as to be occupied by what is, only bigger, and, as it were, a larger container for a body, or is it what has space for a larger body? Anyway, the void is said to be unlimited. For what is outside the cosmos is like this and place is limited because no body is unlimited. Just as the bodily is limited, so the incorporeal is unlimited, for time is unlimited and so is void. For just as the nothing is no limit, so [there is no limit] of the nothing, which is what the void is like. For it is unlimited in its own substance. And again, this is limited by being filled. If what fills it is removed, it is not possible to conceive of a limit for it.

TEXT 48: Sextus Empiricus *M* 8.11–12

11. . . . And there was yet another quarrel among the dogmatists; for some located the true and false in the thing signified, some located it in the utterance, and some in the motion of the intellect. And the Stoics championed the first view, saying that three things are linked with one another: the thing signified, the signifier, and the object. **12.** Of these, the signifier is the utterance, for example, 'Dion'. The thing signified is the thing indicated by the utterance and which we grasp when it subsists in our intellect and which foreigners do not understand although they hear the utterance. The object is the external existent, for example, Dion himself. Two of these are bodies, the utterance and the object, and one incorporeal, the signified thing, i.e., the thing said [*lekton*] which is true or false. This last point is not of unrestricted application, but some *lekta* are incomplete and some complete. One kind of complete *lekton* is the so-called proposition, which they describe thus: a proposition is that which is true or false.

Text 49: Sextus Empiricus *M* 8.70

They say that what subsists in accordance with a rational presentation is a thing said [*lekton*] and that a rational presentation is one according to which the content of a presentation can be made available to reason.

Text 50: Ammonius *Commentary on Aristotle's De*
                Interpretatione 16a3 (*CIAG* 4.5 pp. 17.24–28)

Here [*De Interpretatione*] Aristotle teaches what is primarily and immediately signified by utterances, saying that it is thoughts and that through these as intermediaries, objects are signified. And we need think of nothing beyond these which is between the thought and the object. But the Stoics hypothesized that such a thing exists and thought it should be called a 'thing said'.

Text 51: Seneca *Letters on Ethics* 117.2–3

2. Our school believes that the good is a body because that which is good acts and whatever acts is a body. What is good benefits [someone], but for something to benefit [someone] it ought to act, and if it acts, it is a body. They say that wisdom is good; it follows that it is also necessary to say that it is corporeal. **3.** But being wise is not in the same category. It is an incorporeal attribute of something else, namely, wisdom; consequently, it neither acts nor benefits [anyone]. "What then?" he says, "Do we not say that being wise is good?" We do say so but only by reference to that on which it depends, i.e., to wisdom itself.

Text 52: Stobaeus *Anthology* 1.13.1c (vol. 1, pp. 138.14–22 W-H)

Zeno says that a cause is "that because of which." That of which it is the cause is an event [or accident]. And the cause is a body and that of which it is the cause is a predicate. It is impossible for the cause to be present and that of which it is the cause not to be the case. What is said amounts to this: a cause is that because of which something comes about; for example, prudent thinking occurs because of prudence, living because of soul, and temperate behavior because of temperance. For if someone has temperance or soul or prudence, it is impossible for there not to be temperate behavior, life, or prudent thinking.

Text 53: Sextus Empiricus *M* 9.211

. . . The Stoics say that every cause is a body which causes something incorporeal in a body. For example, a scalpel, which is a body, causes in flesh, which is a body, the incorporeal predicate 'being cut'. Again, fire, which is a body, causes in wood, which is a body, the incorporeal predicate 'being burned'.

TEXT 54: Sextus Empiricus *PH* 3.13–16

13. In order that the dogmatists should not turn to slander against us because of a poverty of substantive counterarguments, we shall consider in a more general way the efficient cause after first attempting to understand the conception of cause. As far as concerns what is said by the dogmatists, it would not be possible for someone to conceive of the cause if, at any rate, account is taken of their disagreements and strange conceptions of the cause, but also given that they have made its existence undiscoverable because of their disagreement regarding it. **14.** For some say that the cause is a body and some say it is incorporeal. Generally, according to them, the cause would seem to be that because of whose activity the effect comes about, for example, the sun or the sun's heat is the cause of the fact that the wax melts or of the melting of the wax. And even on this they have disagreed: some saying the cause is the cause of nouns, for example, 'the melting'; others saying that the cause is the cause of predicates, for example, 'the wax melts'. Therefore, as I just said, generally, the cause would be that because of whose activity the effect comes about.

15. The majority of them think that some of these causes are sustaining, some joint causes, and some auxiliary. Sustaining causes are those whose presence makes the effect present, whose absence brings about the absence of the effect, and whose diminution diminishes the effect (thus they say that the binding of the halter is the cause of the strangulation). A joint cause is one that brings to bear a force equal to that of another joint cause for the effect's existence (thus they say that each of the oxen drawing the plow is a cause of the plow's being drawn). An auxiliary cause is one that brings to bear a little force and so makes easy the existence of the effect, for example, whenever two men are lifting a heavy load with difficulty, when a third comes along, his assistance lightens the load.

16. Some, however, have said that things present are causes of things future, so as to be antecedents, for example, intensive exposure to the sun producing fever. Some reject this, since cause is relative to something [presently] existing, i.e., to the effect, and is not able to precede it as its cause.

TEXT 55: Simplicius *Commentary on Aristotle's Categories*
1b25 (*CIAG* vol. 8, pp. 66.32–67.2)

The Stoics think it right to reduce the number of primary categories. And among this reduced number they include some which have been changed. For they divide them into four: substrates [underlying things], and qualities [qualified things], dispositions [things in a certain state], and relative dispositions [things in a certain state with respect to something]. . .

TEXT 56: Galen *On Incorporeal Qualities* 1

There was a discussion of qualities and of all accidents, which the Stoics say are bodies.

TEXT 57: Aëtius 1.15.6 (Pseudo-Plutarch *On the Doctrines of the Philosophers* 883c = *Dox. Gr.* p. 313)

Zeno the Stoic says that colors are primary arrangements of matter.

TEXT 58: Galen *Commentary on Hippocrates on Humors* 1

Zeno of Citium believed that, like qualities, substances were totally mixed.

TEXT 59: Aëtius 4.20.2 (Pseudo-Plutarch *On the Doctrines of the Philosophers* 902f–903a = *Dox. Gr.* p. 410)

The Stoics say that voice is a body. For everything which acts or has effects is a body. And voice acts and has effects. For we hear it and perceive it striking our ears and making an impression like a seal-ring on wax. Again, everything which stimulates or disturbs is a body; and good music stimulates us and bad music disturbs us. Again, everything which is in motion is a body; and voice is in motion and strikes smooth surfaces and is reflected as in the case of a ball thrown against a wall. At any rate, inside the Egyptian pyramids, one utterance produces four or even five echoes.

Structures and Powers

TEXT 60: Origen *On Principles* 3.1.2–3

2. Of things that move, some have the cause of motion in themselves, whereas others are moved only from the outside. Thus things which are moved by being carried, such as sticks and stones and every form of matter held together by *hexis* [condition] alone, are moved from the outside. . . . Plants and animals, and in a word everything held together by nature and soul have within themselves the cause of motion. They say that this category includes veins of metal and, in addition, that fire and perhaps springs of water are also self-moved. Of things which contain the cause of motion in themselves, they say that some move from themselves and others by themselves. 'From themselves' applies to soulless objects, 'by themselves' to things with soul. For ensouled things move by themselves when a presentation occurs that stimulates the impulse. . . . **3.** But the rational animal has reason too in addition to the power of presentation. Reason judges the presentations and rejects some and admits others.

TEXT 61: Origen *On Prayer* 6.1

Of things that move, some have the mover external to them as do soulless things and those held together by *hexis* [condition] alone. And those things that move by nature or by soul sometimes also move not as beings of this sort but in a manner similar to those held together by *hexis* alone. For stones and sticks, [i.e.,] things which are cut off from a vein of metal or have lost the power to grow, are held together only by *hexis* and have their motive power external to them. And the bodies of animals and the moveable parts of plants that are shifted by someone are not shifted qua animal or plant but in a manner similar to sticks and stones which have lost the power to grow. . . . After those, second are those objects moved by the nature or the soul within them, which are also said to move 'from themselves' by those who use words in their stricter senses [i.e., the Stoics]. Third is the motion in animals which is termed motion 'by itself'. I think that the motion of rational animals is motion 'through themselves'. And if we deprive an animal of motion 'by itself' it is impossible to go on thinking of it as an animal. Rather, it will be similar either to a plant moved only by nature or to a stone carried along by an external agent. And if the animal is aware of its own motion, this animal must be rational since we have called this motion 'through itself'.

TEXT 62: Simplicius *Commentary on Aristotle's Categories*
1b1 (*CIAG* vol. 8, pp. 306.19–27)

They [the Stoics] say that the differences between kinds [of motion] are [1] moving 'from themselves', as a knife has the ability to cut because of its special structure (for the doing is carried out in accordance with its shape and form); [2] and the activation of motion 'through oneself', as natural organisms and curative powers carry out their action (for the seed is sown and unfolds its proper [rational] principle and attracts the matter nearby and fashions the principles in it); [3] and also doing 'by oneself', which in general terms is doing by a thing's own impulse. But another sense [4] is doing by a rational impulse, which is called 'action'. And [5] even more specific than this is activity according to virtue.

TEXT 63: Plutarch *On Stoic Self-Contradictions* 1053f–1054b

(**1053f**) . . . again in *On Conditions* [Chrysippus] says that conditions [*hexeis*] are nothing but [parcels] of air. For bodies are held together by these, and it is air which holds together and is responsible for the quality of each of the things held together by a condition. They call this air 'hardness' in iron, 'denseness' in stone, 'whiteness' in silver. (**1054a**) . . . And yet they claim all the time that matter, which is in itself inactive and unmoving, underlies the qualities and that the qualities, which are *pneumata* and airy tensions, produce forms and shapes **(1054b)** in whatever parts of matter they are in.

TEXT 64: Pseudo-Galen *Introduction* 9, 13

9. According to the ancients, there are two [forms of] *pneuma:* that of the soul and that of nature. And the Stoics add a third, that of *hexis,* which they call a condition. . . .

13. There are two forms of the inborn *pneuma,* that of nature and that of soul; and some add a third, that of *hexis.* The *pneuma* which holds things is what makes stones cohere [hold together], whereas that of nature is what nourishes animals and plants and that of the soul is that which, in animate objects, makes animals capable of sense-perception and of every kind of movement.

TEXT 65: Calcidius *Commentary on Plato's Timaeus* (selections)

c. 290

But several philosophers distinguish matter and substance, such as Zeno and Chrysippus. They say that matter is that which underlies all those things which have qualities; however, the primary matter of all things or their most primeval foundation is substance—being in itself without qualities and unformed. For example, bronze, gold, iron, etc. are matter of those things that are manufactured from them, but are not substance. But that which is cause of the existence of both the former and the latter is itself substance.

c. 292

Then Zeno said that this substance itself is finite and that only this substance is common to all things which exist, but that it is divisible and changeable in every place. Its parts change but do not perish in such a way that they turn into nothing from being existents. But he thinks that there is no form or shape or quality which is proper to the foundation of the matter of all things (just as there is no proper shape for the innumerable shapes which wax too takes on) but that nevertheless this matter is always joined with and inseparably bonded to some quality. And since it is as birthless as it is deathless because it neither comes into being from the non-existent nor turns into nothing, it does not lack an eternal spirit [*pneuma*] and liveliness that will move it in a rational manner—sometimes all of it, sometimes a proportional part of it— and that is the cause of such frequent and powerful changes in the universe. Moreover, this spirit that moves will not be nature but soul—and indeed rational soul, which gives life to this sentient cosmos and gave it the beauty that is now visible. And they call this [i.e., the cosmos] a happy animal and a god.

c. 294

[The Stoics say] that god is that which matter is or that god is the inseparable quality of matter and that he moves through matter just as semen moves
through the genital organs.

TEXT 66: Stobaeus *Anthology* 1.11.5a (vol. 1, pp. 132.27–133.5 W-H)

Zeno: The primary matter of all things which exist is substance and all of this
is everlasting and becomes neither greater nor smaller. Its parts do not always
stay the same but are divided and fused together. Through this runs the rational principle of the universe, which some call 'fate', being just like the seed in
seminal fluid.

TEXT 67: Alexander of Aphrodisias *On Mixture*
(*CIAG* 2.2, pp. 224.32–225.9)

At this point in the argument one might charge that, while saying that there
are two principles for all things, matter and god, the latter being active and the
former passive, they [the Stoics] also say that god is mixed with matter,
extending through all of it and shaping it, forming it, and making it into a
cosmos in this manner. If, according to them, god is a body, being intelligent
and everlasting *pneuma,* and matter too is a body then in the first place a body
once more will extend through a body. And second, this *pneuma* will either be
one of the four simple bodies which they also call 'elements' or a compound
mixture of them, as they themselves also seem to say, I suppose (for they postulate that the substance of the *pneuma* is composed of air and fire); or if it is
something else, then the divine body will be some fifth substance.

TEXT 68: Alexander of Aphrodisias *On Mixture*
(*CIAG* 2.2, pp. 223.25–224.14)

. . . This being so, how could it be true that the totality is unified and held
together because some *pneuma* extends through all of it? Next, it would be reasonable that the coherence produced by the *pneuma* should be found in all bodies; but this is not so. For some bodies are coherent and some discrete. Therefore,
it is more reasonable to say that each of them is held together and unified with
itself by the individual form in virtue of which each of them has its being and
that their sympathy with each other is preserved by means of their communion
with the matter and the nature of the divine body that surrounds it, rather than
by the bond of the *pneuma.* For what is this 'pneumatic tension' by which things
are bound and so both possess coherence with their own parts and are linked to
adjacent objects? For [according to the Stoics] it is when *pneuma* is forced by
something that it takes on a kind of strength as a result of the concentrated

movement, because it is naturally suited to this (since owing to its flexibility it can offer no resistance to what moves it). And being flexible in its own nature it is fluid and easily divisible, and so too is the nature of all other things with which *pneuma* is mixed; it is in virtue of *pneuma* above all that they are divided so very easily. For this reason, at any rate, some thought it was something void and an intangible nature, whereas others thought it had a lot of void in it.

Moreover, if the *pneuma,* which holds bodies together, is the cause of their persistence and not disintegrating, it is clear that bodies which do disintegrate would not possess *pneuma* binding them together.

And how, in the first place, could the divisibility of bodies be preserved if division is the separation of what is united, and according to them all things stay united with each other, all the same even when they are divided? And how could one avoid the inconsistency of saying that objects which are adjacent to each other and can easily be separated from each other are all the same united with each other, being coherent and never being able to be separated from each other without division?

TEXT 69: Plotinus *Enneads* 2.4.1.6–14

And those who postulate that the only things that exist are bodies and that substance consists in them say that matter is one and that it underlies the elements and that matter itself is substance. All other things are, as it were, modifications of matter and even the elements are matter in a certain state. Moreover, they dare to bring matter into the realm of the gods. And finally, they say that their god himself is this matter in a certain state, and they give it [matter] a body, saying that body itself is qualitiless, and magnitude too.

TEXT 70: Aristocles, in Eusebius *Prep. Ev.* 15.14

They say that fire is an element of the things that exist, as does Heraclitus, and that the principles of this are matter and god (as Plato said). But he [Zeno] said that both (the active and the passive) were bodies, whereas Plato's first active cause was said to be incorporeal. And then, at certain fated times, the entire cosmos goes up in flames and then is organized again. And the primary fire is like a kind of seed, containing the rational principles and cause of all things and events, past, present, and future. And the interconnection and sequence of these things is fate and knowledge and truth and an inescapable and inevitable law of what exists. Thus, all things in the cosmos are organized extremely well, as in a very well-managed government.

TEXT 71: Stobaeus *Anthology* 1.10.16c (vol. 1, pp. 129.1–130.20 W-H)

Chrysippus. Concerning the elements which come from substance, he holds views of this sort, following Zeno the leader of the school. He says there are four elements, <fire, air, water, and earth, from which all animals are formed> and plants and the whole cosmos and the things contained in it and into which these same things are resolved. And <fire> is said to be an element par excellence because the others are first formed from it by qualitative change and finally are dissolved and resolved into it, whereas fire itself is not subject to dissolution or breakdown into anything else. So, on this theory fire is said independently to be an element, since it is not formed together with another one, whereas according to the earlier theory fire is formed with other elements. For first there occurs the change in form from fire to air, second occurs the analogous change from water to earth. Again, from earth as it is resolved and dissolved, the first dissolution is into water, second from water to air, third and last to fire. Everything fiery is called 'fire', and everything airy 'air', and so forth. 'Element' is used in three senses by Chrysippus: in one sense fire is the element since the others are formed from it by change of quality and the breakdown is back into fire. In another sense there are said to be four elements (fire, air, water, and earth) since from one or more of these or all of them everything else is formed: through the four, for example, animals and all terrestrial compounds; through two, for example, the moon is formed of fire and air; or through one, as the sun which is formed of only fire, the sun being pure fire. And a third sense [There is a lacuna here.] to be what was first formed in this way, so that it methodically produced generation from itself until the end [was reached] and [then returning] from that point it received the breakdown into itself by the same method. And he said that there have also been the following descriptions of the element: that it is most mobile on its own, and the principle <and the spermatic> principle and the eternal power, which has a nature such as to move itself both downward toward conversion and upward away from the conversion again in a complete circle, both absorbing all things into itself and again restoring them from itself in a regular and methodical way.

TEXT 72: Seneca *Letters on Ethics* 92.30

Why shouldn't you think that there is something divine in him who is a part of god? All of that which contains us is one and is god. And we are his allies and parts.

The Soul

TEXT 73: Nemesius *On Human Nature* 2 (pp. 16.12–16 Morani)

Practically all the ancients disagree on the theory of the soul. For Democritus and Epicurus and the entire Stoic school claim that the soul is a body. And these same people who claim that the soul is a body disagree about its substance. For the Stoics say it is a warm and fiery *pneuma*.

TEXT 74: Eusebius *Prep. Ev.* 15.20.6–7

... They say the soul is generated and destroyed; it is not destroyed as soon as it leaves the body but lasts for a while on its own. The soul of the virtuous man lasts until the breakdown of everything into fire but that of fools [only] for a certain length of time. They say that the enduring of souls works like this, i.e., that we last by becoming souls separated from the body, changing into a more limited substance, that of the soul. But the souls of imprudent and irrational animals are destroyed together with their bodies. . . .

TEXT 75: Nemesius *On Human Nature* 2 (pp. 22.3–6 Morani)

And Chrysippus says: Death is a separation of soul from body. But nothing incorporeal can be separated from a body. For neither does anything incorporeal touch a body, and the soul both touches and is separated from the body. Therefore the soul is not incorporeal.

TEXT 76: Tertullian *On the Soul* 5.3

Then Zeno, defining the soul as the inborn *pneuma* [*spiritus*], teaches as follows: that, he says, because of the departure of which the animal dies, is a body. But when the inborn *pneuma* departs, the animal dies. But the inborn *pneuma* is the soul. Therefore, the soul is a body.

TEXT 77: Alexander of Aphrodisias *De Anima* (*CIAG* 2.1, pp. 18.27–19.1) and *De Anima Mantissa* (*CIAG* 2.1, pp. 117–118.2; selections)

De Anima (*CIAG* 2.1, pp. 18.27–19.1)

[Alexander cites and rejects Stoic arguments.]
   Nor does the argument which says, 'That of which a part is a body is itself also a body; but perception is a part of soul and is a body; so [the soul] itself is a body', prove anything.

De Anima Mantissa (*CIAG* 2.1, pp. 117–118.2; selections)

117.1–2. For it [the soul] is not a body just because the same thing is predicated of it [as of the body].—**117.9–11.** But the argument which says that something incorporeal does not share an experience with a body and purports to show that the soul is not incorporeal, is also false.—**117.21–23.** Nor is the argument sound that says that nothing incorporeal is separated from a body, but the soul is separated from the body, so that it is not incorporeal. —**117.28–29.** Nor is it true to say that only those things which touch each other can be separated from each other.—**117.30–118.2.** Nor is this true: 'we are animate because of that by which we breathe; but we are animate because of the soul'. Not even if [it is true] that animals cannot exist without inborn *pneuma* does it follow that this is the soul.

TEXT 78:   Galen *On the Habits of the Soul* 4

For they [the Stoics] claim that the soul is a kind of *pneuma*, as is nature too; the *pneuma* of nature is more fluid and cool, whereas that of the soul is drier and hotter. Consequently, [they also think this]: that *pneuma* is a kind of matter proper to the soul, and in form the matter is a qualified blend of airy and fiery substance that comes to be in symmetry. For it is not possible to say that it is either air alone or fire alone, since the body of an animal does not appear to be either extremely cold or extremely hot, but rather it is not even dominated by a great excess of either of these. For if there is even a minor deviation from symmetry [in the blend] the animal becomes feverish because of the unmeasured excess of fire, and it becomes chilled and livid, or completely incapable of sense-perception as a result of blending [excessively] with the air. For [air] itself in its own right is cold and becomes temperate as a result of mixture with the fiery element. So, it is immediately clear that the substance of the soul is a certain kind of blend of air and fire, according to the Stoics, and that Chrysippus was rendered intelligent because of a temperate mixture of these [elements].

TEXT 79:   Nemesius *On Human Nature* 2 (pp. 20.14–21.9 Morani)

Cleanthes weaves a syllogism of this sort: "Not only," he says, "are we like our parents in respect to the body but also in respect to the soul, in our passions, characters, and dispositions; but similarity and dissimilarity are [properties] of body and not of the incorporeal; therefore, the soul is a body." . . . Again, [Cleanthes] says, "Nothing incorporeal shares an experience with a body, nor does a body with an incorporeal; but the soul suffers with the body when it is ill and when it is cut, and the body [suffers] with the soul—at any rate when [the soul] is ashamed it [the body] turns red, and pale when [the soul] is frightened; therefore, the soul is a body."

TEXT 80:   Aëtius 4.21.1–4 (Pseudo-Plutarch *On the Doctrines of the Philosophers* 903a–c = *Dox. Gr.* pp. 410–11)

   1. The Stoics say that the leading part [of the soul], i.e., that which produces presentations and assents and sense-perceptions and impulses, is the highest part of the soul. And they call this 'reason'. **2.** Seven parts grow out of the leading part and extend to the body, just like the tentacles from the octopus. Of the seven parts of the soul, five are the senses—sight, smell, hearing, taste, and touch. **3.** Of these, sight is a *pneuma* extending from the leading part to the eyes, hearing a *pneuma* extending from the leading part to the ears, smell a *pneuma* extending from the leading part to the nostrils, taste a *pneuma* extending from the leading part to the tongue, and touch a *pneuma* extending from the leading part to the surface [of the skin] for the sensible contact with objects. **4.** Of the remaining parts, one is called 'seed', which is itself a *pneuma* extending from the leading part to the testicles and the other, which was called 'vocal' by Zeno (which they also call 'voice'), is a *pneuma* extending from the leading part to the throat and tongue and the related organs. The leading part itself, like <the sun> in the cosmos, dwells in our head, which is round.

TEXT 81: Calcidius *Commentary on Plato's Timaeus*

c. 220

The Stoics grant that the heart is the seat of the leading part of the soul but nevertheless that it is not the blood which is created together with the body. To be sure, Zeno argues that the soul is *pneuma* thus: that whose withdrawal from the body causes the animal to die is certainly the soul; furthermore, the animal dies when the inborn *pneuma* withdraws; therefore, the inborn *pneuma* is the soul.

TEXT 82: Plotinus *Enneads* 4.7.7.2–5

When a human is said to be in pain with respect to his finger, the pain is surely in the finger, whereas surely they [the Stoics] will admit that the perception of pain is in the leading part of the soul. Though the distressed part is different from the *pneuma,* it is the leading part which perceives and the whole soul suffers the same experience. How then does this happen? They will say, by a transmission of the *pneuma* of the soul in the finger which suffered first and passed it on to the next *pneuma* and this one to another, until it arrives at the leading part.

TEXT 83: Philo *On the Posterity of Cain* 126

No one, at least no one in his senses, would say that the eyes see but rather that the mind [sees] through the eyes, nor that the ears hear, but that the mind [hears] through the ears, nor that the nostrils smell but that the leading part of the soul [smells] through the nostrils.

TEXT 84: Cicero *Tusculan Disputations* 1.79–80

79. . . . So, are we to believe Panaetius when he disagrees with his hero Plato? He refers to Plato everywhere as being divine, most wise, most holy, the very Homer of philosophers, but even so he does not accept this one view of Plato's: the immortality of souls.[17] He holds—and this no one denies—that everything which is born passes away. But souls are born, as is shown by resemblance to the parents that is manifest not just in bodies but also in mental attributes. He uses another argument: everything which feels pain can become ill, and what gets sick will also die; but souls feel pain and so they die. **80.** These arguments can be rebutted. For they come from someone who does not know that when we are discussing the eternity of souls we are discussing a mind which is always free of all violent movements and not about the parts in which grief, anger, and lust arise. My opponent in this debate thinks that these feelings are separated and shut out from the mind.

TEXT 85: Nemesius *On Human Nature* 15 (pp. 72.9–11 Morani)

The philosopher Panaetius holds that the vocal capacity is part of the voluntary movement [of the soul], and he is quite right. And the reproductive capacity is not a part of soul but rather of nature.

Fate

TEXT 86: Aëtius 1.29.7 (Pseudo-Plutarch *On the Doctrines of the Philosophers* 885c = *Dox. Gr.* p. 326)

Anaxagoras and the Stoics say that chance is a cause non-evident to human calculation. For some things happen by necessity, some by fate, some by intention, some by chance, and some automatically.

TEXT 87: Theodoretus *Graecarum Affectionum Cura* 6.14

And Chrysippus the Stoic said that what is necessitated is no different from what is fated and that fate is an eternal, continuous, and ordered motion [or change]. Zeno of Citium called fate a power capable of moving matter and gave to the same [force] the names 'providence' and 'nature'. His successors

---

17. The term here is *animus*, normally translated as "mind," but here it is contrasted with *mens* in § 80, a term that must be translated as "mind." Cicero's argument here is difficult, but it does seem safe to conclude that Panaetius rejected Platonic immortality (either of the soul as a whole or of the mind) on the grounds that mental capacities are born (proven by the apparent inheritance of mental traits from our parents) and so are mortal. Cicero, on behalf of Plato, dismisses this view as the result of failure to understand that the emotive part of the soul is separate from the purity of the mind and that the mind does not inherit mental traits from one's parents. Evidently Panaetius held that no part of the soul or mind is immortal because he held that all parts of it (if it has parts) are born and therefore can die. Cicero's view here is important for the history of Platonist psychological theories, whereas Panaetius seems to hold a standard Stoic view about the mortality of the entire soul whether or not he followed his predecessors on the issue of its radical unity.

said that fate was a rational principle for the things administered by providence within the cosmos, and again in other treatises they called fate a string of causes.

TEXT 88: Aëtius 1.28.4 (Pseudo-Plutarch *On the Doctrines*
of the Philosophers* 885b = *Dox. Gr.* p. 324)

The Stoics say it is a string of causes, i.e., an ordering and connection which is inescapable.

TEXT 89: Alexander of Aphrodisias *De Anima Mantissa*
(*CIAG* Supp. 2.1, pp. 185.1–5)

But it is conceded that all things which happen by fate occur in a certain order and sequence and have an element of logical consequence in them. . . . Anyway, they say that fate is a string of causes.

TEXT 90: Epictetus *Discourses* 2.19.1–5

1. The Master Argument [of Diodorus Cronus] seems to be based on premises of this sort. There is a general conflict among these three statements: [1] everything past and true is necessary; [2] the impossible does not follow from the possible; [3] there is something possible which neither is nor will be true. Seeing this conflict, Diodorus used the plausibility of the first two statements to establish that only that which is or will be true is possible. **2.** But from among the [consistent] pairs [of statements] one man will retain these: [3] that there is something possible which neither is nor will be true and [2] that the impossible does not follow from the possible; but [he would not concede] that [1] everything past and true is necessary. This seems to be the position of Cleanthes and his followers, and Antipater generally agreed with it. **3.** Others [will accept] the other two, [3] that there is something possible which neither is nor will be true and [1] that everything past and true is necessary; [and they will concede] that the impossible follows from the possible. **4.** But it is impossible to retain all three of those statements because of their general conflict with each other. **5.** So if someone asks me, "Which pair do you retain?" I will answer him by saying that I do not know. I have learned from research that Diodorus retained one pair, the followers of Panthoides and Cleanthes another, and the followers of Chrysippus another.

TEXT 91: Simplicius *Commentary on Aristotle's Categories*
13a37 (*CIAG* vol. 8, pp. 406.34–407.5)

Concerning [pairs of] contradictories that bear on the future, the Stoics accept the same principle as they do for other statements. For what is the case for [pairs of] contradictories concerning things present and past is also the case, they say, for future contradictories themselves and their parts. For either 'it will be' or 'it will not be' is true if they must be either true or false. For according to them, future events are determined. And if there will be a sea battle tomorrow, it is true to say that there will be. But if there will not be a sea battle, it is false to say that there will be. Either there will or there will not be a battle; therefore, each statement is either true or false.

TEXT 92: Pseudo-Plutarch *On Fate* 574e–f

(547e) According to the opposing argument, the first and most important point would seem to be that nothing happens uncaused but according to prior causes. Second, that this cosmos, which is itself coordinated and sympathetic with itself, is administered by nature. Third, which would seem rather to be additional evidence, is the fact that divination is in good repute with all human beings because it really does exist, with divine cooperation, and second, that wise men are contented in the face of events, (547f) since all of them occur according to [divine] allotment; and third, the much discussed point, that every proposition is true or false.

TEXT 93: Plutarch *On Stoic Self-Contradictions* 1045b–1056d (selections)

(1045b) . . . Some philosophers think that they can free our impulses from being necessitated by external causes if they posit in the leading part of the soul an adventitious motion which becomes particularly evident in cases where things are indistinguishable. For when two things are equivalent and equal in importance and it is necessary to take one of the two, there being no cause which leads us to one or the other since they do not differ from each other, this adventitious cause generates a swerve in the soul all by itself (1045c) and so cuts through the stalemate. Chrysippus argues against them, on the grounds that they are doing violence to nature by [positing] something which is uncaused, and frequently cites dice and scales and many other things which cannot fall or settle in different ways at different times without some cause or difference, either something which is entirely in the things themselves or something which occurs in the external circumstances. For he claims that the uncaused and the automatic are totally non-existent and that in these adventitious [causes] which some philosophers make up and talk about there are hidden certain non-evident causes, and they draw our impulse in one direction or another without our perceiving it. . . .

(1049f) But nevertheless one will have not just one or two occasions but thousands to address to Chrysippus this remark, which is now praised, "You have said the easiest thing in blaming the gods." For first, in book 1 of his

Physics he compares the eternity of motion to a posset,[18] which spins and agitates the various things which come to pass in various ways. Then he says, **(1050a)** "Since the organization of the universe proceeds thus, it is necessary for us to be such as we are, in accordance with it, whether we are ill or lame, contrary to our individual nature, or whether we have turned out to be grammarians or musicians." And again, a bit further on, "And on this principle we will say similar things about our virtue and our vice and, in general, about our skills or lack of them, as I have said." And a bit further on, removing all ambiguity, "For it is impossible for any of the parts, even the smallest one, to turn out differently than according to the common nature and its reason." That the common nature and the **(1050b)** common reason of nature are fate and providence and Zeus, even the Antipodeans know this; for the Stoics prattle on about this everywhere and he says that Homer correctly said,[19] "And Zeus' plan was being fulfilled," referring it to fate and the nature of the universe according to which everything is ordered.

How, then, can it be the case at one and the same time that god is not partly responsible for anything shameful and that not even the smallest thing can occur otherwise than according to the common nature and its reason? For in everything that occurs surely there are some shameful things too. And yet, Epicurus twists this way and that and exercises his ingenuity **(1050c)** in his attempt to free and liberate voluntary action from the eternal motion, so as not to leave vice free of blame, whereas Chrysippus gives vice blatant freedom to say not only that it is necessary and according to fate but even that it occurs according to god's reason and the best nature. And this too is plain to see, when we provide the following literal quotation: "For since the common nature extends into everything, it will be necessary that everything that occurs in any way in the universe and in any of its parts should occur according to it [the common nature] and its reason, in proper and unhindered fashion, because there is nothing outside it which could hinder its organization nor **(1050d)** could any of its parts be moved or be in a state otherwise than according to the common nature." . . .

(1055d) . . . Surely his [Chrysippus'] account of possibility is in conflict with his account of fate. **(1055e)** For if Diodorus' view of the possible as "what either is or will be true" is not right but [Chrysippus' view is] that "everything that permits of occurring even if it is not going to occur is possible," then many things are possible which are not according to fate. <Therefore, either> fate loses its character as unconquerable, unforceable, and victorious over all things, or, if fate is as Chrysippus claims, then, "What permits of occurring" will often turn out to be impossible. And everything true

18. A drink composed of a suspension of solid particles in a fluid base.
19. *Iliad* 1.5.

will be necessary, being gripped by the most sovereign of necessities; whereas everything false will be impossible since the greatest cause opposes its being true. . . .

(1055f) . . . Moreover, what is said about presentations is also in powerful opposition to [Chrysippus' view of] fate. For wanting to prove that presentation is not a sufficient cause of assent, he has said that wise men will be doing harm by producing false presentations in others if presentations are sufficient to produce acts of assent; for wise men often use a falsehood when (1056a) dealing with base men and produce a persuasive presentation which is, however, not the cause of assent (since in that case [a presentation] would also be the cause of false belief and deception). So, if someone transfers this statement from the wise man to fate and should say that the assents do not arise because of fate, since in that case false assents and beliefs and deceptions would arise because of fate and people would be harmed because of fate, then the argument that exempts the wise man from doing harm demonstrates at the same time that fate is not the cause of everything. For if people do not hold opinions and are not harmed because of fate, (1056b) it is clear that they also do not act correctly or have correct opinions or hold stable beliefs or receive benefit because of fate, but instead the claim that fate is the cause of everything goes up in smoke. And someone who says that Chrysippus did not make fate the sufficient cause of these things but only the initiating cause will also prove that he is in contradiction with himself where he extravagantly praises Homer,[20] who is speaking about Zeus, "So accept whatever he sends to each of you, of evil" or of good; and Euripides,[21] [who says], "O Zeus, why then should I say that miserable men have any intelligence? For we depend on you and do whatever you happen to think."

(1056c) And Chrysippus himself writes many things in agreement with these views and finally says that nothing, not even the smallest thing, is in any state or motion otherwise than according to the reason of Zeus, who is the same as fate.

Again, then, the initiating cause is weaker than the sufficient and is feeble when it is dominated by other causes which impede it, but by claiming that fate is an unconquerable, unhinderable, and unswerving cause, he calls it 'Unturning', 'Inevitable', 'Necessity', and 'Firmly Fixed' (since it sets a limit on everything).

Should we, then, say that assents are not in our power and neither are virtues, vices, (1056d) [morally] perfect actions, and [moral] errors; or should we say that fate is deficient and that the Firmly Fixed is indeterminate and that Zeus' motions and dispositions are unfulfilled? For some of these result from

20. *Iliad* 15.109.
21. *Suppliants* 734–36, slightly altered.

fate being a sufficient cause, some from it merely being an initiating cause. For if it is a sufficient cause of all things, it destroys what is in our power and the voluntary, and if it is initiating, it ruins the unhinderable and fully effective character of fate. For not once or twice but everywhere, and especially in all his treatises on physics, he has written that there are many hindrances to particular natures and motions but that there are no obstacles to the nature and motion of the universe as a whole.

TEXT 94: Cicero *On Fate* 28–44 (selections)

28. . . . Nor will the so-called 'Lazy Argument' stop us. For a certain argument is called the *argos logos* by the philosophers, and if we listened to it we would never do anything at all in life. For they argue in the following fashion: 'if it is fated for you to recover from this illness whether you call the doctor or not, you will recover; **29.** similarly, if it is fated for you not to recover from this illness whether you call the doctor or not, you will not recover. And one of the two is fated; therefore, there is no point in calling the doctor'. It is right to call this kind of argument 'lazy' and 'slothful' because on the same reasoning all action will be abolished from life. One can also change the form of it, so that the word 'fate' is not included and still keep the same sense in this way: 'if from eternity this has been true, "you will recover from that disease whether you call a doctor or not," you will recover; similarly, if from eternity this has been false, "you will recover from that disease whether you call the doctor or not" you will not recover, etc.'.

30. Chrysippus criticizes this argument. "For," he says, "some things are simple, some conjoined. 'Socrates will die on that day' is simple. Whether he does anything or not, the day of death is fixed for him. But if it is fated, 'Oedipus will be born to Laius', it cannot be said 'whether Laius lies with a woman or not'. For the events are conjoined and co-fated." For that is how he refers to it since it is fated thus *both* that Laius will lie with his wife *and* that Oedipus will be produced by her. Just as, if it had been said, "Milo will wrestle at the Olympics" and someone reported, "Therefore, he will wrestle whether or not he has an opponent," he would be wrong. For 'he will wrestle' is conjoined, because there is no wrestling match without an opponent. "Therefore, all the sophistries of that type are refuted in the same way. 'Whether you call a doctor or not, you will recover' is fallacious; for calling the doctor is fated just as much as recovering." Such situations, as I said, he calls 'co-fated'.

31. Carneades [the Academic] did not accept this entire class [co-fated events] and thought that the above argument had been constructed with insufficient care. And so he approached the argument in another way, not using any fallacious reasoning. This was the result: 'If there are antecedent causes for everything that happens, then everything happens within a closely knit web of natural connections. If this is so, then necessity causes everything. And if this is true there is nothing in our power. There is, however, something in our power. But if everything happens by fate, everything happens as a result of antecedent causes. Therefore, it is not the case that whatever happens, happens by fate'. **32.** This argument cannot be made tighter. For if someone wished to turn the argument around and say, 'If every future event is true from eternity so that whatever should happen would certainly happen, then everything happens within a closely knit web of natural connections', he would be speaking nonsense. For there is a great difference between a natural cause making future events true from eternity and future events which might be understood to be true, without natural [cause] from eternity. Thus Carneades said that not even Apollo is able to pronounce on any future events unless it were those the causes of which are already contained in nature so that they would happen necessarily. **33.** On what basis could even a god say that Marcellus, who was three times a consul, would die at sea? This was indeed true from eternity, but it did not have efficient causes. Thus [Carneades] was of the opinion that if not even past events of which no trace existed would be known to Apollo, how much less would he know future events; for only if the efficient causes of anything were known would it then be possible to know what would happen in the future. Therefore, Apollo could not predict anything regarding Oedipus, there not being the requisite causes in nature owing to which it was necessary that he would kill his father or anything of this sort. . . .

39. Since there were two opinions of the older philosophers—one belonging to those who believed that everything occurred by fate in such a way that the fate in question brought to bear the force of necessity (this was the view of Democritus, Heraclitus, Empedocles, and Aristotle), the other of those who held that there were voluntary motions of the mind without fate—Chrysippus, it seems to me, wanted to strike a middle path, like an informal arbitrator, but attached himself more to the group which wanted the motions of the mind to be free of necessity. But while employing his own terms, he slipped into such difficulties that he wound up unwillingly confirming the necessity of fate.

40. And, if you please, let us see how this occurs in the case of assent, which we discussed at the start of our discourse. For the older philosophers who held that everything occurred by fate said that it occurred by force and necessity. Those who disagreed with them freed assent from fate and denied that if fate applied to assent it could be free of necessity, and so they argued thus, 'If everything happens by fate, everything occurs by an antecedent cause, and if impulse [is caused], then also what follows from impulse [is caused]; therefore, assent too. But if the cause of impulse is not in us then impulse itself is not in our own power; and if this is so, not even what is produced by impulse is in our power; therefore, neither assent nor action is in our power.

From which it follows that neither praise nor blame nor honors nor punishments are fair'. Since this is wrong, they think that it is a plausible conclusion that it is not the case that whatever happens, happens by fate.

41. Chrysippus, however, since he both rejected necessity and wanted that nothing should occur without prior causes, distinguished among the kinds of causes in order both to escape from necessity and to retain fate. "For," he said, "some causes are perfect and principal, whereas others are auxiliary and proximate. Therefore, when we say that all things occur by fate by antecedent causes, we do not want the following to be understood, namely, that they occur by perfect and principal causes; but we mean this: that they occur by auxiliary and proximate causes." And so his response to the argument which I just made is this: 'If everything occurs by fate it does indeed follow that everything occurs by antecedent causes, but not by principal and perfect causes. And if these are not themselves in our power, it does not follow that not even impulse is in our power. But this would follow if we were saying that everything occurred by perfect and principal causes with the result that, since these causes are not in our power, <not even [impulse] would be in our power>'. **42.** Therefore, those who introduce fate in such a way that they connect necessity to it are subject to the force of that argument; but those who will not say that antecedent causes are perfect and principal will not be subject to the argument at all.

As to the claim that assents occur by antecedent causes, he says that he can easily explain the meaning of this. For although assent cannot occur unless it is stimulated by a presentation, nevertheless since it has that presentation as its proximate cause and not as its principal cause, it can be explained in the way that we have been discussing for some time now, just as Chrysippus wishes. It is not the case that the assent could occur if it were not stimulated by a force from outside (for it is necessary that an assent should be stimulated by a presentation); but Chrysippus falls back on his cylinder and cone. These cannot begin to move unless they are struck; but when that happens, he thinks that it is by their own natures that the cylinder rolls and the cone turns.

43. "Therefore," he says, "just as he who pushed the cylinder gave it the start of its motion, he did not, however, give it its 'rollability', so a presentation which strikes will certainly impress its object and, as it were, stamp its form on the mind, but our assent will be in our own power and the assent, just as was said in the case of the cylinder, when struck from without will henceforth be moved by its own force and nature. But if something were produced without an antecedent cause, then it would be false that everything occurs by fate. But if it is probable that a cause precedes all things that occur, what could block the conclusion that all things occur by fate? Let it only be understood what difference and distinction there is among causes."

44. Since Chrysippus has clarified this, if his opponents who say that assents do not occur by fate were nevertheless to concede that they do not occur without a presentation as antecedent [cause], then that is a different argument; but if they grant that presentations precede and nevertheless that assents do not occur by fate, on the grounds that it is not that proximate and immediate [kind of] cause that moves the assent, note that they are really saying the same thing [as Chrysippus].

For Chrysippus, while granting that there is in the presentation a proximate and immediate cause of assent, will not grant that this cause necessitates assent in such a way that, if all things occur by fate, all things would occur by antecedent and *necessary* causes. And similarly the opponents, who disagree with him while conceding that assents do not occur without prior presentations, will say that if everything occurs by fate in the sense that nothing occurs without a prior cause, it must be granted that all things occur by fate.

From this it is easy to understand since both sides get the same result once their opinions are laid out and clarified, that they disagree verbally but not in substance.

TEXT 95: Aulus Gellius 7.2.1–15 (selections)

1. Chrysippus, the chief Stoic philosopher, defines fate (*heimarmenē* in Greek) roughly as follows: "Fate," he says, "is a sempiternal and unchangeable series and chain of things, rolling and unraveling itself through eternal sequences of cause and effect, of which it is composed and compounded." . . .
4. But authors from other schools make this objection to this definition. **5.** "If," they say, "Chrysippus thinks that everything is moved and governed by fate and the sequences and revolutions of fate cannot be turned aside or evaded, then people's sins and misdeeds should not rouse our anger, nor should they be attributed to them and their wills but to a kind of necessity and inevitability which comes from fate, mistress and arbiter of all things, by whose agency all that will be is necessary. And therefore the penalties applied by the law to the guilty are unfair, if people do not turn to misdeeds voluntarily but are dragged by fate."
6. Against this position Chrysippus made many sharp and subtle arguments. But this is the gist of all he said on the topic: **7.** "Although," he said, "it is true that by fate all things are forced and linked by a necessary and dominant reason, nevertheless the character of our minds is subject to fate in a manner corresponding to their nature and quality. **8.** For if our minds were originally formed by nature in a sound and useful manner then they pass on all the force of fate which imposes on us from outside in a relatively unobjectionable and more acceptable way. But if, on the other hand, they are rough and untrained and uncouth, supported by no good training, then even if the blows of fated misfortune which strike them are trivial or non-existent they will plunge headlong into constant misdeeds and errors because of their own

ineptitude and their voluntary impulse. **9.** But this state of affairs is itself brought about by that natural and necessary sequence of cause and effect which is called fate. **10.** For it is by the very nature of the case fated and determined that bad characters should not be free of misdeeds and errors."

11. He then uses a quite appropriate and clever illustration of this state of affairs. "Just as," he says, "if you throw a cylindrical stone down a steep slope, you are indeed the cause and origin of its descent, nevertheless the stone afterward rolls down not because you are still doing this, but because such is its nature and the 'rollability' of its form; similarly, the order and reason and necessity of fate set in motion the general types and starting points of the causes, but each person's own will [or decisions] and the character of his mind govern the impulses of our thoughts and minds and our very actions."

12. He then adds these words, which are consistent with what I have said: "So, the Pythagoreans too said, 'You shall know that human beings have woes which they chose for themselves,' since the harm suffered by each is in his own power and since they err and are harmed voluntarily and by their own plan and decision."

13. Therefore, he says that we ought not to tolerate or listen to people who are wicked or lazy and guilty and shameless, who when convicted of misdeeds take refuge in the necessity of fate as in the asylum of a religious sanctuary and say that their worst misdeeds should be laid at the door, not of their own recklessness, but of fate.

14. And that most wise and ancient poet [Homer] was the first to make this point in the verses that follow:

> It makes me furious! how mortals blame the gods! For they
> say that their troubles come from us; but they incur pains on
> their own beyond their allotment because of their wickedness.[22]

15. And so Cicero, in his book entitled *On Fate,* when he said that the question was very obscure and complex, says also in these words that even the philosopher Chrysippus did not get clear on the problem: "Chrysippus, sweating and toiling to discover how he might explain that everything happens by fate and yet that there is something in our own power, gets tangled up in this manner."

TEXT 96: Alexander of Aphrodisias *De Anima Mantissa*
(*CIAG* Supp. 2.1, pp. 179.6–18)

To say that chance is a cause non-evident to human calculation is not the position of those who posit some nature called 'chance' but of those who say that chance consists in the relational disposition of human beings to the causes. . . .

---

22. *Odyssey* 1.32–34.

For if they were to say not that chance is the cause which is non-evident to some human beings, but [that chance is] the cause which is universally non-evident to all humans, they would not be admitting that chance exists at all, although they grant that divination exists and suppose that it is able to make known to others the things that seemed to be non-evident.

TEXT 97: Cicero *On Divination* 1.6

But Panaetius, the leader of the school, the teacher of Posidonius, and a student of Antipater, deviated from the Stoics, but even so he did not dare to *deny* that there is a power of divination; rather, he said that he had *doubts* about it. Will the Stoics not grant to us in other matters the same permission that was given (though very reluctantly) to that Stoic on one issue? Especially since the matter that was not so clear to Panaetius seems clearer than the light of the sun to the rest of the school.

TEXT 98: Alexander of Aphrodisias *On Fate* 26
            (*CIAG* Supp. 2.2, pp. 196.21–197.3)

Perhaps it would not be a bad idea for us to take in hand and examine how matters stand with the puzzles they put most confidence in; for perhaps they will appear not too difficult to solve. One of these [difficulties] is as follows: if, they say, things are in our power when we can also do the opposite of those things, and it is upon such things that praise and blame and encouragement and discouragement and punishment and honors are bestowed, then it follows that being prudent and virtuous will not be in the power of those who are prudent and virtuous; for [such people] are no longer capable of receiving the vices opposite to their virtues. And the same point applies to the vices of bad people; for it is no longer in the power of such people to cease being bad. But it is absurd to say that the virtues and vices are not in our power and that they are not the objects of praise and blame. Therefore, 'what is in our power' is not like that.

TEXT 99: Hippolytus *Refutation of All Heresies* 1.21

They [Zeno and Chrysippus] support the claim that everything happens by fate, by using this example. It is as though a dog is tied behind a cart. If he wants to follow, he is both dragged and follows, exercising his autonomy in conjunction with necessity. But if he does not wish to follow, he will nevertheless be forced to. The same thing happens in the case of human beings. Even if they do not want to follow, they will nevertheless be forced to go along with what has been destined.

TEXT 100: Eusebius *Prep. Ev.* 6.8

So, in book 1 of his [Chrysippus'] *On Fate,* he used proofs of this nature, and in book 2 he tries to resolve the absurdities that seem to follow on the thesis that all things are necessitated, which we listed at the beginning, for example, the destruction of our own initiative concerning criticism and praise and encouragement and everything which seems to happen by our own agency.

So, in book 2 he says that it is obvious that many things occur by our own initiative, but nonetheless these are co-fated with the administration of the universe. And he uses illustrations like these.

The non-destruction of one's coat, he says, is not fated simply but co-fated with its being taken care of; and someone's being saved from his enemies is co-fated with his fleeing those enemies; and having children is co-fated with being willing to lie with a woman. For just as if, he says, someone says that Hegesarchus the boxer will leave the ring completely untouched, it would be strange for him to think that Hegesarchus should fight with his fists down because it was fated that he should get off untouched (the one who made the assertion saying this because of the fellow's extraordinary protection from being punched), so too the same thing holds in other cases. For many things cannot occur without our being willing and indeed contributing a most strenuous eagerness and zeal for these things, since, he says, it was fated for these things to occur in conjunction with this personal effort. . . . But it will be in our power, he says, with what is in our power being included in fate.

Ethics

The General Account in Diogenes Laërtius

TEXT 101: Diogenes Laërtius 7.84–131

84. They divide the ethical part of philosophy into these topics: on impulse, on good and bad things, on passions, on virtue, on the goal, on primary value, on actions, on appropriate actions, and on encouragements and discouragements to actions. This is the subdivision given by the followers of Chrysippus, Archedemus, Zeno of Tarsus, Apollodorus, Diogenes, Antipater, and Posidonius. For Zeno of Citium and Cleanthes, as might be expected from earlier thinkers, made less elaborate distinctions in their subject matter. But they did divide both logic and physics.

85. They say that an animal's first [or primary] impulse is to preserve itself, because nature gave it an affinity to itself from the beginning, as Chrysippus says in book 1 of *On Goals,* stating that for every animal its first [sense of] affinity is to its own constitution and the reflective awareness of this. For it is not likely that nature would make an animal alienated from itself, nor having made the animal, to give it neither affinity to itself nor alienation from itself. Therefore, the remaining possibility is to say that having constituted the animal she gave it an affinity to itself. For in this way it repels injurious influences and pursues that to which it has an affinity.

The Stoics claim that what some people say is false, namely, that the primary [or first] impulse of animals is to pleasure. **86.** For they say that pleasure is, if anything, a byproduct which supervenes when nature itself, on its own, seeks out and acquires what is suitable to [the animal's] constitution. It is like the condition of thriving animals and plants in top condition. And nature, they say, did not operate differently in the cases of plants and of animals; for it directs the life of plants too, though without impulse and sense-perception, and even in us some processes are plantlike. When, in the case of animals, impulse is added (which they use in the pursuit of things to which they have an affinity), then for them what is natural is governed by what is according to impulse. When reason has been given to rational animals as a more perfect governor [of life], then for them the life according to reason properly becomes what is natural for them. For reason supervenes on impulse as a craftsman.

87. Thus Zeno first, in his book *On Human Nature,* said that the goal was to live in agreement with nature, which is to live according to virtue. For

113

nature leads us to virtue. And similarly Cleanthes in *On Pleasure* and Posidonius and Hecaton in their books *On the Goal.*

Again, "to live according to virtue" is equivalent to living according to the experience of events which occur by nature, as Chrysippus says in book 1 of his *On Goals.* **88.** For our natures are parts of the nature of the universe. Therefore, the goal becomes "to live consistently with nature," i.e., according to one's own nature and that of the universe, doing nothing which is forbidden by the common law, which is right reason, penetrating all things, being the same as Zeus, who is the leader of the administration of things. And this itself is the virtue of the happy man and a smooth flow of life, whenever all things are done according to the harmony of the *daimōn* in each of us with the will of the administrator of the universe. So, Diogenes says explicitly that the goal is reasonable behavior in the selection of things according to nature, and Archedemus [says it is] to live carrying out all the appropriate acts.

89. By nature, in consistency with which we must live, Chrysippus understands both the common and, specifically, the human nature. Cleanthes includes only the common nature, with which one must be consistent, and not the individual. And virtue is a disposition in agreement. And it is worth choosing for its own sake, not because of some fear or hope or some extrinsic consideration. And happiness lies in virtue, insofar as virtue is the soul [so] made [as to produce] the agreement of one's whole life.

And the rational animal is corrupted, sometimes because of the persuasiveness of external activities and sometimes because of the influence of companions. For the starting points provided by nature are uncorrupted.

90. Virtue in one sense is generally a sort of completion [or: perfection] for each thing, for example, of a statue. And there is also non-intellectual virtue, for example, health; and intellectual virtue, for example, prudence. For in book 1 of his *On Virtues,* Hecaton says that those virtues which are constituted out of theorems are knowledge-based and intellectual, for example, prudence and justice; but those which are understood by extension from those which are constituted out of theorems are non-intellectual, for example, health and strength. For it turns out that health follows on and is extended from temperance, which is intellectual, just as strength supervenes on the building of an arch. **91.** They are called non-intellectual because they do not involve assent, but they supervene even in base people, as health and courage do.

Posidonius (in book 1 of his *Ethical Discourse*) says that a sign that virtue exists is the fact that the followers of Socrates, Diogenes, and Antisthenes were making [moral] progress; and vice exists because it is the opposite of virtue. And that it is teachable (virtue, I mean) Chrysippus says in book 1 of his *On the Goal,* and so do Cleanthes and Posidonius in their *Protreptics* and Hecaton too. It is clear that it is teachable because base men become good.

92. Panaetius, anyway, says that there are two [kinds of] virtues, theoretical and practical; others [divide virtue into] logical, physical, and ethical. Posidonius' followers [say there are] four, and those of Cleanthes and Chrysippus and Antipater [say there are even] more. But Apollophanes says there is one virtue, namely, prudence.

Of virtues, some are primary and some are subordinate to these. The primary are these: prudence, courage, justice, and temperance. Forms of these are magnanimity, self-control, endurance, quick-wittedness, and deliberative excellence. And prudence is the knowledge of which things are good and bad and neither; courage is knowledge of which things are to be chosen and avoided and neither; and . . . [There is a lacuna here.]

93. Magnanimity is knowledge or a condition which makes one superior to those things which happen alike to base and virtuous men; self-control is an unsurpassable disposition [concerned with] what accords with right reason or a condition which cannot be defeated by pleasures; endurance is knowledge of or a condition [concerned with] what one is to stand firmly by and what one is not to stand firmly by and what is neither; quick-wittedness is a condition which instantly finds out what the appropriate action is; and deliberative excellence is a knowledge of how to consider the type and manner of actions which we must perform in order to act advantageously.

Correspondingly, of vices, too, some are primary and some are subordinate. For example, imprudence, cowardice, injustice, and wantonness are primary, and lack of self-control, slow-wittedness, and poor deliberation are subordinate. Those vices whose [counterpart] virtues are forms of knowledge are forms of ignorance.

94. Good is in general that from which there is something beneficial; in particular it is either the same as or not different from benefit. Hence, virtue itself and the good, which participates in it, are spoken of in these three ways: [1] the good is that *from which* being benefited is a characteristic result; [2] it is that *according to which* [being benefited] is a characteristic result, for example, action according to virtue; [3] it is he *by whom* [being benefited is a characteristic result]; and 'by whom' means, for example, the virtuous man who participates in virtue.

They give another particular definition of the good, as follows: 'that which is perfectly in accord with nature for a rational being, qua rational'. And virtue is such a thing, so that virtuous actions and virtuous men participate [in it]; and its supervenient byproducts are joy and good spirits and the like. **95.** Similarly, of bad things some are imprudence, cowardice, injustice, and the like; and vicious actions and base men participate in vice; and its supervenient byproducts are low spirits and depression and the like.

Again, some goods are in the soul, some are external, and some are neither in the soul nor external. The ones in the soul are virtues and virtuous actions.

The external are having a virtuous fatherland and a virtuous friend and their happiness. Those which are neither external nor in the soul are for someone, in and for himself, to be virtuous and to be happy. **96.** Conversely, some bad things are in the soul, i.e., vices and vicious actions. The external ones are having an imprudent fatherland and an imprudent friend and their unhappiness. Those which are neither external nor in the soul are for someone, in and for himself, to be base and to be unhappy.

Again, of goods some are final and some are instrumental and some are both final and instrumental. So, a friend and the benefits derived from him are instrumental; but confidence and prudence and freedom and enjoyment and good spirits and freedom from pain and every virtuous action are final. **97.** <The virtues> are both instrumental and final goods. For in that they produce happiness they are instrumental goods, and in that they fulfill it, such that they are parts of it, they are final goods. Similarly, of bad things some are final and some are instrumental and some are both. For an enemy and the harm derived from him are instrumental; but feelings of shock and lowliness and servitude and lack of enjoyment and low spirits and pain and every vicious action are final. <The vices> are both, since in that they produce unhappiness they are instrumental, and in that they fulfill it, such that they are parts of it, they are final.

98. Again of goods in the soul some are conditions and some are dispositions and some are neither conditions nor dispositions. The virtues are dispositions, practices are conditions, and activities are neither conditions nor dispositions. Generally, having good children and a good old age are mixed goods, whereas knowledge is a simple good. And the virtues are constant [goods], but there are ones that are not constant, such as joy and walking.

Every good is advantageous and binding and profitable and useful and well used and honorable and beneficial and worth choosing and just. **99.** [A good is] advantageous because it brings such things as we are benefited by when they occur; binding because it holds together in cases where this is needed; profitable because it pays back what is expended on it, so that it exceeds in benefit a mere repayment of the effort; useful because it makes available the use of a benefit; well used because it renders the use [of it] praiseworthy; honorable because it is symmetrical with its own use; beneficial because it is such as to benefit; worth choosing because it is such that it is reasonable to choose it; just because it is consonant with law and instrumental to a [sense of] community.

100. They say that the perfect good is honorable because it has all the features sought by nature or because it is perfectly symmetrical. There are four forms of the honorable: just, courageous, orderly, knowledgeable. For honorable actions are completed in these [forms]. Analogously, there are also four forms of the shameful: the unjust, the cowardly, the disorderly, and the senseless. The honorable uniquely means that which makes those who possess it praiseworthy; or a good which is worthy of praise; otherwise: what is naturally well suited for its own function; otherwise: that which adorns [its possessor], [as] when we say that only the wise man is good and honorable. **101.** They say that only the honorable is good, according to Hecaton in book 3 of his *On Goods* and Chrysippus in his book *On the Honorable;* and this is virtue and that which participates in virtue; this is the same as [saying] that everything good is honorable and that the good is equivalent to the honorable—which is equal to it. For "since it is good, it is honorable; but it is honorable; therefore, it is good." They think that all goods are equal and that every good is worth choosing in the highest degree and does not admit of being more or less intense. They say that of existing things, some are good, some bad, and some neither. **102.** The virtues—prudence, justice, courage, temperance, and the others—are good; and their opposites—imprudence, injustice, and the others—are bad; neither good nor bad are those things which neither benefit nor harm, such as life, health, pleasure, beauty, strength, wealth, good reputation, noble birth, and their opposites death, disease, pain, ugliness, weakness, poverty, bad reputation, low birth, and such things, as Hecaton says in book 7 of his *On the Goal,* and Apollodorus in his *Ethics* and Chrysippus. For these things are not good, but things indifferent in the category of preferred things. **103.** For just as heating, not cooling, is a property of the hot, so benefitting, not harming, is a property of the good; but wealth and health do not benefit any more than they harm; therefore, neither wealth nor health is good. Again, they say that what can be used [both] well and badly is not good; but it is possible to use wealth and health [both] well and badly; therefore, wealth and health are not good. Posidonius, however, says that these things too are in the class of goods. But Hecaton in book 9 of *On Goods* and Chrysippus in his *On Pleasure* deny even of pleasure that it is a good; for there are also shameful pleasures, and nothing shameful is good. **104.** To benefit is to change or maintain something in accordance with virtue, whereas to harm is to change or maintain something in accordance with vice.

Things indifferent are spoken of in two senses. In the simple sense, those things which do not contribute to happiness or unhappiness [are indifferent], as is the case with wealth, reputation, health, strength, and similar things. For it is possible to be happy even without these things since it is a certain kind of use of them that brings happiness or unhappiness. But in another sense, things indifferent are what do not stimulate an impulse either toward or away from something, as is the case with having an odd or even number of hairs on one's head or with extending or retracting one's finger; the first sort [of indifferents] are no longer called 'indifferent' in this sense; for they do stimulate impulses toward or away from [themselves]. **105.** That is why some of them are selected <and some> are rejected, whereas those others leave one equally balanced between choice and avoidance.

Of things indifferent, they say that some are preferred and some rejected; preferred are those which have value, rejected are those which have disvalue. They say that one sort of value is a contribution to the life in agreement, which applies to every good; but another sort is a certain intermediate potential or usefulness which contributes to the life according to nature, as much as to say, just that [value] which wealth and health bring forward for [promoting] the life according to nature. And another sense of value is the appraiser's value, which someone experienced in the facts would set, as when one says that wheat is exchanged for barley with a mule thrown in.

106. Preferred things are those which also have value; for example, among things of the soul, natural ability, skill, [moral] progress, and similar things; among bodily things life, health, strength, good condition, soundness, beauty, and the like; among external things wealth, reputation, noble birth, and similar things. Rejected are, among things of the soul, natural inability, lack of skill, and similar things; among bodily things death, disease, weakness, bad condition, being maimed, ugliness, and similar things; among external things poverty, lack of reputation, low birth, and the like. Those things which are in neither category are neither preferred nor rejected.

107. Again, of preferred things, some are preferred for themselves, some because of other things, and some both for themselves and because of other things. For themselves, natural ability, [moral] progress, and similar things; because of other things, wealth, noble birth, and similar things; for themselves and because of other things, strength, good perceptual abilities, soundness. [Those which are preferred] for themselves [are preferred] because they are according to nature; [those which are preferred] because of other things [are preferred] because they produce a significant amount of utility; the same applies to the rejected conversely.

Again, an appropriate [action], they say, is that which, when done, admits of a reasonable defense, such as what is consistent in life, and this extends also to plants and animals. For appropriate [actions] are observable in these too.

108. The appropriate was first so named by Zeno and the term is derived from [the expression] 'extending [or applying] to certain people'.[1] It is an action which has an affinity with arrangements that are according to nature. For of actions performed according to impulse [i.e., voluntarily], some are appropriate and some inappropriate <and some are neither appropriate nor inappropriate>.

Appropriate [actions], then, are those which reason constrains [us] to do, such as honoring our parents, brothers, [and] fatherland and spending time with friends. Inappropriate are those which reason constrains [us] not [to do],

---

1. "Appropriate" (*kathēkon*) from *kata tinas hēkein;* the etymological wordplay is not readily translatable.

such as things like this: neglecting our parents, ignoring our brothers, being out of sympathy with our friends, overlooking [the interests of] our fatherland, and such things. **109.** Neither appropriate nor inappropriate are those which reason neither constrains us to perform nor forbids, such as picking up a small stick, holding a writing instrument or scraper, and things similar to these. And some are appropriate without regard to [special] circumstances, whereas some are conditioned by circumstances. Those which [are appropriate] without regard to [special] circumstances are these: looking out for one's health and sense organs, and similar things. Those which are conditioned by circumstances are maiming oneself and throwing away one's possessions. The analogous [distinctions apply] too for the things which are contrary to what is appropriate. Again, of appropriate [actions], some are always appropriate and some not always. And living according to virtue is always appropriate, but asking questions and answering and walking and similar things are not always [appropriate]. The same reasoning applies to inappropriate [actions]. **110.** And there is also a kind of appropriate [action] among intermediates, such as the obedience of boys to their attendants.

They say that the soul has eight parts; for its parts are the five sense organs and the vocal part and the thinking part (which is the intellect itself) and the generative part. And corruption afflicts the intellect because of falsehoods, and from [such a mind] there arise many passions and causes of instability. Passion itself is, according to Zeno, the irrational and unnatural movement of a soul or an excessive impulse.

According to Hecaton in book 2 of his *On Passions* and Zeno in his *On Passions,* the most general [classification] of the passions is into four types: **111.** pain, fear, desire, pleasure. They believe that the passions are judgments, as Chrysippus says in his *On Passions;* for greed is a supposition that money is honorable, and similarly for drunkenness and wantonness and the others.

And pain is an irrational contraction; its forms are pity, grudging, envy, resentment, heavyheartedness, congestion, sorrow, anguish, confusion. Pity is a pain [felt] for someone who is suffering undeservedly; grudging is a pain at the goods of other people; envy is a pain at someone else having things which one desires oneself; resentment is a pain at someone else too having what one also has oneself; **112.** heavyheartedness is a pain which weighs one down; congestion is a pain which crowds one and makes one short of room; sorrow is a persistent or intensifying pain caused by brooding on something; anguish is a laborious pain; confusion is an irrational pain which gnaws at one and prevents one from getting a comprehensive view of one's current circumstances.

Fear is the expectation of something bad. These [forms] are brought under fear: dread, hesitation, shame, shock, panic, agony. Dread is a fear which produces fright; shame is a fear of bad reputation; hesitation is a fear of future action; shock is a fear arising from the appearance of an unfamiliar thing;

113. panic is a fear in conjunction with a hastening of the voice; agony is a fear. . . . [There is a lacuna here.]

Desire is an irrational striving, and these [forms] are ranged under it: want, hatred, quarrelsomeness, anger, sexual love, wrath, spiritedness. Want is an unsuccessful desire and is as though it were separated from its object yet vainly straining for and drawn to it; hatred is a progressive and increasing desire for things to go badly for someone; quarrelsomeness is a desire concerned with a [philosophical] school; anger is a desire for revenge on one who seems to have done an injustice inappropriately; sexual love is a desire which does not afflict virtuous men, for it is an effort to gain love resulting from the appearance of [physical] beauty.

114. Wrath is long-standing and spiteful anger that just waits for its chance, as is apparent in these lines:[2]

> For even if he swallows his resentment for today,
> still he will retain his spite in the future, until it is satisfied.

And spiritedness is anger just beginning.

Pleasure is an irrational elation over what seems to be worth choosing; under it are ranged enchantment, mean-spirited satisfaction, enjoyment, rapture. Enchantment is a pleasure which charms one through the sense of hearing; mean-spirited satisfaction is pleasure at someone else's misfortunes; enjoyment is, as it were, a turning,[3] a kind of incitement of the soul to slackness; rapture is a breakdown of virtue.

115. As there are said to be ailments in the body, such as gout and arthritis, so too in the soul there are love of reputation and love of pleasure and the like. For an ailment is a disease coupled with weakness and a disease is a strong opinion about something which seems to be worth choosing. And as in the body there are certain predispositions [to disease], for example, catarrh and diarrhea, so too in the soul there are tendencies, such as proneness to grudging, proneness to pity, quarrelsomeness, and the like.

116. There are also three good states [of the soul]: joy, caution, and wish. And joy is opposite to pleasure, being a reasonable elation; and caution to fear, being a reasonable avoidance. For the wise man will not be afraid in any way, but will be cautious. They say that wish is opposite to desire, being a reasonable striving. So, just as there are certain passions that are forms of the primary ones, so too there are good states subordinate to the primary; forms of wish are goodwill, kindliness, acceptance, contentment; forms of caution are respect, sanctity; forms of joy are enjoyment, good spirits, tranquillity.

---

2. Homer *Iliad* 1.81–82.

3. *Terpsis* and *trepsis*. The pun is untranslatable.

117. They say the wise man is also free of passions, because he is not disposed to them. And the base man is 'free of passions' in a different sense, which means the same as hard-hearted and cold. And the wise man is free of vanity since he is indifferent to good and ill repute. And there is another type of freedom from vanity, i.e., heedlessness; such is the base man. And they say that all virtuous men are austere because they do not consort with pleasure nor do they tolerate hedonistic [actions and attitudes] from others; and there is another kind of austerity, in the same sense that wine is said to be 'austere' [harsh] (which is used medicinally but not much for drinking).

118. The virtuous are sincere and protective of their own improvement by means of a preparation which conceals what is base and makes evident the good things which are there. And they are not phony; for they have eliminated phoniness in their voice and appearance. And they are uninvolved; for they avoid doing anything which is not appropriate. And they will drink wine but not get drunk. Again, [the wise man] will not go mad, although he will get strange presentations because of an excess of black bile or delirium—not in accordance with the account of what is worth choosing, but rather contrary to nature. Nor indeed will the wise man feel pain (since pain is an irrational contraction of the soul), as Apollodorus says in his *Ethics*.

119. And they are godly; for they have in themselves a kind of god. And the base man is godless. And the godless are of two kinds: the one opposite to him who is godly and the one who denies that the godly exists [i.e., the atheist]— and this is not a feature of every base man. The virtuous are also pious, for they have experience of what is lawful with respect to the gods and piety is a knowledge of how to serve the gods. And indeed they will also sacrifice to the gods and be sanctified since they will avoid [moral] mistakes concerning the gods. And the gods admire them since they are holy and just toward the divine. And only wise men are priests, for they have conducted an investigation into sacrifices, foundations, purifications, and the other matters that are proper for the gods.

120. The [Stoics] think that he [the wise man] will honor his parents and brothers in the second place, after the gods. They also say that love for one's children is natural to them and does not exist among the base. They also see fit to believe that [moral] mistakes are equal, according to Chrysippus, in book 4 of his *Ethical Investigations,* and Persaeus and Zeno. For if one truth is not more [true] than another, then neither is one falsehood [falser] than another. So, neither is one deception [more of a deception] than another nor is one [moral] mistake more [of a moral mistake] than another. For he who is a hundred stades from Canopus and he who is one stade away are [both] equally not in Canopus. So too he who makes a larger [moral] mistake and he who makes a smaller one are [both] equally not acting correctly. **121.** But Heracleides of Tarsus, the student of Antipater of Tarsus, and Athenodorus say that [moral] mistakes are not equal.

They say that the wise man will participate in politics unless something prevents him, according to Chrysippus in book 1 of *On Ways of Life;* for he will restrain vice and promote virtue. And he will marry, as Zeno says in his *Republic,* and have children. Again, the wise man will not hold opinions, i.e., he will not assent to anything that is false. And he will live like a Cynic. For the Cynic, life is a short road to virtue, as Apollodorus says in his *Ethics.* And he will even taste human flesh in special circumstances. He alone is free, and the base men are slaves; for freedom is the authority to act on one's own, whereas slavery is the privation of [the ability] to act on one's own. **122.** There is also another kind of slavery, in the sense of subordination [to another]; and a third, in the sense of subordination [to] and possession [by another]. Its opposite is mastery [or: despotism], and this too is base. Not only are the wise free, but they are also kings since kingship is a form of rule not subject to review, which only the wise could have, as Chrysippus says in his book *On the Fact That Zeno Used Terms in Their Proper Senses.* For he says that the ruler must know about good and bad things and that none of the base understands these things. Similarly they alone are fit for office or for jury duty, and [they alone are] public speakers, but none of the base are. Again, they are also free of [moral] mistakes since they are not subject to making [moral] mistakes. **123.** And they do no harm; for they harm neither others nor themselves. But they are not prone to pity and forgive no one. For they do not relax the penalties which the law fixes as relevant since giving in and pity and equity itself are the vapidity of a soul that aims to substitute niceness for punishment; nor does he think that [such punishments] are too severe. Again, the wise man is astonished at none of the things which appear to be wonders, such as the caves of Charon or tidal ebbs or hot springs or fiery exhalations [from the earth]. Moreover, the virtuous man will not, they say, live in solitude; for he is naturally made for [living in a] community and for action. He will, moreover, submit to training for the sake of [building] bodily endurance.

124. They say that the wise man will pray, asking for good things from the gods, according to Posidonius in book 1 of his *On Appropriate Actions* and Hecaton in book 3 of *On Paradoxes.* And they say that friendship exists only among virtuous men, because of their similarity. They say that it is a sharing [or: community] of things needed for one's life since we treat our friends as ourselves. They declare that one's friend is worth choosing for his own sake and that having many friends is a good thing and [that] there is no friendship among base men and that no base man has a friend. And all the imprudent are mad; for they are not prudent, but do everything in accordance with madness, which is equivalent to imprudence.

125. The wise man does everything well, as we also say that Ismenias plays all the flute tunes well. And everything belongs to wise men; for the law has given them complete authority. Some things are *said* to belong to the base, just as things are also *said* to belong to men who are unjust; in one sense we say they belong to the state, in another sense to those who are using them.

They say that the virtues follow on each other and that he who has one has them all. For their theoretical principles are common, as Chrysippus says in book 1 of his *On Virtues*, and Apollodorus in his *Physics in the Early [Stoic] School*,[4] and Hecaton in book 3 of *On Virtues*. **126.** For he who has virtue has a theoretical knowledge of what is to be done and also practices it. And what one is to do and choose is also what one is to endure for and stand firmly by and distribute, so that if he does some things by way of choosing and others by way of enduring and others by way of distributing and others by standing firmly by [something], one will be prudent and courageous and just and temperate. Each of the virtues is demarcated by a particular sphere of relevance, such as courage which is concerned with what is to be endured for, prudence with what is to be done and what not and what is neither; similarly, the other virtues revolve around their proper objects. Deliberative excellence and understanding follow on prudence, organization and orderliness on temperance, evenhandedness and fairness on justice, constancy and vigor on courage.

127. They believe that there is nothing in between virtue and vice, whereas the Peripatetics say that [moral] progress is between virtue and vice. For, they say, just as a stick must be either straight or crooked, so must a person be either just or unjust and neither 'more just' nor 'more unjust'; and the same for the other virtues. And Chrysippus says that virtue can be lost, whereas Cleanthes says that it cannot be lost; [Chrysippus says] that it can be lost owing to drunkenness and an excess of black bile, whereas [Cleanthes says it] cannot, because [it consists in] secure [intellectual] grasps and it is worth choosing for its <own> sake. At any rate, we are ashamed at things we do badly, as though we knew that only the honorable is good. And it is sufficient for happiness, as Zeno says, and Chrysippus in book 1 of *On Virtues* and Hecaton in book 2 of *On Goods*. **128.** "For if," he says, "magnanimity is sufficient for making one superior to everything and if it is a part of virtue, virtue too is sufficient for happiness, holding in contempt even those things which seem to be bothersome." Panaetius, however, and Posidonius say that virtue is not sufficient [for happiness] but that there is a need for health and material resources and strength.

They think that one employs virtue constantly, as the followers of Cleanthes say. For it cannot be lost and the virtuous man always employs a soul which is in perfect condition. And justice is natural and not conventional, as are the law and right reason, as Chrysippus says in *On the Honorable*. **129.** They think that

4. The title may also be translated *Physics in the Ancient Style*. The consequent uncertainty is whether the book was about early Stoic physics or about the physics of earlier philosophers generally.

one [should] not give up philosophy because of disagreement [among philosophers] since by this argument one would give up one's whole life, as Posidonius too says in his *Protreptics*. And Chrysippus says that general education is very useful.

Again, they think that there is no justice between us and the other animals because of the dissimilarity [between us and them], as Chrysippus says in book 1 of *On Justice* and Posidonius in book 1 of *On Appropriate Action* and that the wise man will fall in love with young men who reveal through their appearance a natural aptitude for virtue, as Zeno says in the *Republic* and Chrysippus in book 1 of *On Ways of Life* and Apollodorus in his *Ethics*.

130. And sexual love is an effort to gain friendship resulting from the appearance of beauty; and it is not directed at intercourse, but at friendship. At any rate Thrasonides, although he had his beloved in his power, kept his hands off her because she hated him. So, sexual love is directed at friendship, as Chrysippus says in his *On Sexual Love;* and it is not to be blamed; and youthful beauty is the flower of virtue.

There being three ways of life, the theoretical, the practical, and the rational, they say that the third is to be chosen; for the rational animal was deliberately made by nature for theory and action. And they say that the wise man will commit suicide reasonably [i.e., for a good reason], both on behalf of his fatherland and on behalf of his friends and if he should be in very severe pain or is mutilated or has an incurable disease.

131. They think the wise men should have their wives in common, so that anyone might make love to any woman, as Zeno says in the *Republic* and Chrysippus says in his *On the Republic* and, again, so do Diogenes the Cynic and Plato. And we shall cherish all the children equally, like fathers, and the jealousy occasioned by adultery will be removed. The best form of government is that which is a blend of democracy and monarchy and aristocracy. And this is the sort of thing they say in their ethical opinions and even more than this, together with the accompanying proofs. But let this be our summary and elementary account.

The Account Preserved by Stobaeus

TEXT 102: Stobaeus *Anthology* 2.5–12 (vol. 2, pp. 57–116 W-H)[5]

5. The views of Zeno and the rest of the Stoics about the ethical part of philosophy.

5a. Zeno says that whatever participates in substance exists and that of things which exist some are good, some bad, and some indifferent. Good are

5. We encourage readers to consult Arthur J. Pomeroy, ed. *Arius Didymus: Epitome of Stoic Ethics* (Atlanta: Society of Biblical Literature, 1999), which has fuller notes.

things like this: prudence, temperance, justice, courage, and everything which either is virtue or participates in virtue. Bad are things like this: imprudence, wantonness, injustice, cowardice, and everything which either is vice or participates in vice. Indifferent are things like this: life and death, good and bad reputation, pleasure and pain, wealth and poverty, health and disease, and things similar to these.

5b. Of goods, some are virtues, some are not. Prudence, then, and temperance <and justice> and courage <and great-heartedness and strength of body and soul> are virtues; joy and good spirits and confidence and wish and such things are not virtues. Of virtues, some are kinds of knowledge of certain things and crafts, and some are not. Prudence, then, and temperance and justice and courage are kinds of knowledge of certain things and crafts; greatheartedness and strength of body and soul are neither kinds of knowledge of certain things nor crafts. Analogously, of bad things some are vices and some are not. Imprudence, then, and injustice and cowardice and pusillanimity and powerlessness are vices; pain and fear and such things are not vices. Of vices, some are kinds of ignorance of certain things and the absence of skill, some are not. Imprudence, then, and wantonness and injustice and cowardice are kinds of ignorance of certain things and the absence of skill. Pusillanimity and powerlessness <and weakness> are neither kinds of ignorance nor lacks of skill.

5b1. Prudence is knowledge of what one is to do and not to do and what is neither or the knowledge in a naturally social <and rational> animal of good things, bad things, and what is neither (and they say that this [definition] is to be understood [to apply] in the case of the rest of the virtues too). Temperance is knowledge of what is to be chosen and avoided and what is neither. Justice is knowledge of the distribution of proper value to each person. Courage is knowledge of what is terrible and what is not terrible and what is neither. Folly is ignorance of good things, bad things, and what is neither, or ignorance of what one is to do and not to do and what is neither. Wantonness is ignorance of what is worth choosing and worth avoiding and what is neither. <Injustice is ignorance of the distribution of proper value to each person>. Cowardice is ignorance of what is terrible and what is not terrible and what is neither. They define the other virtues and vices similarly, following what has been said.

5b2. Of virtues some are primary, some subordinate to the primary. There are four primary virtues: prudence, temperance, courage, justice. And prudence concerns appropriate acts; temperance concerns human impulses; courage concerns instances of standing firm; justice concerns distributions. Of those subordinate to these, some are subordinate to prudence, some to temperance, some to courage, some to justice. To prudence are subordinate deliberative excellence, good calculation, quick-wittedness, good sense, <a good sense of purpose>, resourcefulness. To temperance: organization, orderliness, modesty, self-control. To courage: endurance, confidence, great-heartedness, stout-heartedness, love of work. To justice: piety, good-heartedness, public-spiritedness, fair dealing. They say, then, that deliberative excellence is a knowledge of the type and manner of actions which we must perform in order to act advantageously. Good calculation is knowledge which draws up a balance and summarizes [the value of] what happens and is produced. Quick-wittedness is knowledge which instantly finds out what the appropriate action is. Good sense is knowledge <of what is better and worse; a good sense of purpose is knowledge> that achieves its goal in each action; resourcefulness is knowledge that discovers a way out of difficulties; organization is knowledge of when one is to act and what [to do] after what and in general of the ordering of actions; orderliness is <knowledge> of appropriate and inappropriate motions; modesty is knowledge which is cautious about proper criticism; self-control is an unsurpassable knowledge of what is revealed by right reason; endurance is knowledge which stands by correct decisions; confidence is knowledge in virtue of which we know that we shall meet with nothing which is terrible; great-heartedness is knowledge which makes one superior to those things which naturally occur among both virtuous and base men; stout-heartedness is knowledge in a soul which makes it [the soul] invincible; love of work is a knowledge which achieves its goal by labor, not being deterred by hard work; piety is knowledge of service to the gods; good-heartedness is knowledge which does good [to others]; public-spiritedness is knowledge of fairness in a community; fair dealing is knowledge of how to deal with one's neighbors blamelessly.

5b3. The goal of all these virtues is to live consistently with nature. Each one enables a human being to achieve this [goal] in his own way; for [a human] has from nature inclinations to discover what is appropriate and to stabilize his impulses and to stand firm and to distribute [fairly]. And each of the virtues does what is consonant [with these inclinations] and does its own job, thus enabling a human being to live consistently with nature.

5b4. They say, then, that these virtues just listed are perfect in our lives and consist of theorems; but others supervene on them, which are no longer crafts but rather certain capabilities that come as a result of practice, for example, health of the soul and its soundness and strength and beauty. For just as the health of the body is a good blend of the hot and cold and wet and dry elements in the body, so too the health of the soul is a good blend of the beliefs in the soul. And similarly, just as strength of the body is a sufficient tension in the sinews, so too the strength of the soul is a sufficient tension in judging and acting and in not doing so. And just as beauty of the body is a symmetry of its limbs constituted with respect to each other and to the whole, so too the beauty of the soul is a symmetry of reason and its parts with respect to the whole of it and to each other.

5b5. All the virtues which are forms of knowledge and crafts have common theorems and the same goal, as was said, and consequently they are inseparable; for he who has one has them all, and he who acts with one virtue acts with all. They differ from each other in their topics. For the topics of prudence are, in the first instance, considering and doing what is to be done and, in the second instance, considering what one should distribute <and what one should choose and what one should endure>, for the sake of doing what is to be done without error. The topic of temperance is, in the first instance, to make the impulses stable and to consider them and, in the second instance, [to consider] the topics of the other virtues for the sake of behaving without error in one's impulses. And similarly courage, in the first instance, [considers] everything which one should endure and, in the second instance, the topics of the other virtues; and justice, in the first instance, looks to what is due to each person and, in the second instance, the other topics too. For all the virtues consider the topics of all [the virtues] and those which are subordinate to each other. For Panaetius used to say that what happened in the case of the virtues was like what would happen if there were one target set up for many archers and this target had on it lines that differed in color; and then each were to aim at hitting the target—one by striking the white line, it might be, another by striking the black, and another by striking another colored line. For just as these [archers] make their highest goal the hitting of the target, but each sets before himself a different manner of hitting it, in the same way too all the virtues make being happy their goal (and this lies in living in agreement with nature) but each [virtue] achieves this in a different manner.

5b6. Diogenes [of Babylon] says that there are two senses of 'things worth choosing for their own sake and worth choosing in the final sense':[6] those set out in the previous division and those which have in themselves the cause of being worth choosing (and this is a property of every good thing).

5b7. They say that there are several virtues and that they are inseparable from each other. And that in substance they are identical with the leading part of the soul; accordingly, [they say] that every virtue is and is called a 'body'; for the intellect and the soul are bodies. For they believe that the inborn *pneuma* in us, which is warm, is soul. And they also want [to claim] that the soul in us is an animal since it lives and has sense-perception, and especially so the leading part of it, which is called 'intellect'. That is why every virtue too is an animal since in substance it is the same as the intellect; accordingly, they say also that prudence acts prudently. For it is consistent for them to speak thus.

6. *Telika,* which probably means "having the character of an ultimate goal." The two senses seem to be a narrow one, which applies only to the virtues (below at 5g the virtues are again said to be *telika* as well as instrumental), and a broader sense, which includes all good things, even the prudent man and the friend excluded from this category at 5g. We dissent from Wachsmuth-Hense's correction of the evidently corrupt text and follow Heeren's emendation.

5b8. There is nothing between virtue and vice. For all human beings have from nature inclinations toward virtue and, according to Cleanthes, are like half lines of iambic verse; hence, if they remain incomplete they are base, but if they are completed [or: perfected] they are virtuous. They also say that the wise man does everything in accordance with all the virtues; for his every action is perfect and so is bereft of none of the virtues.

5b9. Consistently with this they hold also that he [the wise man] acts with good sense and dialectically and sympotically and erotically; but the erotic man is so called in two senses, the one who is virtuous and gets his quality from virtue, and the one who is blamed, who gets his quality from vice—a sort of sex fiend. And sexual love is . . . [There is a lacuna here.] And being worthy of sexual love means the same as being worthy of friendship and not the same as being worthy of being enjoyed;[7] for he who is worthy of virtuous sexual love is [properly] worthy of sexual love. They understand virtue exercised at a symposium as similar to virtue in sexual matters, the one being knowledge that is concerned with what is appropriate at a symposium, namely, of how one should run symposia and how one should drink at them; and the other is knowledge of how to hunt for talented young boys, which encourages them to virtuous knowledge, and in general, knowledge of proper sexual activity. That is why they say that the sensible man will engage in sexual activity. And sexual activity just by itself is an indifferent since at times it also occurs among base men. But sexual love is not desire nor is it directed at any base object but is an effort to gain friendship resulting from the appearance of beauty.

5b10. And they also say that the wise man does everything which he does well—obviously. For in the sense that we say that the flute player or kithara player does everything well, it being understood that we refer to what the one does in his flute playing and the other in his kithara playing, in the same sense we say that the prudent man does everything well, both what he does and, by Zeus, what he does not do too.[8] For they thought that the opinion that the wise man does everything well follows from his accomplishing everything in accordance with right reason and, as it were, in accordance with virtue, which is a craft concerned with one's entire life. Analogously, the base man too does everything which he does badly and in accordance with all the vices.

5b11. They call 'practices' the love of music, of letters, of horses, of hunting, and, broadly speaking, the so-called general crafts; they are not knowledge, but they leave them in the class of virtuous conditions, and consistently they say

---

7. See TEXT 101.130.

8. The text is corrupt here and we translate the emendation of Hense. With their own emendation, Long and Sedley (*The Hellenistic Philosophers* [Cambridge: Cambridge University Press, 1987] vol. 1, 61G1, p. 380) translate: "does everything well, so far as concerns what he does, and not of course also what he does not do." Pomeroy has: "does everything well with respect to whatever he does, and not, by Zeus, with respect to what he does not do."

that only the wise man is a music lover and a lover of letters, and analogously in the other cases. They give an outline [definition] of a 'practice' as follows: a method using a craft or some part [of a craft] that leads [us] to what is in accord with virtue.

5b12. They say that only the wise man is a good prophet and poet and public speaker and dialectician and critic, but not every [wise man] since some of these [crafts] also require a mastery of certain theorems. And prophecy is a theoretical knowledge of signs significant for human life given by the gods or daimons. The forms of prophecy are similarly [described].

They say that only the wise man is a priest but that no base man is. For the priest must be experienced in the laws concerning sacrifices and prayers and purifications and foundations and all such things, and in addition he also needs ritual sanctity and piety and experience of service to the gods and [needs] to be intimate with the nature of divinity. And the base man has not one of these features, and that is why all imprudent men are impious. For impiety, being a vice, is ignorance of the service to the gods, whereas piety is, as we said, a knowledge of service to the gods.

Similarly they say that the base are not holy either; for holiness is defined in outline as justice toward the gods, whereas the base deviate in many respects from just action toward the gods, which is why they are unholy and impure and unsanctified and defiled and to be barred from festivals.

For they say that participating at a festival is a [prerogative] of the virtuous man, a festival being a time in which one should be concerned with the divine for the sake of honoring [the gods] and for the sake of the appropriate observations; and that is why the participant in a festival should accommodate [himself] to this sort of role with piety.

5b13. Again, they say that every base man is mad, being ignorant of himself and his own concerns; and that is madness. And ignorance is the vice opposite to prudence; and a certain relative disposition of this, which makes one's impulses unstable and fluttery, is madness. That is why they give an outline [definition] of madness as follows: a fluttery ignorance.

5c. Again, of good things, some are attributes of all prudent men all the time, and some are not. Every virtue and prudent sense-perception and prudent impulse and the like are attributes of all prudent men on every occasion; but joy and good spirits and prudent walking are not attributes of all prudent men and not all the time. Analogously, of bad things too, some are attributes of all imprudent men all the time, and some are not. Every vice and imprudent sense-perception and imprudent impulse and the like are attributes of all imprudent men all the time; but pain and fear and imprudent answering are not attributes of all imprudent men and not on every occasion.

5d. All good things are beneficial and well used and advantageous and profitable and virtuous and fitting and honorable; there is an affinity to them.

Conversely, all bad things are harmful and ill used and disadvantageous and unprofitable and base and unfitting and shameful, and there is no affinity to them.

They say that 'good' is used in many senses; the primary sense, which plays a role like that of a source [for the other senses], is that which is stated as follows: that from which it characteristically results that one is benefited or he by whom [it results that one is benefited] (and what is good in the primary sense is the cause). The second sense is that in accordance with which it characteristically results that one is benefited.

A more general sense and one extending also to the previous cases is that which is such as to benefit. Similarly, the bad too is defined in outline by analogy with the good: that from which or by whom it characteristically results that one is harmed and that in accordance with which it characteristically results that one is harmed; more general than these is that which is such as to harm.

5e. Of good things, some are in the soul, some external, and some neither in the soul nor external. In the soul are the virtues and virtuous conditions and in general praiseworthy activities. External are friends and acquaintances and things like that. Neither in the soul nor external are virtuous men and in general those who have the virtues. Similarly, of bad things, some are in the soul, some external, and some neither in the soul nor external. In the soul are the vices together with wicked conditions and in general blameworthy activities. External are enemies together with their various forms. Neither in the soul nor external are base men and all those who have the vices.

5f. Of the goods in the soul, some are dispositions, some are conditions but not dispositions, and some are neither conditions nor dispositions. All the virtues are dispositions, whereas practices are only conditions but not dispositions, for example, prophecy and the like. Virtuous activities—for example, prudent action and the possession of temperance and the like—are neither conditions nor dispositions. Similarly, of the bad things in the soul, some are dispositions, some are conditions but not dispositions, and some are neither conditions nor dispositions. All the vices are dispositions, whereas tendencies, such as enviousness, resentfulness, and such things, are only conditions and not dispositions; so too for diseases and ailments, such as greed, love of drink, and the like. Vicious activities such as imprudent action, unjust action, and things like that are neither conditions nor dispositions.

5g. Of good things, some are final, some are instrumental, and some are both. For the prudent man and one's friend are only instrumental goods, but joy and good spirits and confidence and prudent walking are only final goods; all the virtues are both instrumental and final goods since they both produce happiness and fulfill it, becoming parts of it. Analogously, of bad things some are instrumental to unhappiness, some are final, and some are both. For the imprudent man and one's enemy are only instrumental bad things, but pain and fear and theft and imprudent questioning and similar things <are only> final <bad things>; the vices are both instrumental and final bad things since they produce unhappiness and fulfill it, becoming parts of it. **5h.** Again, of good things, some are worth choosing for their own sakes, whereas some are instrumental. All those which are subject to reasonable choice for the sake of nothing else are worth choosing for their own sakes, whereas those [which are subject to reasonable choice] because they produce other things are said [to be worth choosing] in the instrumental sense. **5i.** And every good is worth choosing; for it is pleasing and approved of and praiseworthy. And every bad thing is worth avoiding. For the good, insofar as it stimulates reasonable choice, is worth choosing; and insofar as it is subject to choice without suspicion, it is pleasing.[9] And, moreover, insofar as one would reasonably suppose that it is one of the products of virtue, <it is praiseworthy>. **5k.** Again, of good things some consist in motion and some consist in a state. For such things as joy, good spirits, and temperate conversation consist in motion, whereas such things as a well-ordered quietude, undisturbed rest, and a manly attention consist in a state. Of things which consist in a state, some also consist in a condition, such as the virtues; others are only in a state, such as the above mentioned. Not only the virtues consist in a condition but also the crafts which are transformed in the virtuous man by his virtue and so become unchangeable; for they become quasi-virtues. And they say that the so-called practices are also among the goods which consist in a condition, such as love of music, love of letters, love of geometry, and the like. For there is a method which selects those elements in such crafts which have an affinity to virtue by referring them to the goal of life. **5l.** Again, of good things, some are [things which exist] in themselves and some are relative dispositions. Knowledge, just action, and similar things are [things which exist] in themselves. Honor, goodwill, friendship, and <agreement> are relative. And knowledge is a grasp which is secure and unchangeable by argument; another definition: knowledge is a complex system of grasps of this sort, such as knowledge of the particulars, which is, in the virtuous man, rational; another definition: a complex system of craftsmanlike knowledge, which provides its own stability, which is what the virtues are like; another definition: a condition receptive of presentations which is unchangeable by argument, which they say consists in a tension and power [of the soul]. Friendship is a community of life. Agreement is a sharing of opinions about things relevant to life. Within friendship, familiarity is friendship with people who are well known to you; habituation is friendship with people you have become accustomed to; companionship is friendship by choice, such as that

---

9. Some suspect a lacuna here.

with one's contemporaries; guest-friendship is friendship with foreigners; there is also a kind of family friendship between relatives; and an erotic friendship based on sexual love. And painlessness and organization are the same as temperance, just as insight and wits are [the same] as prudence and sharing and generosity are [the same] as good-heartedness; for they have been given names by reference to their relative dispositions. And one must note this too in each of the other virtues.

5m. Again, of good things, some are unmixed, such as knowledge, whereas others are mixed, such as having good children, a good old age, a good life. Having good children is the natural and virtuous possession of children; good old age is the natural and virtuous use of old age; and similarly for a good life.

5n. It is always clear in these cases that there will be similar divisions of [the corresponding] bad things.

5o. They say that what is worth choosing and what is worth taking are different. For what stimulates an unconditional impulse is worth choosing, <whereas what is worth taking is what we reasonably select>. Insofar as what is worth choosing differs from what is worth taking, to the same degree what is in itself worth choosing differs from what is in itself worth taking and, in general, for what is good by comparison with what has value.

6. Since a human being is a rational, mortal animal, social by nature, they say also that all human virtue and happiness constitute a life which is consistent and in agreement with nature.

6a. Zeno defined the goal thus: 'living in agreement'. This means living according to a single and consonant rational principle since those who live in conflict are unhappy. Those who came after him made further distinctions and expressed it thus: 'living in agreement with nature', supposing that Zeno's formulation was an incomplete predicate. For Cleanthes, who first inherited [the leadership of] his school, added 'with nature' and defined it thus: 'the goal is living in agreement with nature'. Chrysippus wanted to make this clearer and expressed it in this way: 'to live according to experience of the things which happen by nature'. And Diogenes: 'to be reasonable in the selection and rejection of natural things'. And Archedemus: 'to live completing all the appropriate acts'. And Antipater: 'to live invariably selecting natural things and rejecting unnatural things'. He often defined it thus as well: 'invariably and unswervingly to do everything in one's power for the attainment of the principal natural things'.

6b. 'Goal' is used in three senses by the members of this school: for the final good is said to be the goal in standard scholarly language, as when they say that agreement is the goal; and they say that the target is the goal, for example, they speak of the life in agreement by reference to the associated predicate; in the third sense they say that the ultimate object of striving is a goal, to which all others are referred.

6c. They think that the goal and the target are different. For the target is the physical state [lit., body] set up [for people] to try to achieve . . . [There is a lacuna here.] those who aim at happiness since every virtuous man is happy and every base man is, by contrast, unhappy.

6d. And of good things, some are necessary for happiness and some are not. And all the virtues and the activities which employ them are necessary; joy and good spirits and the practices are not necessary. Similarly, of bad things, some are necessary as being bad for the existence of unhappiness, and some are not necessary. All the vices and the activities based on them are necessary; all the passions and ailments and things like this are not necessary.

6e. They say that being happy is the goal for the sake of which everything is done and that it is itself done for the sake of nothing else; and this consists in living according to virtue, in living in agreement, and again (which is the same thing) in living according to nature. Zeno defined happiness in this manner: 'happiness is a smooth flow of life'. Cleanthes too used this definition in his treatises, and so did Chrysippus and all their followers, saying that happiness was no different from the happy life, although they do say that while happiness is set up as a target, the goal is to achieve happiness, which is the same as being happy.

So, it is clear from this that [these expressions] are equivalent: 'living according to nature' and 'living honorably' and 'living well' and again 'the honorable and good' and 'virtue and what participates in virtue'; and that every good thing is honorable and similarly that every shameful thing is bad. That is also why the Stoic goal is equivalent to the life according to virtue.

6f. They say that what is worth choosing differs from what is to be chosen. For every good is worth choosing, but every advantage is to be chosen, and [advantage] is understood with reference to having the good. That is why we choose what is to be chosen, for example, being prudent, which is understood with reference to having prudence; but we do not choose what is worth choosing, but if anything, we choose to have it. Similarly too all goods are worth enduring [for] and worth standing firmly by and analogously in the case of the other virtues, even if there is no name for them. And all advantages are to be endured [for] and to be stood firmly by. And in the same manner for the others which are in accordance with the vices.

7. After giving a sufficient account of good things and bad things and what is worth choosing and what is worth avoiding and the goal and happiness, we think it necessary to go through in their proper order what is said about things indifferent. They say that things indifferent are between good things and bad things, saying that the indifferent is conceived of in two ways: in one way, it is what is neither good nor bad nor worth choosing nor worth avoiding; in the other, it is what is stimulative of impulse neither toward nor away from [itself]. In this sense some are said to be absolutely indifferent, such as <having

an odd or even number of hairs on one's head or> extending one's finger this
way or that way, or picking off some annoying object, such as a twig or a leaf.
In the first sense one must say that, according to the members of this school,
what is between virtue and vice is indifferent but not [indifferent] with respect
to selection and rejection; and that is why some have selective value and some
have rejective disvalue but make no contribution at all to the happy life.

7a. And some are natural, some unnatural, and some neither unnatural nor
natural. Natural, then, are such things: health, strength, soundness of one's
sense organs, and things like this. Unnatural are such things: disease, weakness, impairment, and such things. Neither unnatural nor natural are a stable
condition of soul and body according to which the one is receptive of false
presentations and the other receptive of wounds and impairments and things
like these. They say that the account of these matters is based on the primary
natural and unnatural things. For what makes a difference and the indifferent
are relative. That is why, they say, even if we say that bodily matters and external things are indifferent, we [also] say that they are indifferent with respect to
living a beautifully ordered life (and in this consists a happy life) but not, by
Zeus, [indifferent] with respect to being in a natural state nor with respect to
impulse toward or away from [something].

7b. Again, of indifferent things, some have more value and others have less;
and some are [valuable] in themselves and some instrumentally; and some are
preferred and some are rejected, and some neither. Preferred are all things
indifferent which have a lot of value as indifferents; rejected are all things
indifferent which have a lot of disvalue in the same sense; neither preferred
nor rejected are all which have neither a lot of <value nor> a lot of disvalue.

Of preferred things, some are in the soul, some in the body, and some
external. In the soul are things like this: natural ability, [moral] progress, good
memory, mental sharpness, a condition which enables one to stand firm in
appropriate actions, and the crafts which can contribute substantially to the
natural life. Preferred things in the body are health, good sense-perception,
and things like these. Among externals are parents, children, possessions in
due measure, acceptance among men.

The opposites of those mentioned are rejected things in the soul. [Rejected
things] in the body and externally are those which are similarly opposed to the
above-mentioned preferred things in the body and externally.

Neither preferred nor rejected in the soul are presentation, assent, and
things like that; in the body, fair or dark complexion, having blue eyes, and all
pleasure and pain and anything else of this sort; in external things, what is
neither preferred <nor rejected> are things like this: whatever, being cheap
and bringing nothing useful, provides by itself an utterly tiny amount of usefulness. Since the soul is more important than the body, they also say that the
things of the soul which are natural and preferred have more value for the

natural life than bodily and external things; for example, natural ability in the soul is more helpful for virtue than natural ability in the body, and similarly for the others.

7c. Again, of things indifferent, they say that some are stimulative of impulse toward [themselves], some stimulative of impulse away from [themselves], and some stimulative of impulse neither toward nor away from [themselves]. Those things which we said are natural are stimulative of impulse toward [themselves]; those which are unnatural are stimulative of impulse away from [themselves]; those which are neither are stimulative of impulse neither toward nor away from [themselves], for example, having an odd or even number of hairs.

7d. Of things which are indifferent and natural, some are primary natural things, some natural by participation. Primary natural things are a motion or state which occurs in accordance with the spermatic principles, such as <soundness and> health and sense-perception (I mean an act of grasping) and strength. By participation: everything which participates in a motion or state which is in accordance with the spermatic principles, for example, a sound hand and a healthy body and senses which are not impaired. Similarly, for the unnatural things [the situation is] analogous.

7e. Everything which is natural is worth taking and everything which is <un>natural is worth not taking. Of natural things, some are worth taking in themselves, some because of other things. In themselves: everything which is stimulative of impulse in such a manner as to encourage [someone] to pursue it or to hang on to it, such as health, good sense-perception, freedom from pain, bodily beauty. Instrumentally: everything which is stimulative of impulse by reference to other things and not in such a manner as to encourage [someone to pursue] it, such as wealth, reputation, and things like these. Similarly, of unnatural things some are in themselves not worth taking and some because they are instrumental to things which are in themselves not worth taking.

7f. Everything which is natural has value and everything which is unnatural has disvalue. Value has three senses: [1] the estimation and honor [for something] in itself, and [2] the exchange-value of its appraised worth, and [3] third what Antipater calls 'selective value', according to which when circumstances permit we choose these things rather than those, for example, health rather than disease and life rather than death and wealth rather than poverty. Analogously, they also say that disvalue has three senses if one inverts the senses [of the definitions] given for the three kinds of value.

Diogenes says that the 'estimation' is a judgment of the extent to which something is natural or provides something useful to nature. 'Appraised worth' is not interpreted in the sense in which the things [themselves] are said to have 'appraised worth' but as we say that he who puts an appraisal on things is the 'appraiser'. For he says that such a person is the 'appraiser' of exchange-value. And these are the two [senses of] value according to which we say that something is preferred in value, and he says that the third is that according to which we say that something has valuable merit and value, which does not apply to things indifferent but only to virtuous things. He says that we sometimes use the word 'value' in place of 'what is fitting' as it was used in the definition of justice when it is said to be a condition which distributes to each person what is in accordance with his value; for this is like saying 'what is fitting' for each person.

7g. Of things which have value, some have a lot of value, some have little. Similarly, of things which have disvalue, some have a lot of disvalue, some have little. Those which have a lot of value are called preferred things, whereas those which have a lot of disvalue are called rejected, Zeno being the first one to apply these terms to the things. They say that the preferred is that which, being indifferent, we select in accordance with the principal reason. The same kind of account applies to what is rejected, and the examples are the same by analogy. None of the good things is preferred since they have the greatest value. The preferred, which holds the second rank and has value, is in a way close to the nature of good things. For at a court the king is not among those who are preferred, but those below him in rank are. They are called preferred, not because they contribute to happiness and help to produce it, but because it is necessary to select them in preference to the rejected things.

8. The topic of appropriate action follows [naturally] on the discussion of the preferred things. Appropriate action is defined [thus]: 'what is consistent in life, which when done admits of a reasonable defense'. What is contrary to the appropriate is the opposite. This extends even to irrational animals, for they too do thing[s] consistently with their nature. In rational animals it is expressed thus: 'what is consistent in a life'. And of appropriate actions, some are complete [or perfect], and they are called [morally] perfect actions. [Morally] perfect actions are activities in accordance with virtue, such as being prudent and acting justly. Things which are not of this character are not [morally] perfect actions, and they do not call them complete appropriate actions either, but intermediate ones, such as getting married, going on an embassy, engaging in dialectic, and similar things.

8a. Of [morally] perfect actions some are requirements and some not. Requirements are advantages, expressed in predicate form, such as being prudent and being temperate. Things which are not of this character are not requirements. The same technical distinctions apply similarly to inappropriate actions. Every inappropriate action which occurs in a rational <animal> is a [moral] mistake; and an appropriate action when perfected [or completed] is a [morally] perfect action. The intermediate appropriate action is measured by [reference to] certain indifferent things, which are selected according to or contrary to nature, and which bring prosperity of such a sort that if we were not to take them or were to reject them, except under abnormal circumstances, we would not be happy.

9. They say that what stimulates impulse is nothing but a hormetic presentation of what is obviously [or: immediately] appropriate. And impulse is, in general, a movement of the soul toward something. Its species are understood to be the impulse occurring in rational animals and the impulse occurring in irrational animals; but they have not been named. For striving is not rational impulse but a form of rational impulse. And one would properly define rational impulse by saying that it is a movement of intellect toward something which is involved in action. Opposed to this is an impulse away from [something], a movement <of intellect away from something involved in action.> They say in a special sense too that planning is impulse, being a form of practical impulse. And planning is a movement of intellect to something in the future.

So, thus far impulse is used in four senses, and impulse away from in two. When you add the hormetic condition too, which indeed they also call impulse in a special sense and which is the source of the active impulse, then 'impulse' is [seen to be] used in five senses.

9a. There are several forms of practical impulse, among which are these: purpose, effort, preparation, endeavor, <choice,> forechoice, wish, wanting. So, they say that purpose is an indication of accomplishment; effort is an impulse before an impulse; preparation is an action before an action; endeavor is an impulse in the case of something already in hand; choice is wish based on analogy; forechoice is a choice before a choice; wish is a rational striving; wanting is a voluntary wish.

9b. All impulses are [acts of] assent; and the practical ones[10] also include the power to set [the agent] in motion. Now, [acts of] assent are directed at one thing and impulses at another; and [acts of] assent are directed at certain propositions, whereas impulses are directed at predicates which are, in a way, included in the propositions to which assent is given.

Since passion is a form of impulse, let us speak next about the passions.

10. They say that a passion is an impulse which is excessive and disobedient to the reason which constrains, or an <irrational>, unnatural motion of the soul (and all passions belong to the leading part of the soul). And that is why every 'flutter' is a passion <and> again <every> passion is a 'flutter'. Since this is what a passion is like, one must suppose that some are primary and principal, and the others are referred to these. The primary are these four kinds: desire, fear, pain, and pleasure. Desire and fear, then, are principal, one

---

10. Either "practical assents" (see Brad Inwood *Ethics and Human Action* [Oxford: Oxford University Press, 1985], n. 271, pp. 287–88, though we no longer believe that the textual emendation is necessary to get this sense) or "practical impulses" (see Long and Sedley 33I with discussion in vol. 2, p. 200). The text and interpretation are both uncertain.

[being concerned with] the apparent good, the other with the apparent bad. Pleasure and pain supervene on these, pleasure when we achieve what we desired or escape what we were afraid of, pain when we miss achieving what we desired or meet with what we were afraid of. With all the passions of the soul, since they say that they are opinions, the [word] 'opinion' is used instead of 'weak supposition', and 'fresh' is used instead of 'what stimulates irrational contraction <or> elation'.

10a. The terms 'irrational' and 'unnatural' are not used in their common senses, but 'irrational' means the same as 'disobedient to reason'. For every passion is violent since those who are in a state of passion often see that it is advantageous not to do this but are swept away by the vehemence [of the passion], as though by some disobedient horse,[11] and are drawn to doing it; in this connection people often concede [that this is going on] when they cite that familiar tag: "Nature compels me, though I am aware [of what I am doing]."[12] For he here calls the realization and consciousness of what is right 'awareness'. And the term 'unnatural' was used in the outline [definition] of passion since it is something which happens contrary to the right and natural reason. Everyone in a state of passion turns his back on reason, not like those who are deceived on some point or other, but in a special sense. For those who are deceived, about atoms being principles for instance, when they are taught that they do not exist, then abandon their belief. But those who are in a state of passion, even if they do learn and are taught that one should not suffer pain or fear or generally experience any of the passions of the soul, still do not abandon them but are drawn by the passions into being dominated by their tyrannical rule.

10b. They say, then, that desire is a striving which is disobedient to reason; its cause is believing that a good is approaching and that when it is here we shall do well by it; this opinion itself <that it really is worth striving for> has a <fresh> [power] to stimulate irregular motion. Fear is an avoidance disobedient to reason, and its cause is believing that a bad thing is approaching; this opinion that it really is worth avoiding has a 'fresh' [power] to stimulate motion. Pain is a contraction of the soul disobedient to reason, and its cause is believing that a 'fresh' bad thing is present for which it is appropriate to <suffer contraction [in the soul]. Pleasure is an elation of the soul disobedient to reason, and its cause is believing that a fresh good thing is present, for which it is appropriate to> suffer elation [in the soul].

Under desire are subsumed such [passions] as these: anger and its forms (spiritedness and irascibility and wrath and rancor and bitterness and such things), vehement sexual desire, and longing and yearning and love of pleasure and love of wealth and love of reputation and similar things. Under pleasure

11. An allusion to Plato's *Phaedrus* and the myth of the charioteer (246a–247c).

12. Euripides fr. 837 Nauck.

are mean-spirited satisfaction, contentment, charms, and similar things. Under fear are hesitation, agony, shock, shame, panic, superstition, fright, and dread. Under pain are envy, grudging, resentment, pity, grief, heavyheartedness, distress, sorrow, anguish, and vexation.

10c. Anger, then, is a desire to take revenge on someone who appears to have wronged [you] contrary to what is appropriate; spiritedness is anger just beginning; irascibility is swollen anger; wrath is anger laid by or saved up for a long time; rancor is anger which watches for an opportunity for vengeance; bitterness is anger which breaks out immediately; sexual desire is an effort to gain love resulting from the appearance of [physical] beauty; longing is a sexual love for someone who is absent; yearning is a desire for contact with a friend who is absent; love of pleasure is a desire for pleasures; love of wealth [is a desire] for wealth; love of reputation for reputation.

Mean-spirited satisfaction is pleasure at someone else's misfortunes; contentment is pleasure at what is unexpected; charm is deceptive pleasure which comes via vision.

Hesitation is a fear of future action; agony is a fear of failure or, otherwise, a fear of defeat; shock is a fear arising from a presentation of something unfamiliar; shame is a fear of bad reputation; panic is [a] fear which hastens with the voice; superstition is a fear of gods and daimons; fright is a fear of something dreadful; dread is a fear which produces fright.[13]

Grudging is a pain at the goods of other people; envy is a pain at the other fellow getting what one desires oneself and not getting it oneself; there is another sense of 'envy' [zeal], i.e., the congratulation of someone who is [there is a corrupt word here] or the imitation of someone thought of as better [than oneself]; resentment is a pain at the other fellow also getting what one desired oneself; pity is a pain at someone's seeming to suffer undeservedly; grief is a pain at an untimely death; heavyheartedness is a pain which weighs one down; distress is a pain which makes one unable to speak; sorrow is a pain which comes by brooding [on something]; anguish is a pain which penetrates and settles in; vexation is a pain accompanied by tossing about.

10d. Of these passions, some indicate the object they are concerned with, such as pity, grudging, mean-spirited satisfaction, shame; some indicate the peculiar qualities of the motion, such as anguish and dread.

10e. A predisposition is a tendency toward [having a] passion, such as one of the activities contrary to nature, for example, proneness to pain, proneness to grudging, proneness to irascibility, and similar things. There are also predispositions to other activities which are contrary to nature, such as to theft and adultery and arrogant behavior; it is in virtue of these that people are said to become thieves, adulterers, and arrogant. A disease is an opinion connected to

---

13. Restored from Diogenes Laërtius 7.112 (TEXT 101).

a desire which has settled and hardened into a condition, in virtue of which people think that things not worth choosing are extremely worth choosing, for example, love of women, love of wine, love of money; there are also certain states opposite to <these> diseases which turn up as antipathies, such as hatred of women, hatred of wine, hatred of humanity. Those diseases which occur in conjunction with weakness are called ailments.

11a. They say that a [morally] perfect action is an appropriate action which covers all the features[14] or, as we said before, a complete [perfect] appropriate action. What is done contrary to right reason is a [moral] mistake; or, an [action] in which something appropriate has been omitted by a rational animal [is a moral mistake].

11b. They say that all good things belong <in common> to the virtuous, in that he who benefits one of his neighbors also benefits himself. Concord is a knowledge of common goods, and that is why all virtuous men are in concord with each other, because they are in agreement about matters concerned with life. The base are enemies and do harm to each other and are hostile, because they are in discord with each other.

They say that justice exists by nature and not by convention. Consequent on this is [the belief] that the wise man participates in political life, especially in the sort of governments which show some [moral] progress toward becoming perfect governments. Again, the virtuous have an affinity to legislating and to educating people and again to composing [books] which can help those who encounter their writings; and so they condescend to marry and have children, both for their own sake and for that of the fatherland; and they will endure both pain and death for the sake of [the fatherland], if it is moderate. Juxtaposed to these traits are base ones, courting the people and practicing sophistry and composing books which are harmful to those who read them. These are traits which would not occur in virtuous men.

11c. There are three senses of friendship. In one sense it is for the sake of common benefit that people are said to be friends; this kind of friendship is not that of good men, because for them there is no good which is composed out of separate components. They say that friendship in the second sense, a friendly attitude from one's neighbors, is one of the external goods. They claim that a personal friendship, according to which one is a friend of one's neighbors, is one of the goods in the soul.

11d. There is another sense in which all good things are common. For they believe that anyone who benefits anyone, by that very fact, receives equal benefit but that no base man either benefits or is benefited. For benefiting is <to change> or maintain something in accordance with virtue, and being benefited is to be changed in accordance with virtue.

---

14. Literally, "numbers."

They say that only the virtuous man is a household economist and a good household economist, and again a moneymaker. For household economy is a condition which contemplates and practices what is advantageous to a household; and economy is an arranging of expenditures and tasks and a care for possessions and for the work that is done on the farm. And moneymaking is experience of acquiring money by means of the actions by which one should do so and a condition which causes one to behave 'in agreement' in the collection and preservation and expenditure of money with the aim of [achieving] prosperity. And some think that moneymaking is an intermediate [activity], others that it is virtuous. And no base man is a good guardian of a household, nor can he arrange it that a house is well run. And only the virtuous man is a moneymaker since he knows the sources from which one is to get money and when and how and up to what point [one should continue doing so].

They say that <the sensible man> forgives <no one; for it is characteristic of the same man to forgive>, and to think that someone who has made a [moral] mistake did not do so because of himself, although [in fact] everyone who makes a [moral] mistake does so because of his own vice. And that is why it is quite proper for them to say that he does not even forgive those who make [moral] mistakes. Nor, they say, is the good man equitable since the equitable man is prone to ask for a reduction of the punishment which is due; and it is characteristic of the same person to be equitable and to suppose that the punishments established by the law for wrongdoers are too harsh and to believe that the lawgiver established punishments which are unduly [severe].

They say that the law is virtuous, being right reason which commands what is to be done and forbids what is not to be done. And since the law is virtuous, the lawful man would be virtuous; for he is someone who is lawful and follows the law and does what is commanded by it. He who interprets the law is a man of the law; and none of the base is either lawful or a man of the law.

11e. Again, they say that some activities are [morally] perfect actions, some are [moral] mistakes, and some are neither. [Morally] perfect actions are such things: being prudent, being temperate, acting justly, feeling joy, doing good works, being in good spirits, walking prudently, and everything which is done in accordance with right reason. [Moral] mistakes are: being imprudent, being wanton, unjust action, feeling pain and fear, stealing, and in general whatever is done contrary to right reason. Such things as these are neither [morally] perfect actions nor [moral] mistakes: speaking, asking, answering, walking, going out of town, and similar things. All [morally] perfect actions are just actions and lawful actions and orderly actions and good practices and acts of good fortune and acts of a happy life and opportune actions and beautifully ordered actions. They are, however, not yet acts of prudence but only those which are performed on the basis of prudence and similarly for all the other virtues— even if they do not have proper names, such as acts of temperance which are performed on the basis of temperance and acts of justice which are performed on the basis of justice. By contrast, [moral] mistakes are unjust actions and unlawful actions and disorderly actions.

11f. They say that just as there is a difference between what is worth choosing and what is to be chosen, so there is a difference between what is worth striving for and what is to be striven for and what is worth wishing for and what is to be wished for and what is worth accepting and what is to be accepted. For <good things> are worth choosing and wishing for and striving for <and accepting; but advantages are to be chosen and wished for and striven for> and accepted since they are predicates corresponding to the good things. For we choose what is to be chosen and want what is to be wanted and strive for what is to be striven for. For acts of choice and striving and wishing are directed at predicates, just as impulses are. But we choose and wish, and similarly strive, to *have* good things, which is why good things are worth choosing and wishing for and striving for. For we choose to have prudence and temperance but not, by Zeus!, being prudent and being temperate since these are incorporeals and predicates.

Similarly, they say that all goods are worth abiding in and cleaving to and analogously for the other virtues, even if they do not have proper names. But all the advantages and similar things are to be abided in and cleaved to. In the same way they suppose there is a difference between things worth being cautious over and things which one is to be cautious over and things which are not worth abiding in and things which are not to be abided in; the same account applies to the other terms which go with the vices.

11g. They say that every honorable and good man is complete [perfect] because he lacks none of the virtues. The base man, by contrast, is incomplete since he participates in none of the virtues. That is why good men are always and under all conditions happy, and the base unhappy. And <their> happiness does not differ from divine happiness; and Chrysippus says that momentary [happiness] does not differ from the happiness of Zeus, <and> that the happiness of Zeus is in no respect more worth choosing or more honorable or more majestic that that of wise men.

Zeno and the Stoic philosophers who follow him believe that there are two classes of men, the virtuous and the base. And men of the virtuous class employ all the virtues throughout their entire life, whereas the base [employ] the vices. Hence, the one group is always [morally] perfect in everything they apply themselves to, but the other group [always] makes [moral] mistakes. And the virtuous man always uses his experience of life in what he does, and so does everything well, insofar [as he acts] prudently and temperately and in accordance with the other virtues. And the base man by contrast [does everything] badly. And the virtuous man is big and powerful and lofty and strong. Big, because he is able to achieve his purposes and aims; powerful, because he is well developed in all respects; lofty, because he participates in the height fitting for someone who is noble and wise; and strong, because he has acquired the fitting strength, being invincible and unbeatable in contests. Accordingly, he is not compelled by anyone nor does he compel anyone; he neither hinders nor is hindered; he is forced by no one and forces no one; he neither dominates nor is dominated; neither harms nor is himself harmed; neither meets with misfortune <nor makes others do so>; is neither deluded nor deceives another; is neither deceived nor ignorant nor unaware of himself nor, in general, believes anything that is false. He is happy most of all, and fortunate and blessed and prosperous and pious and god loving and worthy, like a king and a general, a politician and a household economist and a moneymaker. And the base are the opposite of all of these.

In general, the virtuous have all good things and the base have all bad things. One must not suppose that they mean it in this sense: that if there exist good things, they belong to the virtuous, and similarly for the base; but rather [they mean that] they have so many good things that they are in no way lacking with respect to having a perfect [complete] <and happy> life, and the others have so many bad things that their life is incomplete [imperfect] and unhappy.

11h. They call virtue by many names.[15] For they say that it is something good because it draws us to the correct life; and pleasing, because it is approved of without suspicion; and worth a lot, <because> its value is unsurpassable; and virtuous, for it is worth much virtuous effort; and worthy of praise, for one would be reasonable in praising it; and honorable, because by nature it summons to itself those who strive for it; and advantageous, for it brings the sort of things which contribute to living well; and useful, because it is advantageous when used; and worth choosing, for its characteristic results are those things which one would reasonably choose; and necessary, because when it is present it benefits and when it is absent it is not possible to be benefited; and profitable, for the advantages which come from it are greater than the effort which produces them; and self-sufficient, for it suffices for the person who possesses it; and not lacking, because it removes one from all lack. And it suffices, because when used it is sufficient and applies to every kind of use relevant to one's life.

11i. The base participate in none of the good things since the good is virtue or what participates in virtue; and the requirements which correspond to the good things, being benefits, occur only in the virtuous; just as the non-requirements corresponding to the bad things [occur] only in the base; for they are forms of harm, and for this reason all good men are free of harm in both senses, unable either to do harm or to suffer it; and conversely for the base.

15. Most of these appellations and their explanations exploit fanciful and inimitable etymological connections.

They say that true wealth is a good thing and that true poverty is a bad thing; and that true freedom is a good thing and true slavery a bad thing. That is why the virtuous man is also the only wealthy and free man, and the base man, conversely, is a pauper (since he is deficient in the requirements for wealth) and a slave (because of his suspect disposition).

All good things are common to the virtuous, and bad things to the base. That is why he who benefits someone else is also benefited himself, and he who harms someone also harms himself. All virtuous men benefit each other, even though they are not in all cases friends of each other or well disposed [to each other] or in good repute [with each other] or receptive [of each other], because they do not have a [cognitive] grasp of each other and do not live in the same place. They, however, are disposed to be well disposed and to be friendly to each other and to hold [each other] in good repute and to be receptive [of each other]. The imprudent are in a condition opposite to this.

Since the law, as we said, is virtuous (because it is right reason which commands what is to be done and forbids what is not be done), they say that only the wise man is lawful, since he does what is commanded by the law and is the only interpreter of it, and that is why he is a man of the law. And silly men are in the opposite condition.

Again, they also assign to the virtuous the supervisory function of a ruler and its forms: kingship, generalship, naval command, and forms of rule like these. Accordingly, only the virtuous man rules, and even if he does not in all circumstances do so in actuality, still in all circumstances he does so by disposition. And only the virtuous man is obedient since he is prone to follow a ruler. But none of the imprudent is like this; for the imprudent man is not able either to rule or to be ruled since he is stubborn and intractable.

The sensible man does everything well since he continuously makes use of his experience of life in a prudent and self-controlled and orderly and organized fashion. But the base man, since he has no experience of the right use [of things], does everything badly, acting in accordance with the disposition he has, being prone to change [his mind] and seized by regret about each thing [he does]. And regret is [a feeling of] pain [one has] about actions which have been performed, because [of the belief that] they were [moral] mistakes made by oneself; and this is a passion of the soul which produces unhappiness and internal strife. For insofar as the regretful man loathes what has happened, to that extent he is angry at himself for having been responsible for these events. And this is why the base man is dishonored since he is neither worthy of honor nor honored. For honor is worthiness of reward and reward is the prize for virtue which does good for others. Thus what does not participate in virtue would justly be called 'dishonored'.

They say that every base man is an exile, insofar as he is deprived of law and a naturally fitting government. For the law is, as we said, virtuous and so too is the [corresponding] state. And it was enough that Cleanthes posed this sort of argument about the [claim that] the state [*polis*] is virtuous: if the state is a contrivance for dwelling in which one takes refuge in order to give and receive justice, is not the state a virtuous thing? But the state is such a dwelling place; therefore, the state is a virtuous thing. And 'state' is used in three senses: as a dwelling place, as a complex system of human beings, and third as the combination of these two senses. In two of these senses the state is said to be virtuous: as a complex system of human beings and in the combination [of the two senses] because <of the> [implicit] reference to its inhabitants.

11k. They say that every base man is a boor; for boorishness is inexperience of the habits and laws of the state, and every base man is subject to this. And he is also wild since he is a man hostile to the lawful way of life, beastlike, and harmful. This same fellow is untamed and tyrannical, having a disposition to perform despotic actions as well as ferocious and violent and illegal actions when he gets the chance. He is also ungrateful, not having an affinity either with returning or with offering gratitude since he does nothing for the common good or for friendship or without calculation.

Nor is the base man a lover of learning [*philologos*] or of listening, because in the first place he is not prepared for the reception of right accounts [or: arguments, *logoi*] because of the imprudence which derives from his corruption and because no base man has been encouraged [to turn] to virtue nor does he encourage [others to turn] to virtue; for he who has been encouraged [to turn] to virtue or who is encouraging others [to turn] to virtue must be prepared for philosophizing, and he who is prepared for it faces no impediments; but none of the base is like that. For it is not the man who listens eagerly and memorizes what philosophers say who is prepared for philosophizing, but the man who is prepared to carry into action what is pronounced in philosophy and to live by it. But none of the base is like that since they are already in the grip of the opinions of vice. For if any of the base had been encouraged to [turn to virtue], he would also have turned away from vice. And no one who possesses vice has turned to virtue; just as no one who is sick has turned to health. Only the wise man has been encouraged to [turn to virtue], and only he is able to encourage [others to turn to virtue], and none of the imprudent—for none of the imprudent lives by the precepts <of virtue>. Nor is he a lover of learning [*philologos*] but rather a lover of talk [*logophilos*], since he only proceeds as far as a superficial [sort of] chatter and does not yet confirm the talk [*logos*] about virtue by means of deeds.

Nor is any of the base a lover of toil; for love of toil is a disposition which produces what is fitting by means of toil in a manner which is unapprehensive; but none of the base is unapprehensive with regard to toil.

Nor does any of the base make the estimation of virtue which is in accordance with its value; for the estimation is a virtuous thing since it is knowledge in accordance with which we think we are acquiring something worth considering. But none of the virtuous things belongs to the base so that none of the base makes the proper estimation of virtue. For if any of the imprudent made the estimation which is in accordance with the value of virtue, then insofar as they honored this, they would regulate vice out [of their lives]. But every imprudent man is pleasantly inured to his own vice. For one should not consider their external [i.e., verbalized] discourse, which is base,[16] but rather the discourse of their actions. For by their actions it is proven that they are not committed to honorable and virtuous actions but rather to slavish and unmeasured pleasures.

They hold that every [moral] mistake is an act of impiety; for to do anything contrary to the wish of god is a sign of impiety. For since the gods have an affinity to virtue and its works and are alienated from vice and its products and since a [moral] mistake is an action in accordance with vice, obviously every [moral] mistake turned out to be displeasing to the gods—and that [sort of thing] is an act of impiety; for in every [moral] mistake the base man does something displeasing to the gods.

Again, since every base man does all that he does in accordance with vice, just as the virtuous man [does all that he does] in accordance with virtue, [it is] also [true that] he who has one vice has all. And among these [vices] one sees impiety, not the impiety which is classified as an activity but the condition opposite to piety. And what is done in accordance with impiety is an act of impiety; <therefore>, every [moral] mistake is an act of impiety.

Again, they also hold that every imprudent man is an enemy to the gods. For hostility is a lack of consonance and lack of concord <concerning> the [practical] concerns of life, just as friendship is consonance and concord. But the base disagree with the gods about the [practical] concerns of life, and that is why every imprudent man is an enemy to the gods. Again, if every one believes that those who are opposed to them are enemies and if the base man is opposed to the virtuous and if god is virtuous, then the base man is an enemy to the gods.

11l. They say that all [moral] mistakes are equal but not, however,[17] similar. For by nature they all derive from vice as from a single source, since in all [moral] mistakes the decision is the same; but [moral] mistakes do differ in quality with regard to the external cause since there are differences among the intermediate things that are the subject of the decisions.

You could get a clear image of the point being demonstrated by attending to the following: every falsehood is equally a falsehood; for one is no more in error than another; for the statement 'it is <always> night' is a falsehood, just

---

16. This word is probably corrupt; perhaps the text should say "deceptive" or something similar.

17. Literally, "not yet" or "no longer."

as is the statement 'a centaur lives'; and it is no more possible to say that the one is a falsehood than to say that the other is. But the falseness in each is not equally false, and those who are in error are not equally in error. And it is not possible to be making a [moral] mistake to a greater or lesser degree since every [moral] mistake is performed in virtue of being in error. Moreover, it is not the case that a [morally] correct action does not admit of being greater or lesser whereas a [moral] mistake does admit of being greater or lesser; for they [i.e., moral mistakes and morally correct actions] are all complete and that is why they could not be deficient or excessive with respect to each other. Therefore, all [moral] mistakes are equal.

11m. As to natural ability and noble birth, some members of this school were led to say that every wise man is endowed with these attributes; but others were not. For some think not only that people are endowed with a natural ability for virtue by nature but also that some are such by training, and they accepted this proverbial saying:[18] "Practice, when aged by time, turns into nature." And they made the same supposition about noble birth, so that natural ability is a condition with an affinity to virtue which comes from nature or training, or a condition by which certain people are prone to acquire virtue readily. And noble birth is a condition with an affinity to virtue which comes from birth or training.

Since the virtuous man is affable in conversation and charming and encouraging and prone to pursue goodwill and friendship through his conversation, he fits in as well as possible with the majority of people; and that is why he is lovable and graceful and persuasive, and again flattering and shrewd and opportune and quick-witted and easygoing and unfussy and straightforward and unfeigned. And the base man is subject to all the opposite traits. And they say that being ironic is a trait of base men and that no free and virtuous man is ironic. Similarly for sarcasm, which is irony combined with a kind of mockery. They say that friendship exists only among the wise since it is only among them that there is concord about the [practical] matters of life; and concord is a knowledge of common goods. For it is impossible for there to be genuine friendship (as opposed to falsely named friendship) without trust and reliability; but since the base are untrustworthy and unreliable and have hostile opinions, there is no friendship among them, although there are certain other kinds of association and bonding which are held together from the outside by necessity and opinions. And they say that cherishing and welcoming and love belong to the virtuous alone.

And only the wise man is a king and regal, but none of the base is. For regal rule is not subject to review and is supreme and is superior to all [other forms of rule].

18. From an unknown tragedy, 227 Nauck.

And they say that the virtuous man is the best doctor of himself; for he is a careful observer of his own nature and is knowledgeable about the factors which contribute to health.

The sensible man cannot get drunk; for drunkenness includes an element of [moral] error, for there is babbling over drink. But the virtuous man makes a [moral] mistake in no situation, which is why he does everything in accordance with virtue and right reason which depends on it.

There are three principal ways of life: the regal, the political, and third, the life devoted to knowledge. Similarly, there are three principal ways to make money: by kingship, in which one is either a king oneself or commands the resources of a monarch; second, by political life, for in accordance with the principal reason, he will participate in political life; for indeed he will also marry and have children <since> these things follow on the <nature> of the rational and social and philanthropic animal. So he will make money both from politics and from his friends, [at least] those who are in elevated positions.

On the topic of being a sophist[19] and doing well financially from sophistry, the members of this school disagreed with respect to what is meant. For they agreed about making money from students and sometimes receiving fees from those who want to learn. But there arose among them a debate about the meaning. Some said that this very practice was sophistry, [i.e.,] sharing the doctrines of philosophy in return for a fee; others surmised that there was something base about the term 'sophistry', as though it meant setting up a retail market in arguments, and so they said that one ought not to make money from the education of whoever came along [to study], that this manner of making money was beneath the dignity of philosophy.

They say that sometimes suicide is appropriate for virtuous men, in many ways, but that for base men, [it is appropriate] to remain alive even for those who would never be wise; for in [their mode of] living they neither possess virtue nor expel vice.[20] And [the value of] life and death is measured by [a reckoning of] appropriate and inappropriate actions.

They say that the wise man is free of arrogance; for he neither suffers arrogant behavior nor inflicts it since arrogance is a shameful act of injustice and harm. And the virtuous man does not suffer injustice or harm (although [it is true that] some people behave unjustly and arrogantly toward him), and in this he acts justly. In addition, arrogance is no ordinary form of injustice, but one which is shameful and arrogant. And the sensible man is immune from

19. A professional intellectual.

20. This probably means that the base should refrain from suicide since it is in general appropriate for all animals to maintain their own lives, and the base (who are not wise) could not *know* when suicide would be appropriate for them; the wise, however, could recognize the exceptional circumstances which justify suicide.

these things and is never shamed. For he has the good and divine virtue within himself, which is why he escapes all vice and harm.

And the sensible man will sometimes be a king and live with a king if he shows natural ability and a love of learning. We said[21] that it is possible for him to participate in political life in accordance with the principal reason but that he will not do so if there is a <hindrance> and especially if it is going to provide no benefit to his fatherland and he supposes that great and difficult risks will follow from political activity.

They say that the wise man does not lie, but is truthful in all [circumstances]; for lying does not consist in saying something false, but in saying something false in order to make someone be in error and with intent to mislead one's neighbors. They believe, however, that he will sometimes employ falsehood in several ways without assenting [to it]; for [he will do so] when a general against his adversaries and in the provision of what is advantageous and in many other aspects of managing life. They say that a wise man will never believe a falsehood nor indeed will he assent at all to anything which is not graspable, because he neither holds [mere] opinions nor is ignorant in any respect. For ignorance is a changeable and weak assent. Nor does he hold any belief weakly, but rather securely and stably, and that is why the wise man holds no [mere] opinion. For there are two [kinds of] opinion: one is assent to something which is not graspable; the other is weak belief. And these are alien to the disposition of the wise man, and that is why hastiness and assenting before he has a grasp are traits of the hasty and base man and are not attributes of the man of natural ability who is perfect [complete] and virtuous. Nor does anything escape his notice, for to fail to notice is to have a belief which asserts a false thing.[22]

Following on these traits, he is not distrustful, for distrust is a belief in a falsehood; and trust is a virtuous thing, for it is a strong grasp which secures what is believed. Similarly, knowledge is unchangeable by argument; and that is why they say that the base man neither knows nor trusts in anything. Consequently, the wise man is not greedy nor does he cheat or deliberately miscount (nor does anyone cheat him by miscounting either); for all of these involve deception and commitment to falsehoods about the topic in question. And none of the virtuous men makes a mistake about the road or his house or his target. But they believe that the wise man neither mis-sees nor mishears nor, generally, makes a mistake when using any of his sense organs; for they believe that each of these depends on false assent. Nor does the wise man make conjectural interpretations, for a conjectural interpretation is in the class

21. 11b above.

22. A difficult sentence. Alternatively, one might emend *apophantikē* to *apophatikē* and translate: "for failure to notice is a belief in a falsehood which [implicitly] denies a fact."

of assent to something which is not grasped. Nor do they suppose that the sensible man changes his mind, for changing one's mind depends on false assent <as though> one had previously made a mistake. Nor does he change in *any* respect or shift his position or err. For all of these are characteristic of those who change their doctrines, and that is alien to the sensible man. Nor, they say, does he have any opinions similar to those discussed.

11n. They believe that a wise man does not at first notice that he is becoming one nor does he strive for anything or believe that he wishes any of the special objects of wishing; [this is] because he does not judge that he has the requirements. Such distinctions also apply in the case of the other crafts and not just to prudence.

11o. Since all [moral] mistakes and [morally] perfect actions are equal, all imprudent men are also equally imprudent since they possess a disposition which is equal and identical. Although all [moral] mistakes are equal, there are some differences among them, insofar as some come from a hardened disposition which is difficult to cure and some do not.

11p. And some virtuous men are better than others at encouraging [people to virtue] and persuading them; again, some are more quick-witted than others, the increases being a result of the inclusion of intermediate steps.

11q. Only the virtuous man fares well with regard to his children, though not all have virtuous children since it is necessary for him who fares well with regard to his children to interact with them as such. Only the virtuous man has a good old age and a good death; for a good old age is conducting oneself virtuously at a certain age, and a good death is to make one's end virtuously with a certain kind of death.

11r. And things are called healthy and unhealthy relative to humans, [as are] what serves as nutriment and what is laxative or astringent and things like these. For things which are naturally inclined to produce or preserve health are healthy; unhealthy are those which are in the opposite condition. A similar account applies to the others.

11s. And only the virtuous man is a prophet since he has a knowledge which distinguishes the signs relevant to human life which come from the gods and daimons. And that is why he also has the forms of the prophetic art, i.e., dream reading and bird interpretation and sacrificial prophecy and any other types like these.

And the virtuous man is said to be austere insofar as he neither uses another nor admits for himself discourse directed at winning gratitude. And they say that the wise man will live a Cynic life, this <being> equal to remaining in one's Cynicism [after becoming wise]; however, once one becomes wise, one will not *begin* to practice Cynicism.

They say that sexual love is an effort to produce friendship resulting from the appearance of [physical] beauty of young men in their prime and that is why the wise man makes sexual advances and will have sexual intercourse with those who are worthy of [true] sexual love, [i.e.,] those who are wellborn and endowed with natural ability.

They say that nothing happens to the wise man which is contrary to his striving and impulse and effort since he does all such things with reservation and none of the events which oppose his [plans] befalls him unexpectedly.

And he is also gentle, gentleness being a condition according to which they are gentle about doing what is fitting in all circumstances and do not get swept away to anger in any circumstances. And he is calm and orderly, orderliness being knowledge of fitting motions and calmness being a proper organization of states of motion and rest of the soul and body in accordance with nature; the opposites of these are traits of all base men.

Every honorable and good man is free of slander since he is immune to slander and so is free of slander in this sense and also in the sense that he does not slander someone else. And slander is a falling out among apparent friends because of a false utterance; this does not happen to good men, but only base men slander and are slandered, and that is why true friends neither slander nor are slandered but [only] seeming and apparent friends.

Nor does the virtuous man ever stall on anything since stalling is a deferral of action because of hesitation; but he defers some things only when the deferral is free of blame; for Hesiod said this of stalling: "Do not stall until tomorrow and the next day" and "A man who puts off his work always wrestles with disaster"[23] since stalling produces an abandonment of one's proper jobs.

12. So much for this. For Chrysippus discussed all the paradoxes in many other works: in his *On Doctrines* and in the *Outline [Definition] of Rational Discourse* and in many other treatises on special topics. But I have already gone through in an adequate fashion as much as I intended to deal with in the summary account of the ethical doctrines of <those> who belong to the Stoic school of philosophy; [so] I shall put an end to this notebook forthwith.

The Account in Cicero *On Goals*

TEXT 103: Cicero *On Goals* 3.16–70 (selections)

16. The school whose views I follow [a Stoic speaks] holds that every animal, as soon as it is born (for this should be our starting point), has an affinity to itself and is inclined to preserve itself and its constitution and to like those things which preserve that constitution; but it is alienated from its own death and those things which seem to threaten it. They confirm this by [noting] that before pleasure or pain can affect them, babies seek what is salutary and spurn what is not, and this would not happen unless they loved their constitution

---

23. *Works and Days* 410, 413.

and feared death. They could not, however, desire anything unless they had a perception of themselves and consequently loved themselves. From this, one ought to see that the principle [of human action] is derived from self-love. **17.** Most Stoics do not think that pleasure should be classed among the primary natural things; and I strongly agree with them for fear that, if nature seemed to have classed pleasure among the primary objects of impulse, then many shameful consequences would follow. It seems, however, to be a sufficient argument as to why we love those things which were first accepted because of nature [to say] that there is no one (when he has a choice) who would not prefer to have all the parts of his body in a sound condition to having them dwarfed or twisted though equally useful.

They think, moreover, that acts of cognition (which we may call 'grasps' or 'perceptions' or, if these terms are either displeasing or harder to understand, *katalēpseis*) are, then, to be accepted for their own sake since they have in themselves something which, as it were, includes and contains the truth. And this can be seen in babies, who, we see, are delighted if they figure something out for themselves, even if it does not do them any good. **18.** We also think that the crafts are to be taken for their own sake, both because there is in them something worth taking and also because they consist of acts of cognition and contain something which is rational and methodical. They think, though, that we are more alienated from false assent than from anything else which is contrary to nature. . . .

20. Let us move on, then, since we began from these natural principles and what follows should be consistent with them. There follows this primary division: they say that what has 'value' (we are to call it that, I think) is that which is either itself in accordance with nature or productive of it, so that it is worthy of selection because it has a certain 'weight' which is worth valuing (and this [value] they call *axia*); by contrast, what is opposite to the above is disvalued. The starting point being, then, so constituted that what is natural is to be taken for its own sake and what is unnatural is to be rejected, the first appropriate action (for that is what I call *kathēkon*) is that it should preserve itself in its natural constitution and then that it should retain what is according to nature and reject what is contrary to nature. After this [pattern of] selection and rejection is discovered, there then follows appropriate selection, and then constant [appropriate] selection, and finally [selection] which is stable and in agreement with nature; and here for the first time we begin to have and to understand something which can truly be called 'good'. **21.** For a human being's first sense of affinity is to what is according to nature; but as soon as he gets an understanding, or rather a conception (which they call an *ennoia*), and sees the ordering and, I might say, concord of things that are to be done, he then values that more highly than all those things that he loved in the beginning. And he comes to a conclusion by intelligence and reasoning, with the result that he decides that this is what the highest good for a human consists in, which is to be praised and chosen for its own sake. And since it is placed in what the Stoics call *homologia*, let us call it 'agreement', if you please. Since, therefore, this constitutes the good, to which all things are to be referred, honorable actions and the honorable itself—which is considered to be the only good—although it arises later [in our lives], nevertheless it is the only thing which is to be chosen in virtue of its own character and value; but none of the primary natural things is to be chosen for its own sake. **22.** Since, however, those things which I called 'appropriate actions' proceed from the starting points [established] by nature, it is necessary that they be referred to them; so it is right to say that all appropriate actions are referred to acquisition of the natural principles, not however in the sense that this is the highest good since honorable action is not among our primary and natural affinities. That, as I said, is posterior and arises later. But [such action] is natural and encourages us to choose it much more than all the earlier mentioned things.

But here one must first remove a misunderstanding, so that no one might think that there are two highest goods. For just as, if it is someone's purpose to direct a spear or arrow at something, we say that his highest goal is to do everything he can in order to direct it at [the target], in the same sense that we say that our highest goal is a good. The archer in this comparison is to do all that he can to direct [his arrow at the target]; and yet doing all that he can to attain his purpose would be like the highest goal of the sort that we say is the highest good in life; actually striking [the target], though, is as it were to be selected and not to be chosen.

23. Since all appropriate actions proceed from the natural principles, it is necessary that wisdom itself proceed from them as well. But just as it often happens that he who is introduced to someone puts a higher value on the person to whom he is introduced than on the person by whom he was introduced, just so it is in no way surprising that we are first introduced to wisdom by the starting points [established] by nature, but that later on wisdom itself becomes dearer to us than the things that brought us to wisdom. And just as our limbs were given us in such a way that they seem to have been given for the sake of a certain way of life, similarly the impulse in our soul, which is called *hormē* in Greek, seems not to have been given for the sake of any old type of life but for a certain kind of living; and similarly for reason and perfected reason. **24.** Just as an actor or dancer has not been assigned just any old [type of] delivery or movement but rather a certain definite [type], so too life is to be lived in a certain definite manner, not in any old [manner]. And we call that manner 'in agreement' and consonant. And we do not think that wisdom is like navigation or medicine, but rather like the craft of acting or dancing that I just mentioned; thus its goal, i.e., the [proper] execution of the craft, depends on it itself and is not sought outside itself. There is also another point of dissimilarity between wisdom and these crafts, namely, that in them proper actions do not contain all the components [lit., parts] which constitute the art; but things called 'right' or 'rightly done', if I may call them that, though the Greeks call them *katorthōmata* [morally perfect actions], contain all the features of virtue. Only wisdom is totally self-contained, and this is not the case with the other crafts. **25.** But it is misguided to compare the highest goal of medicine or navigation with that of wisdom; for wisdom embraces magnanimity and justice and an ability to judge that everything which happens to a [mere] human being is beneath it—and this does not apply to the rest of the crafts. But no one can possess the very virtues that I just mentioned unless he has firmly decided that there is nothing except what is honorable or shameful which makes a difference or distinguishes one [thing or situation] from another.

26. Let us now see how splendidly these further points follow from what I have already expounded. . . . So, since the goal is to live consistently and in agreement with nature, it follows necessarily that all wise men always live happy, perfect, and fortunate lives, that they are impeded by nothing, hindered by nothing, and in need of nothing. The key not only to the doctrines of which I am speaking but also to our life and fortune is that we should judge that only what is honorable is good. This point can be elaborated and developed fully and copiously, with all the choicest words and profoundest sentiments which rhetorical art can produce; but I prefer the short and pointed syllogisms of the Stoics.

27. Their arguments go like this: Everything which is good is praiseworthy; but everything which is praiseworthy is honorable; therefore, that which is good is honorable. Does this argument seem valid enough? Surely it does; for as you see, the argument concludes with a point that is proven by the two premises. Generally speaking, people attack the former of the two premises and claim that it is not the case that everything which is good is praiseworthy; for they concede that what is praiseworthy is honorable. But it is totally absurd [to claim] that something is good but not worth choosing, or worth choosing but not pleasing, or pleasing but not also to be loved; and so it is also to be approved of, so it is also praiseworthy, but that is [the same as] honorable. So, it turns out that what is good is also honorable.

28. Next, I ask who can boast of a life if it is wretched or even just not happy. So we boast only of a happy life. From this it results that the happy life is, if I may put it so, worth boasting about; and this cannot properly [be said to] happen to any life but one that is honorable. So, it turns out that an honorable life is a happy life. Moreover, since someone who is justly praised must have about him something remarkable, either in point of honor or of glory, so that he can justly be called happy on account of these very valuable attributes, the same thing can be said most properly about the life of such a man. So, if the honorable is a criterion for a happy life, one must hold that what is honorable is also good.

29. What? Could anyone deny that we could never have a man who is of steadfast and reliable spirit, a man you could call brave, unless it is firmly established that pain is not a bad thing? For just as someone who regards death as a bad thing cannot help but fear it, in the same way no one can be indifferent to and despise something which he regards as bad. Once this point is established and assented to, our next premise is that magnanimous and strong-hearted men are able to despise and ignore everything which fortune can bring to bear against man. Consequently, it is proven that there is nothing bad that is not also shameful. But the man we refer to is lofty and superior, magnanimous, truly brave, looks down on all merely human concerns; the man, I say, whom we wish to produce, whom we are looking for, should certainly have faith in himself and his life, both past and future, and should think well of himself, believing that nothing bad can happen to a wise man. And from this one can again prove the same old point, that only the honorable is good, i.e., that to live happily is to live honorably, i.e., virtuously.

30. I am not unaware that there is a variety of views held by philosophers, by which I mean those who place the highest good, which I call the goal, in the mind. Even though some of them have gone wrong, still I prefer them, whatever their views, who locate the highest good in the mind and virtue to those three who have separated the highest good from virtue by placing either pleasure or freedom from pain or the primary natural things among the highest goods; I even prefer them to the other three who thought that virtue would be deficient without some addition and so added to it one or other of the three things mentioned above. **31.** But those who think that the highest good is to live with knowledge and who claim that things are absolutely indifferent and that this was why the wise man would be happy, because he did not prefer one thing to any other in even the slightest degree, they are particularly absurd; so too are those who, as certain Academics are said to have held, believe that the highest good and greatest duty of the wise man is to resist his presentations and steadfastly to withhold his assent. Normally one gives a full answer to each of these views separately. But there is no need to prolong what is perfectly clear, and what is more obvious than that the very prudence which we are seeking and praising would be utterly destroyed if there were no grounds for choosing between those which are contrary to nature and those which are according to nature? When we eliminate, therefore, those views I have mentioned and those which are similar to them, all that is left is [the view] that the highest good is to live by making use of a knowledge of what happens naturally, selecting what is according to nature and rejecting what is contrary to nature, i.e., to live consistently and in agreement with nature.

32. When in the other crafts something is said to be craftsmanlike, one must suppose that what is meant is something that is, in a way, posterior and consequent, which they [the Greeks] call *epigennēmatikon* [supervenient]; but when we say that something is done wisely we mean that it is from the outset thoroughly right. For whatever is undertaken by a wise man must immediately be complete in all its parts; for it is in this that we find what we call 'that which is worth choosing'. For just as it is a [moral] mistake to betray one's country, to attack one's parents, to rob temples (and these are [moral] mistakes because of the outcome [of the action]), so too it is a [moral] mistake to fear, to grieve, and to suffer desire, even quite independently of their outcome. Rather, just as the latter are not dependent on their posterior consequences but are [moral] mistakes right from the outset, similarly the actions which proceed from virtue are to be judged to be right from the outset and not by their ultimate completion.

33. 'Good', which has been used so frequently in this discussion, is also explained with a definition. The definitions offered by [the Stoics] do differ from each other, but only very slightly; for all that, they are getting at the same point. I agree with Diogenes who defined 'good' as that which is perfect in its nature. He followed this up by defining the 'beneficial' (let us use this term for *ophelēma*) as a motion or condition which is in accord with what is perfect in its nature. And since we acquire conceptions of things if we learn something either by direct experience or by combination or by similarity or by rational inference, the conception of good is created by the last method mentioned. For the mind attains a conception of the good when it ascends by rational inference from those things which are according to nature. **34.** But the good itself is not perceived to be good or called good because of some addition or increase or comparison with other things but in virtue of its own special character. For honey, although it is the sweetest thing, is nevertheless perceived to be sweet not because of a comparison with other things but because of its own distinctive flavor; in the same way the good, which is the subject of our discussion, is indeed most valuable, but that value derives meaning from its distinctive type and not from its magnitude. For value (which is called *axia*) is not counted as either good or bad; consequently, however much you might increase it, it will still remain in the same general category. Therefore, there is one kind of value which applies to virtue, and it derives its meaning from its distinctive type and not from its magnitude. . . .

62. Again, they think it important to understand that nature has brought it about that children are loved by their parents. For from this starting point we can follow the development of the shared society which unites the human race. One ought to see this first of all from the form and organs of the body which show that nature has a rational scheme for reproduction; but it would be inconsistent for nature to want offspring to be born and yet not to see to it that they are loved once they are born. The power of nature can be seen even in the beasts; when we see the effort they go to in bearing and rearing their offspring, we seem to be listening to the voice of nature herself. So, just as it is obvious that we naturally shrink from pain, so too it is apparent that we are driven by nature herself to love those whom we bear. **63.** From this it develops naturally that there is among human beings a common and natural affinity of people to each other, with the result that it is right for them to feel that other humans, just because they are humans, are not alien to them. . . . So, we are naturally suited to [living in] gatherings, groups, and states.

64. They also hold that the cosmos is ruled by the will of the gods, that it is like a city or state shared by gods and humans, and that each and every one of us is a part of this cosmos. From which it naturally follows that we put the common advantage ahead of our own. For just as the laws put the well-being of all ahead of the well-being of individuals, so too the good and wise man, who is obedient to the laws and not unaware of his civic duty, looks out for the advantage of all more than for that of any one person or his own. . . .

67. But just as they think that the bonds of justice unite human beings with each other, so too they deny that there is any bond of justice between a human being and a beast. Chrysippus expressed it well, saying that everything else was born for the sake of humans and gods, but they were born for the sake of their own community and society, with the result that humans can use beasts for their own advantage without injustice. . . .

70. They also think that friendship should be cultivated because it falls into the class of beneficial things. Although some [Stoics] say that in a friendship a friend's reason is just as dear to the wise man as is his own, whereas others say that each person's reason is dearer to himself, even this latter group admits that to deprive someone of something in order to appropriate it for oneself is inconsistent with justice, which is a virtue we are naturally committed to. So the school I am speaking of does not at all approve of the view that justice or friendship should be welcomed or approved of because of its advantages. For the very same advantages could just as well undermine and overthrow them. Indeed, neither justice nor friendship can exist at all unless they are chosen for their own sakes.

Other Evidence for Stoic Ethics

TEXT 104: Stobaeus *Anthology* 4.39.22 (vol. 5, pp. 906.18–907.5 W-H)

Chrysippus says, "He who makes [moral] progress to the highest degree performs all the appropriate actions in all circumstances and omits none." And he says that his life is not yet happy, but that happiness supervenes on him when these intermediate actions become secure and conditioned and acquire a special sort of fixity.

TEXT 105: Plutarch *On Moral Virtue* 446f–447a

(**446f**) . . . But some say that passion is not something distinct from reason, and that there is no disagreement and strife between two things, but that
the reason which is a single thing turns in both directions, (**447a**) and this
escapes our notice because of the sharpness and speed of the change, since we
do not realize that it is the same thing in the soul that gives us the ability to
desire and to regret, to get angry and to fear, to be drawn to shameful acts by
pleasure, and to fight back against this temptation. For they say that desire and
anger and fear and all such things are bad opinions and judgments and that
they do not arise in some one part of the soul, but are cases of the inclination,
yielding, assent, and impulse of the leading part of the soul, and in general are
activities which can change in a very short time, just as the charging around of
children is violent, very unstable, and uncertain because of their weakness.

TEXT 106: Plutarch *On Stoic Self-Contradictions* 1037c–1038c

(**1037c**) . . . They say that a [morally] perfect action is what the law commands and that a [moral] mistake is what the law forbids, and that is why the
law forbids the foolish to do many things (**1037d**) but commands them to do
nothing; for they are unable to perform a [morally] perfect action. And who is
not aware that it is impossible for someone who cannot perform a [morally]
perfect action to avoid making a [moral] mistake? So, [the Stoics] put the law
in conflict with itself by commanding what they are unable to do and forbidding what they are unable to refrain from. For he who cannot be temperate
cannot avoid being wanton, and he who cannot be prudent cannot avoid acting imprudently. Indeed, they themselves say that those who forbid say one
thing, forbid another, and command yet another. For he who says 'do not
steal' says just this, 'do not steal', (**1037e**) forbids <stealing and commands>
not stealing. So, the law will not be forbidding base men to do anything if it is
not giving them a command. Moreover, they say that the doctor commands
his apprentice to cut and burn, with the omission [of the specification] that he
should do so at the right time and in the right manner, just as the music master [commands his students] to play the lyre or sing, with the omission [of the
specification] that they do so tunefully and harmoniously. The reason why
they punish the students who do these things inartistically and badly is that
they were ordered to act on the understanding that it be done so properly, but
they did not act properly. Therefore, when the wise man commands his ser-
vant to do or say something and punishes him for doing it at the wrong time
or in the wrong manner, obviously he too is commanding him to an intermediate act and not a [morally] perfect act. But if wise men command base men
to perform intermediate acts, (**1037f**) why can the commands of the law not
be like this? And indeed, impulse, according to [Chrysippus] is the reason of a

human being commanding him to act, as he wrote in his treatise *On Law*. Therefore, an impulse away from something is reason forbidding, <and so is avoidance, for it is reasonable since it is the opposite of desire; and according to him caution> is reasonable avoidance. **(1038a)** And caution, then, is reason which forbids the wise man [to do something]. For being cautious is special to the wise man and does not belong to base men. So, if the wise man's reason is distinct from the law, then the wise men will have their caution, i.e., their reason, in conflict with law. But if law is nothing other than the wise man's reason, then the law is found to be forbidding wise men to do those things which they are cautious about.

Chrysippus says that nothing is useful to base men and that the base man makes use of nothing and needs nothing. After saying this in book 1 of his *On [Morally] Perfect Actions,* he goes on to say later that utility and gratitude extend to intermediate actions, none of which is useful according to the Stoics. **(1038b)** Moreover, he also says that the base have no affinity to anything and nothing is fitting for them, in [the] following words: "Similarly, the virtuous person is alien to nothing and the base person has an affinity with nothing since one of these properties is good and the other is bad." So why does he grind on in every single book on physics and even, by Zeus!, on ethics, writing that as soon as we are born we have an affinity to ourselves and to our parts and to our offspring? And in book 1 of *On Justice,* he says that even beasts have an affinity to their offspring in accordance with the needs of the offspring, except in the case of fish, for even the unhatched eggs are nourished by themselves. **(1038c)** But there is no sense-perception for those to whom nothing is perceptible, and there is no state of affinity for those who have an affinity to nothing. For the state of affinity seems to be a perception and grasp of that to which one has an affinity.

TEXT 107: Sextus Empiricus *M* 11.22–73 (selections)

22. The Stoics cling to the common conceptions and define the good as follows: 'Good is benefit or what is not other than benefit'. By 'benefit' they mean virtue and virtuous action, and by 'not other than benefit' they mean the virtuous man and a friend. **23.** For since virtue is the leading part of the soul in a certain state, and virtuous action is an activity in accordance with virtue, they are immediately beneficial. And the virtuous man and the friend, who themselves belong to the class of good things, would not properly be termed 'benefit', but neither would they be other than benefit, for the following reason. **24.** For, the followers of the Stoics say, the parts are not the same as the whole nor are they different in kind from the whole; for example, the hand is not the same as the whole human being (for the hand is not a whole human) nor is it other than the whole since the entire human being is conceived of as a human with the hand included. So, since virtue is a part of the virtuous human being and of the friend, and the parts are neither the same as the whole nor other than the whole, it is said that the virtuous human being and the friend are not other than benefit. Consequently, every good thing is encompassed by the definition, whether it is immediately a benefit or is not other than benefit.

25. Hence and consequently, they say that good is said in three senses; and they outline each of its meanings in its own formulation. For one sense of good, they say, is that by which or from which it is possible to be benefited, which is indeed the most fundamental sense and is [the same as] virtue; for from this as from a spring every other utility naturally flows. **26.** In another sense it is that according to which being benefited is a characteristic result. In this not only will the virtues be called good but also virtuous actions since it is characteristic of them that benefit results. **27.** In the third and final sense, good is said to be that which is such as to benefit, this description encompassing the virtues, virtuous actions, friends, virtuous men and gods, and excellent daimons. . . . **30.** . . . and there were some who said that the good is that which is worth choosing for its own sake; and some who used this definition: 'good is that which contributes to happiness'; and others who said that it is 'that which fulfils happiness'. And happiness is, according to definition given by the followers of Zeno, Cleanthes, and Chrysippus, a smooth flow of life. . . .

40. It suffices to have made these remarks, for the sake of illustration, about the conception of the good. . . . **41.** And intermediate between these, i.e., between the good and the bad, is that which is in neither state, which they also labeled 'indifferent'. From the discussion of the good it is possible to learn what the force of these definitions is and what remarks should be directed against these definitions. . . .

48. So, some hold that health is a good, some that it is not a good; and of those who think that it is a good, some claimed that it is the greatest good and others that it is not the greatest; and of those who said that it is not a good, some said that it is a preferred indifferent and others said that it was an indifferent but not preferred. . . . **59.** Crantor [the Academic] certainly assigned health to the second tier [of goods]. . . . but the Stoics said that it was not a good but an indifferent. But they think that 'indifferent' has three senses. In one sense it is that with respect to which there is neither an impulse toward it nor away from it (for example, whether the number of stars or the number of hairs on one's head is odd or even). **60.** In another sense it is that with respect to which there is an impulse toward or away from it, but no more toward one or the other of two options, for example, if there are two drachmas indistinguishable in their stamp and shininess and you must choose one or the other of them—for one does have an impulse toward one of them but no more to one than the other. **61.** In the third and final sense the indifferent is that which contributes neither to happiness nor to misery, and it is in this sense that they say that health and disease and everything bodily and most external things are indifferent since they tend to produce neither happiness nor misery. For that which can be used well and badly would be indifferent. Virtue is always used well; vice is always used badly; but health and bodily things can be used sometimes well and sometimes badly, and that is why they would be indifferent. **62.** And of indifferents, they say, some are preferred and some are rejected; the preferred are those which have considerable value, the rejected are those which have considerable disvalue, and neither preferred nor rejected are things like holding one's finger straight or crooked and everything like this. **63.** Health and strength and beauty, wealth and reputation, and things like these are counted among the preferred things; disease and poverty and pain and similar things are counted among the rejected. That is what the Stoics say.

64. Ariston of Chios said that health and everything similar to it are not preferred indifferents. For to say that it is a preferred indifferent is tantamount to claiming that it is good since they practically differ only in name. **65.** In general, things which are indifferent as between virtue and vice are indistinguishable nor are some naturally preferred and others naturally rejected; rather [they vary] in accordance with different circumstances and occasions. Thus things which are said to be preferred are not unconditionally preferred nor are things called rejected unconditionally rejected. **66.** Anyway, if it were necessary for healthy men to serve a tyrant and for this reason to be executed, whereas sick men were released from service and so also freed from destruction, the wise man would choose sickness over health on such an occasion. And in this way health is not unconditionally a preferred thing nor is disease rejected. **67.** So, just as when we write words we sometimes put one letter first, sometimes another, fitting them to their different circumstances (we write the D first for Dion's name, the I first for Ion, the O first for Orion); it is not that some letters are naturally preferred to others, but just that circumstances force us to do this. In the same way in matters which are intermediate between virtue and vice, there is no natural preference for one set over the other but this, rather, is determined by circumstances. . . .

73. For example, Epicurus says that pleasure is good, whereas he[24] who said "I'd rather go mad than feel pleasure" thinks it is bad. And the Stoics say that pleasure is indifferent and not preferred, but Cleanthes held that it is not natural and does not have value in life, but, like a makeup brush, it is not natural. Archedemus says that it is natural in the way that armpit hairs are natural but does not have value; and Panaetius says that one kind of pleasure is natural and another kind is unnatural.

---

24. Antisthenes the Cynic.

TEXT 108: Clement of Alexandria *Stromates* 2.21.129.1–6²⁵

Again, Zeno the Stoic thinks that living according to virtue is the goal, Cleanthes that it is living in agreement with nature. <Diogenes situates it> in being reasonable, which he distinguished as being located in the selection of things according to nature, and his collaborator Antipater holds that the goal lies in the invariable and unswerving selection of natural things and rejection of unnatural things. Archedemus, moreover, explained the goal as follows: to live selecting the greatest and most important things according to nature, which cannot be surpassed. In addition to them Panaetius claimed as well that the goal is living according to the inclinations given to us by nature. In addition to all of these Posidonius says that the goal is to live in contemplation of the truth and orderliness of the universe, helping to establish that order as much as one can, being in no respect guided by the irrational part of the soul. And some of the more recent Stoics defined it thus: the goal is to live consistently with the constitution of a human being.

TEXT 109: Cicero *On Duties* 1.9

In the opinion of Panaetius, then, deliberation about what plan of action to adopt has three forms. For people are uncertain about whether the issue under deliberation is honorable or shameful to do, and when assessing this our minds are often torn between opposing views. And next they investigate or consult as to whether what they are deliberating about is advantageous or not for practical convenience and pleasure, for the resources, supplies, money, and influence which they can use to benefit themselves or their friends and family. This whole line of deliberation falls under the heading of 'the useful'. The third kind of deliberation arises when what seems to be useful seems to be in conflict with the honorable. For when the useful seems to draw them to its side and the honorable seems in its turn to summon them back to itself, it transpires that our mind is torn apart in its deliberations and introduces into our thinking a two-edged worry.

TEXT 110: Cicero *On Duties* 1.107–20 (selections)

107. We should understand that we have been clothed, as it were, by nature with two roles [*personae*]. One of these is common and is based on the fact that we all share in reason and in the preeminence which we have over beasts. This is the source from which all that is honorable and fitting is derived and the basis for our search for the right method of discovering what our responsibilities are. But the other role is the one that is assigned to each of us

25. Cf. TEXT 102.6a above.

individually. For just as there are great differences in our bodies (some people, we notice, are fast on the race track and others have the muscles for wrestling) and similarly some bodily types have dignity and others have grace; so too there are even bigger differences among our minds. . . .

110. However, each person should hang on to what is his own, not the faults of course but the distinctive features, so that it will be easier to maintain what we are seeking, i.e., what is fitting. For we must act in such a way that we do not oppose in any respect our general nature, but, providing this is preserved, we should pursue our own individual nature. Thus, even if some activities are better and more serious, we should nevertheless measure our own activities by the standard of our own nature. For it is not appropriate to fight against nature nor to pursue something which you cannot achieve. And from this our sense of what is fitting becomes clearer, precisely because nothing is fitting 'if Minerva is reluctant', as they say, i.e., if nature is opposed or fights against us. **111.** If anything at all is fitting, then nothing is more fitting than a smooth flow of life as a whole and of individual actions; and you cannot preserve this if you neglect your own nature and imitate that of other people. For just as we should employ the style of speech that is familiar to us to avoid being quite justifiably ridiculed like *certain* people who drop in Greek words all over the place, so too we should not admit any inconsistency into our actions and our general way of life. . . .

115. And a third role is added to the two that I mentioned above, the one assigned by some chance event or circumstance; a fourth also, one which we adopt for ourselves in accordance with our own judgment. . . .

117. We should bear all this in mind and reflect on it when we are inquiring into what is fitting. But above all we should decide who we want to be, what we want to be like, and what way of life we want to lead. This is the toughest of all our deliberations. For it is right at the beginning of adolescence when our deliberative capacities are at their weakest that each of us decides to lead the way of life that he finds most attractive. And so one gets entangled in a definite manner and pattern of life before one is able to judge which one is best. **118.** For Prodicus (as Xenophon[26] tells it) told a story about Hercules. When Hercules was a youth (a time assigned by nature for each person to choose which way of life he will embark upon), he went off into the wilderness and sat there for a long time. He saw two paths, one the path of Pleasure and the other the path of Virtue, and pondered long and hard by himself as to which was the better path to take. Now maybe this could happen to Hercules, "born of Jupiter's seed," but not to us. Each of us imitates whomever we think we should imitate, and we are driven to adopt their activities and customs. Now generally we are saturated by parental advice and so we are drawn to

---

26. *Memorabilia* 2.1.21–34.

their habits and character; but others are swept away by the judgment of the masses and make a point of choosing whatever the majority thinks is most attractive. Nevertheless, whether it is by a kind of good luck or by innate goodness or by parental training, some people do pursue the right path through life. **119.** But one type of person is extremely rare: those who, as a result of their outstanding intellectual talent or their distinguished education and training or both, have had the room to deliberate about which path through life they would most want to follow. When deliberating on this question, the decision comes down entirely to each person's individual nature. For in all of our particular actions, we seek out what is fitting in accordance with how each of us is by nature, as I said above; and we must exercise even greater care on this point when we are deciding on our life as a whole, so that we can remain consistent with ourselves throughout our life and not fail in any of our responsibilities. **120.** And since nature has the greatest impact on reasoning about this and luck the next greatest, we should certainly take account of both when we are choosing a mode of life, but take more account of nature. For nature is more solid and more stable. . . .

TEXT 111: Cicero *On Duties* 3.34

First, I must defend Panaetius on this point: he did not say that the useful could ever conflict with the honorable (that would have been very wrong of him) but only what *seemed* to be useful. In fact, he claims frequently that nothing is useful which is not also honorable and that nothing is honorable which is not also useful and he says that no greater plague has infested human life than the notion of those who have driven a wedge between them. And so he introduced this apparent, not real, conflict—not so that we would at any point put the useful ahead of the honorable but so that we could reliably distinguish them when the issue arises.

Passions and the Goal: Criticism within the Stoic School and the Evidence of Galen

TEXT 112: Strabo *Geography* 2.3.8

There is in Posidonius a great deal of causal analysis and Aristotelianism, which our school avoids because the causes are hidden.

TEXT 113: Galen *On the Doctrines of Hippocrates and Plato* 5.6.9–12

Not satisfied with this, Posidonius made a clearer and stronger criticism of Chrysippus for not having given a proper explanation of the goal. This is what he said: "Some ignore this and limit living in agreement to 'doing whatever one can for the sake of the primary natural things'; by doing that, they are doing much the same thing as they would be doing if they claimed that the goal was pleasure or freedom from pain or something else of the sort. There is something which reveals an internal conflict in the very utterance [of this formulation of the goal], but there is nothing which is honorable or could promote happiness. For this is a consequence of the goal but is not the goal. But if one gets [the formulation of] the goal right, one can use it to defeat the puzzles that the sophists advance, but one cannot so use the [formula] 'living according to experience of what happens in the whole of nature', which is equivalent to saying 'living in agreement' since this makes no small contribution to achieving things [that are] indifferent."

TEXT 114: Galen *On the Doctrines of Hippocrates and Plato* 4.2.9–18

We shall see this more clearly if we quote his own [Chrysippus'] utterances. The first passage goes like this: "We must first keep in mind that the rational animal is by nature such as to follow reason and to act according to reason as a guide. Nevertheless, he often moves toward some things and away from some things in another way, disobediently to reason, when he is pushed too far [or to excess]. Both definitions [of passion, the one mentioning] the natural motion which arises irrationally in this way and [the one mentioning] the excessiveness in the impulses, are in terms of this motion. For this irrationality must be taken to be disobedient to reason and turning its back on reason. And it is in terms of this motion that we also say in ordinary usage that some people are 'pushed' and 'moved irrationally without reason and judgment'. For we do not use these expressions as if someone is moved mistakenly and because he overlooks something that is according to reason, but most especially according to the motion he [Zeno?] outlines since the rational animal does not naturally move in accordance with his soul in this way, but rather in accordance with reason. . . . The excess of the impulse was also spoken of in terms of this, because they overstep the symmetry of impulses which is proper to themselves and natural. What I say would be made easier to understand by means of these examples. In walking according to impulse, the motion of the legs is not excessive but is in a sense coextensive with the impulse, so that it can come to a standstill when he [the walker] wishes or change direction. But in the case of those who are running according to impulse, this sort of thing is no longer the case, but the motion of the legs exceeds the impulse so that it is carried away and does not change direction obediently in this way as soon as they start to do so. I think something similar to these motions [of the legs] occurs in the impulses because of the overstepping of the symmetry which is according to reason, so that whenever one has an impulse he is not obedient with respect to it—the excess being beyond the impulse in the case of running and beyond reason in the case of impulse.

For the symmetry of natural impulse is that according to reason and is as far as reason thinks proper. Therefore, since the overstepping is according to this [sc. standard] and in this way, the impulse is said to be excessive and an unnatural and irrational motion of the soul."

TEXT 115: Galen *On the Doctrines of Hippocrates and Plato* 4.4.16–17, 24–25

4.4.16 Chrysippus himself shows this in the following quotation: "That is why it is not off the mark to say, as some people do, that a passion of the soul is an unnatural motion, as is the case with fear and desire and things like that; **4.4.17** for all such motions and conditions are disobedient to reason and reject it. And so we say that such people are irrationally moved, not as though they make a bad calculation, which would be the sense opposite to 'reasonably', but rather in the sense of a rejection of reason." . . . **4.4.24** "That is what such conditions are like, uncontrolled, as though they were not masters of themselves but were carried away in the way that those who run strenuously are swept away and cannot control their motion. **4.4.25** But those who move according to reason, as though it were their leader, and steer their course by it wherever it might lead, these people are in control of this sort of motion and the impulses that go with it."

TEXT 116: Galen *On the Doctrines of Hippocrates and Plato* 5.1.4, 4.3.2

5.1.4 In book 1 of his *On Passions* Chrysippus tries to show that the passions are certain judgments [formed] by the reasoning part of the soul, but Zeno did not believe that the passions were the judgments themselves but contractions, relaxations, elations, and depressions which supervene on the judgments. Posidonius disagreed with both of them and at the same time both praised and accepted the doctrine of Plato and argued against Chrysippus and his followers, showing that the passions are not judgments and do not supervene on judgments but are certain movements of other, irrational powers which Plato called the 'desiderative' and the 'spirited'. . . . **4.3.2** [Chrysippus] is in conflict with Zeno on this point, and with himself, and many other Stoics who did not suppose that the passions of the soul were judgments of the soul but rather the irrational contractions, depressions, 'bites', elations, and relaxations which follow those [judgments].

TEXT 117: Galen *On the Doctrines of Hippocrates*
            and Plato 5.2.49–5.3.5, 5.3.7

5.2.49 [Chrysippus said,] "There do exist parts of the soul out of which the reason in it and the disposition in [the reason] are composed. And the soul is honorable or shameful in accordance with the condition of its leading part with respect to its proper divisions." **5.2.50** What are these proper divisions, Chrysippus, which you will write about next to get us out of our difficulties? **5.2.51** But you did not explain this here or in any of your books; but just as though the whole central issue of the discussion of the passions did not turn on this point, you immediately give up on teaching it and drag out your discussion with irrelevant considerations. But you ought to stick to the point and indicate just what these parts of the reasoning part of the soul are. **5.2.52** But since you have abandoned the argument—whether intentionally or inadvertently I cannot guess—I shall try to follow your doctrines and discover your intention and then to consider its truth, and I shall take my start from the passage just quoted, which is: **5.3.1** "There do exist parts of the soul out of which the reason in it is composed." Perhaps you are reminding us of what you wrote in your *On Rational Discourse,* where you explained that reason is an aggregation of certain conceptions and basic grasps. **5.3.2** But if you think that each of the conceptions and basic grasps is a part of the soul, then you are making two mistakes. First of all, you should not have said that they were parts of soul but parts of reason, just as you have written in your *On Rational Discourse.* **5.3.3** For surely soul and reason are not the same thing; besides, you proved in the preceding discussion that reason, too, is one of the components in the soul—and the soul and a component in it are not the same. **5.3.4** And second, even if we let this first point go by without refutation, still one should not call conceptions and basic grasps *parts* of the soul but rather activities. **5.3.5** But nothing is *composed* of its proper activities, neither the eye nor the ear nor the hand nor the leg nor any other bodily organ. . . . **5.3.7** For conceptions and basic grasps are activities of the soul, but its parts, as you yourself explain elsewhere, are the auditory *pneuma* and the visual *pneuma,* and again the vocal in addition to these and the reproductive, but above all the leading part of the soul, of which you said that the reason is a component and which is the part [of the soul] in virtue of which (more than any other part) you say that the shameful and the honorable come to inhere in it.

TEXT 118: Galen *On the Doctrines of Hipocrates and Plato* 5.6.13

I think it advisable to cite the next portion of what Posidonius said, which is like this: "This absurdity [about the goal of life] was dissolved once the cause of the passions was discerned, for it indicated the way the corruption of our sense of what is to be chosen and what is to be avoided gets started, sorted out what kinds of training were needed, and shed light on the puzzles about the impulse that comes from passion." And he says that when the cause of the passions is discovered, we enjoy benefits which are neither small nor negligible.

TEXT 119: Galen *On the Doctrines of Hipocrates and Plato* 5.5.26

Different blends of bodily elements create 'passionate movements' which are distinctive to each blend (for that is the name Posidonius regularly uses for them).

TEXT 120: Plutarch *On Grief and Desire* 6

Posidonius says that some passions belong to the soul, some to the body; and some do not belong to the soul but <to the body and> affect the soul, <whereas others do not belong to the body but to the soul and affect the body.> He says that the passions which accompany judgments and opinions are <the ones that belong to the soul> without qualification, for example, desires, fears, angry outbursts; the ones that belong to the body without qualification are fevers, chills, constrictions, and openings; those that are bodily but affect the soul are episodes of lethargy, black bile, 'bites', presentations, expansions; contrariwise, those that [belong to the soul] but affect the body are cases of trembling, pallor, and changes of appearance produced by fear or pain.

TEXT 121:   Posidonius fragments 157–62 (various short selections
            from books 4 and 5 of Galen *On the Doctrines of
            Hippocrates and Plato*, as arranged by Kidd)[27]

Fragment 157 (Galen 4.3.3–5)

Posidonius completely abandoned both of these views; for he did not hold that the passions are judgments nor that they supervene on judgments, but he holds that the passions are produced by the spirited and desiderative power, in every respect following the ancient doctrine. And in his own treatise on the passions, he asks Chrysippus and his followers many times what the cause of the excessive impulse is. For reason could not go beyond its own affairs and exceed its bounds. So, it is very clear that there is some distinct irrational power which is the cause of the fact that our impulse exceeds the bounds of reason, just as there is a cause of the fact that running exceeds the bounds of our intent, namely, the weight of the body.

Fragment 158 (Galen 4.7.33–35)

For just as the passionate element in the soul aims at certain objects of desire that are proper to it, so when it gets them it is fulfilled and at that point stabilizes its own motion, which was the one that controlled the animal's

27. In L. Edelstein and I. G. Kidd, eds. *Posidonius Volume 1: The Fragments* (Cambridge: Cambridge University Press, 1972), pp. 141–44.

impulse and on its own led it to its aim (such as it was). And so the causes of the cessation of the passions are not, as Chrysippus said, hard to figure out but are in fact quite clear to anyone who is not intent on competing with the ancients. For nothing is so clear as the fact that there are certain powers in our souls which by nature aim for things—one for pleasure, the other for dominance and victory—and Posidonius says that these are clearly observed in other animals too, as I too pointed out right at the beginning of my first book.

Fragment 159 (Galen 5.1.10)

But on points where he [Chrysippus] defeats himself (along with contradicting the obvious phenomena) there, I think one might perhaps feel a bit of shame and adopt the better theory. That is what even Posidonius did, being ashamed to advocate the obviously false doctrine of the other Stoics. They became so competitive that, because they said that the passions belong to the rational power, they would concede that irrational animals do not participate in the passions; most of them hold that not even children have passions since it is pretty obvious that they are not yet rational.

Fragment 160 (Galen 5.5.8–9)

So, by nature we have these three affinities in each of the parts of the soul: to pleasure because of the desiderative part, to victory because of the spirited part, and to the honorable because of the reasoning part. And Epicurus only took account of the affinity of the worst part of the soul, whereas Chrysippus considered only the affinity of the best part, saying that we have an affinity only to what is honorable, and obviously that is the good. Only the ancient philosophers took account of all three affinities. So Chrysippus neglected two of them and became puzzled about the way vice comes to be since he could not refer to any cause for it nor could he discover its modes of existence nor how children go wrong; and in my view, Posidonius was quite right to criticize him for this and to refute him.

Fragment 161 (Galen 5.6.17–18)

"And once the cause of the passions was discerned it taught us how the corruption of our sense of what is to be chosen and what is to be avoided gets started."[28] For some people are deceived and think that the affinities of the irrational powers of the soul are unqualified affinities, not realizing that pleasure and dominance over one's neighbors are desired by the animalistic part of the soul, but that wisdom and all that is good and honorable belong to the part which is at once both rational and divine.

28. See TEXT 118.

Fragment 162 (Galen 5.6.23–26)

And so Posidonius says that we will get these benefits from knowing the cause of the passions, and in addition, he says, "It shed light on the puzzles about the impulse that comes from passion."[29] And then he himself goes on to explain what these puzzles are in the following way: "I think that you have seen for a long time now how it is that when they are convinced by reason that something bad is present to them or imminent they do not experience fear or pain, but they do so when they have presentations of these very same things. For how could one move one's irrational part by reason, unless one puts before it an image which is virtually perceptual? At any rate, this is how some people fall prey to desire on the basis of a narration and, when urged vividly to flee an approaching lion, they fear it even though they do not see it."

A Critique from the Academic-Peripatetic Point of View

TEXT 122: Cicero *On Goals* 5.16–21

16. Since there is so much disagreement about this [the goal of life], we should employ the division of Carneades, which our friend Antiochus is so fond of using. Carneades discerned not only all the views that philosophers had yet held about the highest good but also all the views that are possible. So, he claimed that no craft took its starting point from itself since there is always something external that is the object of the craft. We need not prolong this point with examples; for it is obvious that no craft is concerned with itself, but the craft is distinct from its object. So, just as medicine is the craft of health and helmsmanship is the craft of navigation, in the same way prudence is the craft of living; therefore, it too must be constituted by and take its principle from something else. **17.** It is a matter of general agreement that the concern of prudence and its goal must be what is adapted and accommodated to nature and such as to stimulate and stir up, all by itself, an impulse in the mind (which the Greeks call *hormē*). But there is no agreement about what it is that thus moves us and that nature seeks from the moment of birth—and that is the source of all the disagreement among philosophers when they are considering what the highest good is. For the source of the entire debate about the limits of good and bad, when they investigate the extreme limits of each, is to be found in the primary natural affiliations; and when that is found, the whole debate about the highest good and [worst] bad [thing] is derived from it as from a source. **18.** Some philosophers think that our first impulse is to pleasure and that our first avoidance is of pain. Others think that freedom from pain is what we first welcome and that pain is the first object of avoidance. Others again take

29. See TEXT 118.

their start from the things which they call 'primary' according to nature—a class in which they include the integrity and preservation of all of our parts, health, sound sense organs, freedom from pain, strength, good looks, and other things of this kind. Similar to these are the primary natural things in the soul, which are, as it were, the sparks and seeds of the virtues. Since it is some one of these three that first stirs nature into action, either to pursue something or to avoid it, and since there can be no additional possibility beyond these three, it follows necessarily that the tasks of pursuit and avoidance are to be referred to one of these. Consequently, that prudence which we called the 'craft of living' is concerned with some one of those three things and takes from it the basic principle for all of life.

19. One's theory of what is right and honorable is derived from whichever of these three one has decided is the thing that stimulates nature into action, and this theory can correspond with any one of the three. As a result, honorableness is either a matter of doing everything for the sake of pleasure, even if you do not achieve it, or for the sake of avoiding pain, even if you cannot manage this, or for the sake of acquiring primary natural things, even if you succeed in getting none of them. So it is that disagreements about the starting points of nature exactly correspond to disagreements about the limits of good and bad things. Others again will start from the same principles and refer every [question about] appropriate action either to [the actual attainment of] pleasure or freedom from pain or to the acquisition of the primary natural things.

20. So six views about the highest good have now been set forth, and the chief spokesman for the last three are for pleasure, Aristippus, for freedom from pain, Hieronymus, and for the enjoyment of those things which we have termed 'primary natural things' it is Carneades himself—not indeed that he believes in the view, but he does defend it for the sake of argument. The other three were views that *could* be held, though only one of them has ever been defended, but it has been defended with great vigor. For no one has said that the plan of acting in such a way that one does everything for the sake of pleasure, even if we do not achieve anything, is nevertheless worth choosing for its sake and honorable and the only good thing. Nor has anyone held that the very act of trying to avoid pain was something worth choosing, unless one could actually escape it. But that doing everything to acquire the primary natural things, even if we do not succeed, is honorable and the only thing worth choosing and the only good thing—that is what the Stoics say.

21. These are the six simple views about the greatest good and bad things—two without spokesmen, four that have actually been defended. There has been a total of three composite or double accounts of the highest good, and if you consider the nature of things carefully you will see that there could not have been any more. For either pleasure can be coupled with the honorable, as Callipho and Dinomachus held, or freedom from pain, as

Diodorus held, and so can the primary natural things, which is the view of the ancients, as we call the Academics and Peripatetics.

Pyrrhonist Critique of Basic Ethical Concepts

TEXT 123: Sextus Empiricus *PH* 3, 168–249 (selections)

168. There remains the ethical part of philosophy, which seems to be concerned with the discernment of things good and bad and indifferent. In order that we may discuss ethics summarily, we shall investigate the existence of things good, bad, and indifferent, first setting forth the conception of each.

169. The Stoics say that good is 'benefit' or 'not other than benefit' meaning by a 'benefit' virtue and virtuous action, and by 'not other than benefit' the virtuous human being and the friend. For 'virtue', being the leading part of the soul in a certain state, and 'virtuous action', being a certain activity according to virtue, are exactly 'benefit', whereas the virtuous human being and the friend are 'not other than benefit'. **170.** For a benefit is a part of the virtuous human, i.e., the leading part of his soul. But, they say, the wholes are not the same as their parts, for a human being is not his hand, nor are they other than their parts, for they do not exist without the parts. Therefore, they say that wholes are not other than their parts. For this reason, the excellent human being, being a whole in relation to his leading part (which they have said is benefit), is not other than benefit.

171. They go on to say that 'good' is spoken of in three ways. In one sense, they say 'good' is that by which something is benefited, which is the principal sense [of good] and is virtue; in another sense it is that in accordance with which being benefited is a characteristic result, as virtue and virtuous actions; in the third sense it is that which is such as to benefit, and this is virtue and virtuous action and the excellent man, and the friend, and gods and excellent *daimōns;* so the second meaning of 'good' includes the first and the third includes the second and first. **172.** Some say that 'good' is that which is worth choosing for its own sake; others say it is that which contributes to happiness or fulfils it. And happiness is, as the Stoics say, a 'smooth flow of life'.

Now these are the sort of things said about the conception of the good. . . .

177. They say that that which is indifferent is spoken of in three ways. In one sense, it is that neither toward which nor away from which an impulse arises, for instance, the question of whether the number of stars or the number of hairs on one's head is even. In another sense it is that toward or away from which an impulse arises, but not more toward this rather than that, for example, two indistinguishable four-drachma coins, whenever one has to choose one of them. For an impulse to choosing one of them does indeed arise, but no more toward this one than that one. In the third sense they say that 'indifferent' is what contributes neither to happiness nor unhappiness, as health or wealth. For that which is sometimes used well and sometimes badly is, they say, indifferent. They say that they discuss especially this sense of 'indifferent' in ethics. . . .

179. Fire, which by nature is hot, appears to everyone as capable of producing heat, and snow, which is by nature cold, appears to everyone as capable of producing cold, and everything that moves something in virtue of its nature moves all people who are in a natural condition in the same way, as they say. But, as we shall suggest, none of the things said to be good move all people as a good. Therefore, there is nothing good by nature. Now, they say it is evident that none of the things said to be good moves all people in the same way. **180.** For leaving aside ordinary people, some of whom believe that a sound bodily condition is good, others fornication, others gluttony, others drunkenness, others gambling, others greed, and others even worse things, some philosophers themselves, like the Peripatetics, say that there are three kinds of goods: those of the soul, such as the virtues, bodily [goods], such as health and the like, and external [goods], such as friends, wealth, and related things. **181.** The Stoics themselves also say that there is a triad of goods: those in the soul, such as the virtues; external, such as the virtuous man and the friend; and some that are neither in the soul nor external, such as the virtuous man in relation to himself. But the bodily things said to be good by the Peripatetics, they say are not good. Some [philosophers] have accepted pleasure as good, some say that this is exactly what the bad is, so that one philosopher [Antisthenes] even cried out, "I would rather be mad than experience pleasure." . . .

188. Again, the Stoics say that the goods of the soul are certain crafts, namely, the virtues. They say that a craft is a complex system of grasps practiced together and that the grasps arise in the leading part of the soul. How, then, there arises in the leading part of the soul that is, according to them, *pneuma,* a deposit of grasps and how an aggregate of so many things becomes a craft, it is not possible to conceive, when each subsequent impression replaces the one before it since the *pneuma* is fluid and is said to be moved totally with each impression. . . .

191. Similarly, there is nothing by nature indifferent, because of the disagreement about things indifferent. For example, the Stoics say that of indifferents some are preferred, some rejected, and some neither preferred nor rejected. Things preferred are those having sufficient value, such as health and wealth. Things rejected are those not having sufficient value, such as poverty and sickness. Things neither preferred nor rejected are such things as extending or bending the finger. **192.** Some say that none of the things indifferent are by nature preferred or rejected, for each of the things indifferent sometimes appears to be preferred, sometimes rejected, depending on different circumstances. Indeed, if, they say, the wealthy are attacked by a tyrant whereas the poor are left in peace, everyone would choose to be poor rather than wealthy, so that wealth would become something rejected. **193.** So, since each of the things said to be indifferent is said by some to be good and others bad and everyone would have similarly believed the same thing to be indifferent, if it really were indifferent by nature, there is nothing indifferent by nature. . . .

239. It is evident from what has been said that there also could not be a craft of living. For if there is such a craft, then it is a craft of contemplating things good and bad and indifferent; and since these are non-existent, the craft of living is non-existent. Moreover, since the dogmatists do not all agree in locating the craft of living in one thing, but some hypothesize one craft, some another, they stand accused of disagreeing, and are held to account by the argument from disagreement, which I expounded previously in what I said about the good. **240.** But even if, for the sake of hypothesis, they were to say that the craft of living is one craft, for example, the notorious craft of 'prudence', which is fantasized about by the Stoics and seems more impressive than the rest, still no less absurd consequences follow. For since prudence is a virtue and only the wise man has virtue, the Stoics, not being wise men, will not possess the craft of living. **241.** And, in general since according to them it is not possible that any craft exists, there will not be a craft of living, as far as what they say is concerned.

For example, they say that a craft is a complex of grasps and a grasping is an assent to a graspable presentation. But the graspable presentation is undiscoverable. For not every presentation is graspable, nor is it possible to decide which one from among the presentations is graspable since we are not able to judge unqualifiedly in the case of every presentation which one is graspable and which one is not. And if we need a graspable presentation to decide what the graspable presentation is, we fall into an infinite regress since we are asking for another graspable presentation to use in deciding whether a received presentation is graspable. **242.** And, further, the Stoics are not on sure footing in their proposal of the conception of a graspable presentation for the following reasons: on the one hand, they say that the graspable presentation arises from something that exists; on the other hand, by 'existing' they mean that which is such as to produce a graspable presentation, and so they stumble into the circular mode for producing an impasse [*aporia*]. If, then, in order for a craft of living to exist there must previously exist a craft, and in order for a craft to exist there must previously exist a grasp, and in order for a grasp to exist, assent to a graspable presentation must be grasped, and the graspable presentation is undiscoverable, the craft of living is undiscoverable.

243. Further, this can be said. Every craft seems to be grasped by means of its peculiar products, but there is no peculiar product of the craft of living. For whatever product someone would say this is, is found to be common to ordinary people also [i.e., those without the craft of living], such as honoring one's parents, paying debts, and all the rest. Therefore, there is no craft of living. For we shall not recognize, as they say, what is a product of prudence from what appears to be something said or done from a prudent disposition by a prudent man. **244.** For the prudent disposition is itself ungraspable, being neither simply apparent by itself nor by its products, these being common to ordinary people. And to say that we grasp that one has the craft of living from the consistency of his actions is to trumpet human nature and to brag more than to tell the truth, for[30]

> The mind of earthborn men is such
> as is the day brought forth by the father of men and gods.

245. The remaining possibility is that the craft of living is grasped from those of its products that they write about in books. I shall set forth a few of these as examples of the rest, which are many and much alike. Zeno, for example, the head of their school, in his writings concerning the rearing of children, along with many other similar statements, says, "It makes no difference whether you spread the thighs of a beloved youth or one who is unbeloved, a female or a male, for between beloved youth and unbeloved, women and men, there is no difference, but it befits and is fitting to do the same thing to either." **246.** The same man says, regarding piety toward parents, in the case of Jocasta and Oedipus, that it was not a bad thing for him to have sex with his mother. "If she had been ailing in some other part of her body and he benefited her by rubbing it with his hands, there would be nothing shameful. So, if he gave her joy by rubbing other parts of her body, and relieved her sorrow, and fathered noble children by her, was that shameful?" Chrysippus agrees with these words. Indeed, in his *Republic* he says, "It seems to me that we should act as many are nowadays accustomed to act blamelessly, so that a mother bears her son's children, a daughter her father's, and a sister her brother's." **247.** In the same works he introduces us to cannibalism. Indeed, he says, "If some part of a living thing is cut off and found to be useful for eating, we should neither bury it nor otherwise dispose of it, but consume it, so that another part might grow from ours." **248.** In his *On Appropriate Actions,* he says literally, regarding the burial of one's parents, "When parents die, the simplest burials should be employed, as if the body were nothing to us, like the nails or teeth or hair, the sort of thing to which we give no care or attention. Therefore, should pieces of flesh be useful for eating, people will make use of them, and so too for their own parts, for example, a foot that is severed; it was right to use it and things like it. Should the parts be useless, they should bury or leave them or burn them and let the ashes lie or throw them away and make no further use of them, like nails or hair." **249.** The philosophers say these and many similar things which they would not dare to carry out unless they were ruled by a Cyclops or Laestrygones.[31] But if their

---

30. Homer *Odyssey* 18.136–37.

31. Uncivilized peoples mentioned in the *Odyssey.*

recommendations are totally ineffectual, what they actually do, which is what everybody else does, is not the peculiar product of those who are supposed to have the craft of living. If, then, the crafts ought certainly to be grasped from their peculiar products and there is observed to be no peculiar product of that which is said to be the craft of living, then it is not grasped. Therefore, no one can assert definitely regarding it that such a craft exists.

TEXT 124: Diogenes Laërtius 9.101

And there is nothing good or bad by nature. For if good and bad exist by nature, then it must be either good or bad for everyone, just as snow is something cold for everyone. But there is nothing that is good or bad for everyone in common; therefore, there is nothing good or bad by nature. For either one should say that everything which is thought [to be good] by anyone is good or not everything. And one cannot say that everything is since the same thing is thought to be good by one person (for example, pleasure [is thought to be good] by Epicurus) and thought to be bad by someone else, namely, Antisthenes. It will turn out, then, that the same thing is both good and bad. But if we say that not everything which is thought [to be good] by anyone is good, it will be necessary for us to make a distinction among opinions. But that is not possible because of the equal force of the arguments. So, what is good by nature is unknowable.

TEXT 125: Sextus Empiricus *M* 11.200–07 (selections)

200. . . . they say that all people have the same functions, though it makes a difference whether they are carried out from a craftsmanlike disposition or an uncraftsmanlike one. For taking care of one's parents and otherwise honoring them is not the special function of a virtuous man but doing so from prudence is. **201.** And just as healing is common to the doctor and the layman but doing so medically is the special function of the craftsman, in the same way, too, honoring one's parents is common to the virtuous man and the nonvirtuous man; but honoring one's parents from prudence is the special function of the wise man; consequently, he has a craft of life whose special function it is to do each of the things which are done from a virtuous disposition. . . .

207. Just as in the intermediate crafts it is the special function of a craftsman to do things regularly and to produce the same results consistently (for even a layman could carry out the function of a craftsman, but rarely and not all the time and certainly not consistently in the same manner), so too it is the function of a prudent man, they say, to be consistent in his [morally] perfect actions, and just the opposite for the imprudent man.

Later Stoic Ethics: A Sampler

Musonius Rufus[1]

TEXT 126: Fragment 3. From "That women too should do philosophy"

When someone asked him whether women too should practice philosophy, he began in roughly this way to expound the view that they should in fact do so. He said,

"Women have received from the gods the same rationality as men have, and it is this that we use [to converse] among ourselves and in accordance with it we think about every matter, [investigating] whether it is good or bad, whether it is honorable or shameful. Similarly, the female has the same senses as the male: sight, hearing, smell, etc. Similarly, the body parts of each are the same—neither has more than the other.[2] Further, the desire for and affinity to virtue are not limited to men but also occur in women; for they, no less than men, are naturally pleased by honorable and just actions and censure their opposites.

"Since all of this is the case, why *would* it be appropriate for men to inquire and investigate how to live honorably (this is what practicing philosophy is) but not for women? Is it appropriate for men to be good but not women? Let us investigate each of the things that is appropriate for a woman who is to become good. It will become apparent that she would acquire each of these from philosophy above all. For a woman must manage her household and assess the things beneficial for the house and also be in charge of the servants. I claim that these abilities will be acquired especially well by the woman who practices philosophy. For if each of these functions is a part of life and knowledge about life is just what philosophy is, then the philosopher too, as Socrates says, continually investigates 'what is good or bad in one's halls'.[3]

"Moreover, it is certainly necessary for a woman to be temperate, too, for example, to be pure of improper sexual activities, pure of any failure of self-control with regard to other pleasures, not to be a slave to her desires, not to

---

1. The fragments of Musonius are presented following Cora Lutz *Musonius Rufus: "The Roman Socrates,"* Yale Classical Studies 10 (New Haven, CT: Yale University Press, 1947), pp. 3–147.

2. This is a striking claim if taken absolutely, but the translation given here is literal. One hopes that Musonius has in mind the body parts pertinent to the various senses, but that is not what he actually says.

3. Homer *Odyssey* 4.392.

be aggressively ambitious, not to be a spendthrift, not to be a fashion plate. These are the functions of a temperate woman and on top of these, the following: to control anger, not to be overpowered by distress, and to be stronger than every passion. Philosophical discourse puts all of this at our disposal. Anyone, whether a man or a woman, who has learned these things and practiced them becomes, in my view, a very orderly person.

"Well then? That's how things are. And would a woman who practices philosophy not be just, blameless in life and cooperative, a good and harmonious collaborator, a supportive caregiver for husband and children, in all respects pure from any grasping or greed? And what woman would be more likely to have these characteristics than a philosophical woman? It is absolutely necessary, if she is really a philosopher, that she hold the view that committing injustice is worse than suffering injustice just insofar as it is more shameful, and to believe that being bested is better than being greedy, and moreover that loving one's children is more important than life. What woman could be more just than someone like this? And, moreover, it is appropriate that the educated woman is more courageous than the uneducated, and the philosophical woman more so than the non-philosopher; and she will not endure anything shameful owing to fear of death or reluctance to work hard, nor will she cower before anyone on the grounds that he is wellborn, powerful, wealthy, or even, by Zeus, that he is a tyrant. She has the trait of having trained herself to think lofty thoughts, to hold that death is not a bad thing, and that life is not a good thing, and similarly trained herself not to avoid hard work and not to pursue freedom from hard work at all costs. Hence it is likely that this woman will be industrious and tough, able to nurse at her own breast any children she bears and to serve her husband with her own hands. She will do without hesitation jobs that some regard as servile. Would a woman like this not be worth having for the man who married her, an ornament to her relatives by birth, a fine example to those who know her?

"But, by Zeus, some will say, women who study with philosophers generally become strong willed and overassertive when they abandon their household duties and mix with men, and they practice argumentation and they develop sophisms and analyze syllogisms when they should be sitting at home with their spinning! For my part, it's not just the women who practice philosophy but the men too—I would not have either group neglect their appropriate activities and spend all their time on arguments. I say they should turn their hand to arguments for the sake of their activities. Just as a doctor has no use for medical argumentation unless it contributes to the health of a human body, so too even if a philosopher has or teaches some argument it is of no use to him unless it contributes to the virtue of a human soul. Above all, one must consider whether the argument which proves that modesty is the greatest good (and this is the one we think that woman philosophers must pursue) can make them overassertive; if the argument which recommends maximal modesty will habituate them to live too aggressively; if the one that proves that wantonness is the worst thing will fail to teach them to be temperate; [and] if the argument that establishes that household management is a virtue will fail to encourage them to manage the household. Philosophical argument will encourage women to love [There is a lacuna here.][4] . . . and to be industrious."

TEXT 127:   Fragment 5. From "Whether habituation
              or reasoning is more effective"

On another occasion we fell to investigating whether habituation or reasoning would be more effective in the acquisition of virtue, if reasoning provided correct teaching about what is to be done, and habituation turned out to be characteristic of those habituated to act in accordance with this sort of reasoning. Musonius thought that habituation was the more effective, and in support of his view he questioned one of his students in this way.

"Suppose there are two doctors; one is able to speak even about medical matters as though he were as experienced as one could be, although he has no practical experience in treating sick people; the other is unable to speak but is accustomed to providing treatment that accords with sound medical reasoning. Which of these," he said, "would you choose to have at your bedside if you were ill?"

The other fellow answered, "The one who is accustomed to providing treatment."

And Musonius said, "What about this? Suppose there are two men; one has often been to sea and has already been captain of quite a few ships; the other has not been to sea much and has never been a captain. And suppose that the one who has not been a captain gives an extremely good speech about how to captain a ship, but the other fellow gives a deficient—in fact, an utterly lame—speech on the topic. Which of these would you employ as a captain when you go to sea?"

And he said, "The one who has frequently been a captain."

And Musonius again said, "Suppose there are two musicians and one knows musical theories and gives extremely persuasive speeches about them, whereas the other is not so good at theories but can play the kithara and the lyre beautifully and can even sing too. To which of these men would you entrust musical activity, or which would you want to become the music teacher for a child who doesn't know any music?"

And he replied, "The one who is good at the <practical> side."

---

4. The gap in the text may have specified her children, hard work, or more generally her lot in life as that which philosophy induces women to love (or be content with).

And Musonius said, "So then? That is the situation in these matters. But when it comes to temperance or self-control isn't it much better to become self-controlled and temperate in all one's actions than just to be able to say what one should do?"

The young man agreed on this point too: speaking adequately about temperance is less important and less valuable than being temperate in practice.

Then Musonius linked this up with his earlier responses and said, "So, in these matters how could it possibly be the case that it is more important to know the reasoning relevant to each topic than to be habituated as well to carry out one's actions in accordance with the explanations provided by reason? For habituation gives us the ability to act, whereas knowing the reasoning on the matter gives us the ability to speak. Reasoning does contribute to action by teaching us how one should act and it is temporally prior to habituation. For one cannot be habituated to anything honorable unless one is habituated in accordance with reason. But nevertheless habituation is prior to reasoning in its impact because it is more effective than reasoning in getting people to act."

TEXT 128: Fragment 14. From "Whether marriage is
         an obstacle to practicing philosophy"

When someone else said that he thought that getting married and living with a wife was an obstacle to practicing philosophy, Musonius replied,

"It wasn't an obstacle for Pythagoras nor for Socrates nor for Crates, each of whom lived with a wife, and you couldn't name any other men who philosophized better than they did. And yet Crates didn't even have a house or possessions, and he was utterly without property; but still he got married. Moreover, he didn't even have a private place to take shelter in, but spent his days and nights with his wife in the public porticoes of Athens. But we have houses as a base of operations, and some of us also have house slaves who serve us, and still we have the nerve to say that marriage is an obstacle to philosophy!

Moreover, the philosopher is surely a teacher and a leader for others with respect to everything that is naturally appropriate for a human being. And getting married is obviously natural, if anything is. For why did the craftsman who made human beings first cut our species in half and then make for it two different kinds of genitals (one for the female and one for the male) and then implant in each sex a powerful desire for intercourse and for sharing their lives? And then mix into both of them a powerful longing for each other, male for female and female for male? So, do we not all realize that the craftsman wanted male and female to have intercourse and to live together and to share with each other the challenge of providing life's necessities and to both produce and rear children so that our species might last forever? What? Tell me, is it sensible for each man to take care of his neighbor's business too in order that there be households in the city, that the city not be unpopulated, and that the republic should thrive? For if you say that one must look only to one's own interests, you will be claiming that a human being is no better than a wolf or any other of the wildest beasts which naturally live by violence and greed and do not refrain from anything by which they might gain some pleasure; they have no share in any common interest, no share in mutual cooperation, no share in any form of justice. But if you agree that human nature is more like that of a bee, which cannot live alone and is doomed if isolated from others and which is inclined toward one task that is shared with its hive mates and works and labors in cooperation with its neighbors; if this is the way things really are and if in addition it is understood that injustice, cruelty, and neglect of the distress of one's collaborators are vice in human beings, whereas our virtues include kindness, decency, justice, and the inclination to be generous and caring to one's neighbors—then on this basis each of us must look out for the interests of one's city and regard his household as part of the city's defenses.

And marriage is the foundation of a household that can serve as a defense. The result is that anyone who eliminates marriage from human life also eliminates the household, eliminates the city, and eliminates the entire human species. For without reproduction the species would not persist and there could be no reproduction if there were no marriage (at least, no just and legitimate reproduction). And it is obvious that a household or a city does not consist of women alone nor of men alone, but consists of their mutual sharing. And you could not find any form of sharing more necessary or more congenial than the sharing between husbands and wives.[5] For what friend is as supportive of his friend as a devoted wife is of her husband? What brother for his brother? What son for his parents? And who is missed in his absence the way a husband is missed by his wife or a wife by her husband? And who by his or her mere presence could better assuage pain, augment joy, or reverse misfortune? For whom is it established by custom that all things are in common (body, soul, and wealth) except a husband and a wife?

This is why all people regard the love of man and wife as the most revered of all. No one with any sense, neither mother nor father, would expect to be dearer to their own child than is the child's wedded spouse. And the priority of a wife's love for her husband over parents' love for their children seems to be indicated by this famous old story: the gods gave Admetus the privilege of living twice his regular life span if he could find someone to die in his place; but he found that his parents were unwilling to die for him, despite their old age,

5. The word for "wife" is the same as the word for "woman" and the word for "husband" is the same as the word for "man." This ambiguity helps Musonius make his point, but one may well ask which of these considerations points to the need for legally sanctioned marriage rather than the simple pairing up of man and woman.

whereas his wedded wife, Alcestis, though she was quite young, readily agreed
to die in place of [her] husband.

This too makes it clear that marriage is something important and worth taking most seriously. For according to human belief, there are great gods who preside over marriage. First of all, Hera—and this is why she is addressed as Hera,
Goddess of Marriage—then Eros and then Aphrodite. For we believe that all
these gods have undertaken the job of bringing man and woman together for
the production of children. For what more proper role is there for Eros than in
the lawful union of husband and wife? Or Hera? Or Aphrodite? And what better time is there to pray to these gods than when one is about to be married?
What could we more appropriately call the 'work of Aphrodite' than the bringing together of bride and groom? So then, why would anyone say that such
great gods oversee and preside over marriage and the production of children
but that these matters are not appropriate for human beings? And why would
one say that these things are appropriate for a human being but not for a philosopher? Would it be because the philosopher is worse than other people? But
he shouldn't be; rather, he should be better and more just and nobler. Or would
one say that a man who does not care for his own city is not worse and more
unjust than a man who does? Or that a man who considers only his own interests is not worse and more unjust than a man who looks out for the republic?
Or that a man who chooses the solitary life is more patriotic, philanthropic,
and sociable than one who manages his household, produces children, and
helps his city to prosper—all of which are things that a married man does?

Hence, it is clear that it is appropriate for the philosopher to devote attention to marriage and the production of children. And if this is appropriate,
then, my young man, how could the argument which you made just now be
right, to the effect that marriage is an obstacle for the philosopher? For the
practice of philosophy is evidently nothing but the rational investigation of
what is fitting and what is appropriate and then the actual doing of those
things."

That is roughly what he said on that occasion.

TEXT 129:   Fragment 15. From "Whether all children
            that are born should be raised"

The lawgivers have made it their particular job to inquire into and investigate
what is good for the city, what is bad for it, what benefits the republic, and
what harms it. And have not all such lawgivers determined that it is very
advantageous for cities that the households of citizens should be more popu-
lous and very harmful that those households be reduced? And have they not
taken the view that it is unprofitable for citizens to have no children or to have
few children, whereas it is advantageous that they should have children—by

Zeus, that they should have lots of children? This is why they forbade women to induce miscarriage and established penalties for those who disobeyed, and this is why they banned the toleration of contraception and the prevention of pregnancy, and this is why they established rewards for both the husband and the wife if they have many children, and why they made childlessness subject to civil penalty.

So, we would, of course, be acting lawlessly and illegally if we acted contrary to the intention of the lawgivers, reverend and god-fearing men, obedience to whom is established as honorable and beneficial. And we would be acting contrary to their intention if we prevented ourselves from having many children. And, of course, we would also be wronging our ancestral gods and Zeus, guardian of family ties, if we did this. For just as one wrongs Zeus, guardian of strangers, if one is unjust to strangers and one wrongs Zeus, guardian of friendship, if one is unjust to friends, in the same way anyone who is unjust to his own family is wronging his ancestral gods and Zeus, guardian of family ties, who oversees crimes against the family. And anyone who wrongs the gods is certainly impious.

And indeed, one might conclude that it is honorable and profitable to raise many children if one reasons as follows: a man with many children is honored in the city, instills respect for himself among his neighbors, is more powerful than all his peers—unless they have just as many children. For, in my view, just as a man with many friends is more powerful than one with no friends, in the same way a man with many children is more powerful than one with no children or just a few children—and this is even more the case since sons are closer to him than friends are. It is worth reflecting on the impression made by a man or a woman with many children, when they are seen in public with all their children massed around them. No procession for the gods could make such a fine impression, nor could any sacred dance by well-trained dancers be so fine to gaze upon as a chorus of many children leading the way in the city for their father or mother <and> taking their parents by the hand or in some other way attending on them with fond concern. What is more honorable than this sight? What is more enviable than parents like this, especially if they are decent people as well? For whom else would we be so eager to add to our prayers when we ask for good things from the gods or to cooperate with on anything they need?

"By Zeus," he says, "but if I am a poor man and lack money and have many children, where would I find the resources to feed them all?"

These little birds—swallows, nightingales, larks, and blackbirds—are poorer than you are, and where do they find the resources to feed their young? Homer says this about them:[6]

6. *Iliad* 9.323–24.

As a bird brings to her featherless chicks
whatever food she finds, and so she fares badly herself.

Do these animals surpass humans in intelligence? No, you would not say
that. Well then? In strength and vigor? Much less so. Well then? Do they keep
food in storage? . . . [There is a lacuna here.][7]
And what seems most dreadful to me is that some people do not even have
poverty to offer as an excuse. They are quite well-off financially, some of them
even rich, but they still have the nerve not to rear later-born children in order
that the ones born earlier might be more prosperous, contriving prosperity for
their children from an unholy source. In order that their children might have a
greater share in their ancestral wealth, they kill off their brothers, not realizing
how much better it is to have many brothers than it is to have a lot of money.
For money stirs up plots among one's neighbors, whereas brothers protect
against the plotters. And the same money needs to be protected, whereas one's
brothers are the most powerful protectors. And one cannot <compare> a good
friend to a brother <nor the protection> one gets from others who are one's
peers and equals with the protection which brothers can provide.[8] And with
respect to one's safety, what fine thing could one compare to the goodwill of a
brother? And whom could one have who would be more generous in sharing
good things than a brother of decent character? In misfortunes, whose presence
would one desire more keenly than that of a brother like that? I certainly think
that someone who lives in the midst of a crowd of like-minded brothers is
most enviable. And I think that this man must be most beloved by the gods
because he has his goods right at home. And so I also think that each of us
should try to leave his children brothers rather than money because in that way
he will leave them more important resources for the acquisition of good things.

TEXT 130: Fragment 38

God put some things in our power and other things not in our power. That
which is most honorable and most virtuous is in our power, and it is exactly
this that makes even god himself happy: the use of presentations. For this,
when it proceeds correctly, is freedom, a smooth flow of life, tranquillity, stability; and this is justice, law, temperance, and virtue as a whole. God put
everything else *not* in our power. We therefore must cast our ballots with god
and divide things in this way: aiming in every way to achieve the things which

---

7. The lacuna here must have said something like, "No, they do not. But they still manage to
provide for their young. So, the claim that one is too poor is no excuse for limiting family size."

8. The supplements are not certain. There has been a good deal of damage to the Greek text
here.

are in our power but surrendering to the cosmos those things which are not in our power and cheerfully yielding them up, whether it is children one wants or one's fatherland or the body or anything at all.

Seneca

TEXT 131: Seneca *On Peace of Mind* 13.2–14.2

13.2. . . . He who does many things frequently puts himself in fortune's power. But the safest course is to tempt fortune rarely and always to be mindful of her and never to put any trust in her promises. Say "I shall set sail unless something intervenes" and "I shall become praetor unless something hinders me" and "My enterprise will be successful unless something interferes." **13.3.** This is why we say that nothing happens to a wise man contrary to his expectations; we free him not from the misfortunes but from the blunders of humankind, nor do all these things turn out as he has wished but as he has thought. But his first thought has been that something might obstruct his plans. Then, too, the suffering that comes to the mind from the frustration of desire must necessarily be much lighter if you have not certainly promised it success. **14.1.** We ought also to make ourselves adaptable, so that we do not become too fond of the plans we have formed, and we should pass readily to the condition to which chance has led us and not dread shifting either purpose or positions, provided we avoid fickleness—a vice which poses a most grave threat to mental equilibrium. For obstinacy, from which fortune often wrests some concession, must be anxious and unhappy, and fickleness is much worse if it does not restrain itself. Both are hostile to peace of mind, being unable to make any change and being unable to endure anything. **14.2.** At all events the mind must be withdrawn from all externals into itself. Let it trust in itself, rejoice in itself, esteem its own possessions, retreat as much as it can from things not its own, devote itself to itself, feel no damage, and even take setbacks in a generous spirit. When he received news of a shipwreck and heard that all his possessions had been lost with the ship, Zeno, the head of our school, said, "Fortune bids me to follow philosophy bearing a lighter load."

TEXT 132: Seneca *On Benefits* 4.34.4

The wise man does not change his mind when all the factors which were in place when he made his decision remain. And so he never experiences regret, because at the time nothing better could have been done than what was done, no better decision could have been made than was made. Rather, he approaches every situation with the reservation, 'if nothing comes up to prevent it'. And so we say that everything is a success for him and that nothing happens contrary to his expectation since he anticipates that something could arise which would interfere with his intentions.

TEXT 133: Seneca *On Anger* 3.36

36.1 . . . The mind should be called to account daily. This is what Sextius[9] used to do: at the end of the day when he retired for the night, he would question his own mind, "Which of your failings have you cured today? Which vice have you resisted? In what respect are you better?" **36.2** An anger which knows that it must come before a judge every day will stop and be more restrained. Is anything more admirable than this habit of critically examining one's entire day? What a wonderful sleep comes after this kind of self-criticism, how calm, how deep, how peaceful it is after the mind has been either praised or chastised, acting as its own inspector and as a private censor and passing judgment on its own habits. **36.3** I make use of this capacity and every day I plead my case in my own internal court. When the light has been taken out of the room and my wife has fallen silent (for she is well aware of this habit of mine), I reflect on my whole day and reconsider what I have done and said. I hide nothing from myself and omit nothing. For why should I shrink before any of my mistakes when I am able to say, "Make sure you don't do that anymore; I forgive you this time. **36.4** You were too combative during that debate; in the future, don't go at it with inexperienced people. Those who have never learned aren't willing to start now. You chastised that fellow more openly than you should have, with the result that you didn't improve him but merely made him angry. From here on in, consider not just whether what you say is true but whether the person you are criticizing can take the truth. A good person is happy to be chastised, but the worse someone is the more bitterly he resents being set straight."

TEXT 134: Seneca *Letters on Ethics* 41

1. You are doing a fine thing and something that will be good for you if, as you write, you persist in your plan of mental improvement. It is foolish to pray for it, when you can get it from yourself. There is no need to raise your hands to the heavens and to implore the temple attendant to let us approach the god's statue and whisper in its ear, as though we could be better heard that way. The god is near you, is with you, is *in* you. **2.** That's right, Lucilius. A sacred spirit[10] dwells within us as an inspector of our good and bad deeds, as a guardian. It treats us just as we have treated it. In fact, a good man is never without god. Can anyone rise above fortune without god's assistance? God gives us strong and noble advice. In each and every good man "there dwells a god (though it is not clear which god it is)."[11] **3.** Suppose you come across a

---

9. A Roman philosopher of the generation before Seneca.

10. The Latin is *spiritus,* normally a translation of the Greek *pneuma.* Here it may represent the Greek term *daimōn.*

11. Virgil *Aeneid* 8.352.

grove, thick with ancient trees of unusual height that block your view of the sky with their <densely> interwoven branches; the lofty dignity of the forest, the isolation of the place, and the wonder aroused by the appearance of such dense, uninterrupted shade amid open spaces will convince you that divinity is present. Suppose a natural cave hollowed out of the rocks supports a mountain; it will impress upon your mind a certain spiritual intuition. We worship the sources of great rivers; altars have been established where a huge stream suddenly erupts from below ground; hot springs are objects of veneration; even some lakes have been sanctified by their darkness or their unfathomable depths. **4.** Suppose you see a person who is fearless despite dangers, immune to desires, prosperous in adversity, tranquil amid the storms, looking upon other humans from a lofty height and upon the gods from their own level; won't you get a feeling of reverence for him? Won't you say, "This is something grander and loftier than one can believe to be at all like the mere body which it is in"? **5.** A godlike power is present from on high; a heavenly power animates the mind which is outstanding and balanced, which glosses over everything as being trivialities, which laughs at the objects of all our hopes and fears. Something this great cannot exist without the help of a divinity. Just as the rays of the sun touch the earth but are still present at their source, so too the great and sacred mind which was sent down to give us a closer familiarity with the divine interacts with us but nevertheless clings to its source. It depends on that source, it looks toward it, it strives for it; but it is among us, being better than we are.

6. So, what kind of mind is this? One that relies only on its own goodness. For what is more foolish than to praise in a human being those things that are foreign to him? Who is crazier than someone who stands in awe of things that can be instantly transferred to someone else? A horse is not improved by a golden bridle. . . . **7.** No one should boast of anything except what is his own. We praise a vine if its branches are heavy with its own fruit. . . . Surely no one will prefer to such a vine one that has golden grapes and golden leaves. Fruitfulness is the proper merit of a vine; in a human being too one should praise what belongs properly to him. 'Oh, this fellow has a handsome stable of slaves and gorgeous house, he has huge estates and a big financial portfolio'. None of those things is *in* him. They are his surroundings. **8.** What you should praise in him is what can neither be taken from him nor given to him, what is proper to a human being. You ask what this is? His mind and perfected reason in that mind. For a human being is a rational animal, and his good is accomplished if he fulfills that for which he is born. And what does this reason demand of him? Something very simple: to live according to his *own* nature. But our public madness makes this a difficult task; we drive each other into vice. But how can they be saved if no one restrains them and the mob drives them on?

TEXT 135: Seneca *Letters on Ethics* 120.3–14 (selections)

3. . . . So now I return to the topic you wish to have discussed, which is how we get our conception of what is good and honorable. **4.** Nature could not have taught us this; she has given us the seeds of knowledge, but not the knowledge itself. Some people say that we stumble onto the notion, but it is unbelievable that anyone should learn the form of virtue by chance. Our view is that it is the result of the observation and comparison to each other of frequently performed actions. Our school thinks the honorable and the good are understood by analogy. . . . Let me explain what this analogy is. **5.** We know what bodily health is; from this we suppose that there is also a kind of health of the soul. We know what bodily strength is; from this we infer that there is also a kind of strength of the soul. Certain generous and humane deeds, certain brave deeds struck us so forcefully that we began to admire them as though they were perfect. They contained many faults, but these were hidden by the shining beauty of a remarkable deed; these we ignored. Nature commands us to magnify what is praiseworthy, and everyone exaggerates what is glorious. It is from such actions that we derive the form of a great good. . . .

8. . . . I shall add a point which will perhaps seem amazing: sometimes bad things contribute to the form of the honorable and what is best shines forth from its opposite. As you know, the virtues are quite close to their opposites, and there is a similarity between what is right and things which are corrupt and shameful. Thus the spendthrift mimics the generous man, though there is a very great difference between someone who knows how to give and someone who does not know how to save. . . . Carelessness imitates easygoingness; rashness imitates bravery. **9.** This similarity forced us to pay attention and to distinguish things which are formally quite close to each other but in fact radically different. While we were watching those who have been made famous by some outstanding deed, we began to note who has done something with a noble spirit and great effort, but only once. We saw a man brave in war, but a coward in politics, a man who endured poverty with spirit, but disgrace with shame. [In these cases] we praised the deed and held the man in contempt.

10. But we have [also] seen a different man, who is kind to his friends, moderate to his enemies, governing public and private affairs in a pious and religious manner. We saw that he did not lack patience in enduring what had to be endured or prudence in doing what had to be done. We have seen his generosity in distributing, his effort and determination (which relieve bodily weariness) in working. Moreover, he was always consistent in every action, not good by some plan but by character the sort of person who was not only able to act properly, but could not act otherwise. **11.** In this man we came to understand perfect virtue, and we distinguished it into parts: the desires were to be held in check, fears repressed, plans made for action, what was owed was to be distributed; so we grasped temperance, courage, prudence, and justice, and we assigned to each its own appropriate role. So, where did we get our understanding of virtue? It was shown to us by his orderliness, fittingness, and consistency, by the mutual harmony of all his actions, and by his greatness which elevated itself above all else. This is the source for our understanding of the happy life that flows smoothly in its own course and is completely in control of itself. **12.** So, how did this make itself apparent to us? I shall tell you. This perfect and virtuous man never cursed fortune, was never sad about what happened, regarded himself as a citizen and soldier of the cosmos, and so endured all his labors as though he were under orders. Whatever happened, he did not scorn it as inflicted upon him by chance but took it as a job assigned to him. He says, "This, whatever it may be, is mine; it is harsh and difficult, but it is to this that I must devote my efforts." **13.** A man who never whined over misfortune and never complained about his fate of necessity appears to be great. He provided many people with an understanding of himself, like a light shining in the darkness; he attracted attention from everyone, though he was quiet and mild, equally able to handle human and divine affairs. **14.** He had a mind which was perfect and had achieved its full potential; there is nothing greater, except the mind of god, from whom some portion was diverted into his mortal breast. This part is never more divine than when contemplating its mortality and realizing that human beings were born for dying, that the body is not a home but a guesthouse—and a brief one at that since it must be vacated when you see that you are a burden to your host.

TEXT 136: Seneca *Letters on Ethics* 121.1–24 (selections)

1. I can see that you will quarrel when I have expounded for you today's theme, which we have already spent quite some time with; yet again you will cry out, "What does this have to do with ethics?" Exclaim away, until I can, first, give you the names of others to quarrel with, Posidonius and Archidemus. . . .

5. Meanwhile let me examine some questions which seem to be a bit too far removed [from your practical concerns]. We were asking whether all animals had an awareness of their own constitution. The best evidence that this is so was that they move their limbs in a fitting and efficient manner, as though they had been trained to do so; each animal has a nimble mastery of his various parts. A craftsman handles his tools with ease; a helmsman controls the rudder with skill; and a painter can very quickly apply the many and varied colors that he sets out on his palette for the purpose of capturing a likeness and moves back and forth between the hot wax and the canvas with a ready hand and eye. In the same way, an animal is expeditious in the use of himself. **6.** We often admire skilled dancers because their hands are capable of expressing all kinds of objects and emotions and their gestures are responsive to the rapidly uttered words. What art gives to them, nature provides to the animals. They do this as soon as they are born; they come into this world with this knowledge; they are born with a sound training.

7. "And so," he says, "animals move their parts in a fitting manner because if they moved them any differently they would feel pain. Thus, on your theory, they are forced [to act as they do] and it is fear that leads them to correct action, not choice." This is false; for things which are driven by necessity are slow; nimbleness belongs to those who move of their own free will. Far from it being fear of pain that drives them to this [behavior], they even strive for their natural motions when pain discourages them. **8.** Consider a baby who is practicing standing up and learning how to walk; as soon as he begins to try his strength he falls and, in tears, gets up again and again until, despite the pain, he trains himself to the [function] demanded by his nature. Some animals who have hard shells can be turned over on their backs and they will strain and push with their feet and twist themselves for a long time until they get back in their [proper] posture. Yet the turtle feels no pain when on its back; it is uneasy, nevertheless, because it desires its natural constitution and does not stop straining and flailing until it gets to its feet. **9.** Therefore, all [animals] have an awareness of their own constitution and that is the source of their very expeditious handling of their limbs. We have no better evidence that they come into life equipped with this knowledge than the fact that no animal is clumsy in handling itself.

10. "The constitution is," he says, "according to you, the leading part of the soul in a certain disposition relative to the body. How can a baby understand this, which is so complex and subtle and hard even for you to explain? All animals ought to be born as dialecticians so that they can understand that definition, which is opaque to most Roman citizens." **11.** Your objection would be valid if I were saying that animals understood the *definition* of constitution and not the constitution itself. Nature is more easily understood than explained. And so that baby does not know what a constitution is but does know his constitution; he does not know what an animal is, but he knows that he is an animal. **12.** Furthermore, he understands that constitution of his vaguely and in outline and dimly. We too know that we have a soul; what the soul is, where it is, what it is like or where it came from—that we do not know. Our awareness of our own soul (despite our ignorance of its nature and location) is to us in the same relation as the awareness of their constitution is to all animals. It is necessary that they be aware of that through which they are also aware of other things; it is necessary that they have an awareness of that thing which they obey, by which they are governed. **13.** Every one of us understands that there is something which sets our impulses in motion; but we do not know what that thing is. Thus babies and animals also have an awareness, neither very clear nor distinct, of the leading part in them.

14. "You say," he says, "that every animal first has an affinity to its own constitution; but a human being's constitution is rational and so a human being has an affinity not to his animality but to his rationality; for a human being is dear to himself in virtue of that part which makes him human. So, how can a baby have an affinity to a rational constitution when he is not yet rational?" **15.** There is a different constitution for every age: one for the baby, one for the child, <one for the teenager,> one for the old man. All have an affinity to the constitution that they are in. A baby lacks teeth; he has an affinity to that constitution. His teeth appear; he has an affinity to that constitution. For the plant which will turn into mature crop has a different constitution when it is tender and barely poking its nose out of the furrow, another when it gains strength and stands, admittedly with an unripe stalk but one able to support its own weight, and another when it ripens and gets ready for the threshing floor and the ear firms up; it looks to and adapts itself to whatever constitution it achieves. **16.** There are different stages of life for a baby, a boy, a teenager, and an old man; yet I am, for all that, the same [person] as the baby and the boy and the teenager I used to be. Thus, although each person's constitution changes [from one stage to another], the affinity he has to his constitution is the same. For nature does not commend to me a boy or a youth or an old man, but myself. Therefore, a baby has an affinity to his own constitution, the constitution he then has and not the one that he will have as a youth; the fact that he will have something greater to change into some day does not mean that the state in which he is born is not according to nature. **17.** First of all, the animal has an affinity to itself; for there must be something to which all else can be referred. I seek pleasure. For whose sake? Mine. Therefore, I am looking out for myself. I flee pain. For whose sake? My own. Therefore, I am looking out for myself. If I do everything in order to look out for myself, then looking out for myself is prior to everything else. This concern for oneself is in all animals. It is not acquired; it is innate. **18.** Nature brings forth her young; she does not abandon them. And since the most certain guardianship is the closest, everyone is entrusted to himself. Thus, as I said in my earlier letter, young animals, even those that have just recently emerged from their mothers' womb or egg, know immediately what is dangerous and they avoid what is life threatening. Animals that are at risk from birds of prey even avoid the shadows cast by predators as they fly over. No animal comes into life without a fear of death.

19. "How," he says, "can a newborn animal understand what is salutary or life threatening?" First of all, the point at issue is whether it understands, not how it understands. It is clear that they do understand from the fact that they behave no differently than [they would] if they did understand. Why is it that a hen does not flee a peacock or a goose but does flee a hawk, which is so much smaller and is not even known to it yet? Why do chicks fear a cat, but not a dog? Obviously, they have a knowledge of what is liable to harm them that is not acquired by experience; for before they can acquire any experience they are already cautious. **20.** Next, in order that you should not think that this is an accident, they neither fear things which they need not fear nor do they ever forget this care and diligence; the avoidance of danger is their lifelong companion. Moreover, they do not become more timid as they live; from this it is obvious that they do not get this characteristic by practice but from a natural love of their own preservation. What practice teaches is late and various; whatever nature passes on is the same for all [members of a species] and instantaneous. **21.** If, however, you insist, I shall tell how every animal is compelled to understand what is dangerous. It is aware that it is made of flesh; and so it is aware of what can cut and burn and bruise flesh. Of the animals which are equipped for hurting it, it regards their appearance as hostile and threatening. These things are closely connected; for as soon as each animal has an affinity to its safety, it seeks what will help it and fears what will harm it. There are natural impulses to what is useful and natural rejections of the opposite. Whatever nature teaches comes without any thought to enunciate it, without planning. **22.** Do you not see how sophisticated bees are in building their hives, how much cooperation there is all around in the division of the necessary tasks? Do you not see that the weaving of a spider cannot be imitated by any mortal, [do you not see] how much work it takes to arrange the threads—some set in a straight line as a kind of framework, others spun in a circle to fill in the pattern, so that smaller animals (for whose destruction such webs are woven) might be caught and held as though in a net? **23.** That craft is born, not learned. Therefore, no one animal is any more skilled than any other; you will see that the webs of spiders are all the same, the cells in all the corners of honeycombs are all the same. What craft passes on is indefinite and uneven. What nature distributes comes equally. She passes on nothing more than care of oneself and skill in that, and that is also why they begin to live and learn at the same time. **24.** And it is not surprising that animals are born with those things without which it would be pointless for them to be born. Nature gave them this as their first tool for survival: affinity to and love for themselves. They could not have been safe if they did not want to be; this would not have been beneficial all on its own, but without it nothing else would have been either. But in no animal will you find contempt for itself, nor even neglect; even silent and brutish animals have the cunning required to live, although they are stupid in all else. You will see that even animals which are useless to others do not let themselves down.

TEXT 137: Seneca *Letters on Ethics* 124.1–20

1. . . . The question is whether the good is grasped with the senses or the mind; connected with this is the fact that the good is not found in dumb animals and infants. **2.** Those who make pleasure supreme hold that the good is perceptible, but we on the other hand attribute it to the mind and hold that it is intelligible. If the senses made judgments about the good, we would not reject any pleasure, for no pleasure fails to attract us and every pleasure pleases us; conversely, we would not willingly suffer any pain, for every pain hurts our senses. **3.** Moreover, those who are excessively pleased by pleasure and who fear pain more than anything else would not deserve criticism. But in point of fact we do disapprove of those who are devoted to their bellies and to pleasure and we hold in contempt those whose fear of pain prevents them from ever daring to act in a manly fashion. What are they doing wrong if they obey their senses, i.e., the judges of what is good and bad? For you have handed over the decision about what is good and bad to the senses. **4.** But surely it is reason which is in charge of that matter; that is what makes the decisions about good and bad, just as it does about the happy life, about virtue, and about the honorable. But [the hedonists] let the lowest part make the decisions about what is better, so that judgment is pronounced on the good by sense-perception, which is blunt and lazy and slower in humans than it is in beasts. **5.** What [would we think] if someone wanted to discriminate tiny things not by the eyes but by touch? . . .

   6. He says, "Just as every branch of knowledge and every craft takes something that is obvious and is grasped by sense-perception as the starting point from which it will develop, similarly, the happy life must take something obvious as its foundation and starting point. Surely you say that the happy life has something obvious as its starting point." **7.** We say that those things which are in accordance with nature are happy. And what is in accordance with nature is out in the open and immediately apparent, just as is the case with what is healthy. I do not call the natural, [i.e.,] what immediately affects a newborn [animal], 'good' but rather the starting point of the good. You give over the highest good, i.e., pleasure, to infancy, so that a newborn starts out from the point which a fully accomplished human being [might hope to] reach. You put the top of the tree where the roots ought to be. **8.** It would be a blatant error if someone said that the fetus hidden in its mother's womb, still of uncertain sex, immature, unfinished, and not yet formed, were already in some good condition. And yet, how small is the difference between one who is just in the act of receiving life and one who lies as a hidden burden inside its mother's body. As far as an understanding of good and bad is concerned, both are equally mature; an infant is no more capable of the good than a tree or some dumb animal! But why is the good not found in a tree or a dumb animal? Because reason is not there either. That is also the reason why it is missing in an infant; for infants too lack reason. It attains the good when it attains reason.

   9. There is such a thing as a non-rational animal, and such a thing as an animal that is not yet rational, and one that is rational but not yet perfect. In none of them can you find the good, which is brought with reason. What is the difference, then, between the [kinds of animal] I have mentioned? In the non-rational the good will never exist; in that which is not yet rational the good cannot exist just then; <in the rational> but imperfect the good is already *able* to <exist> but does not. **10.** I maintain, Lucilius, that the good is not found in just any body, nor in just any age. It is as far from the state of infancy as the last is from the first and as the perfect is from its starting point; so it is not found in a young body, still immature and in the process of formation. Of course it is not found there, any more than it is found in the seed!

11. You could put it like this: we are familiar with the good in a tree or a plant: it does not lie in the first sprouts that are just breaking the soil as they sprout. There is something good in a stalk of wheat, but it is not yet present in the sappy sprout nor when the tender ear [first] emerges from the husk, but when it ripens with the heat of summer and its proper maturity. Just as every nature refuses to bring forth its good until it is finished, so too the good of a human being is not present in him until his reason is perfected. **12.** But what is this good? I shall say: a free and upright mind, superior to other things and inferior to nothing. So far is infancy from having this good that childhood does not hope for it, and adolescence is wrong to hope for it. We are lucky if it comes with old age as a result of long and serious effort. If this is what is good, it is also intelligible.

13. He says, "You said that there was a certain [kind of] good that belongs to a tree and to a plant; so there can also be a certain [kind of] good in an infant." The true good is not in trees or dumb animals; what is good in them is called 'good' by courtesy. "What is this?" you say. [Merely] that which is in accord with the nature of each. But the good can in no way apply to a dumb animal; it belongs to a happier and better nature. Where there is no room for reason, there is no good. **14.** There are these four kinds of natures: that of a tree, of an animal, of a human, and of a god. The latter two are rational and have the same nature and differ [only] in that the one is immortal and the other mortal. Nature perfects the goodness of one of these, i.e., the god, whereas effort perfects the goodness of the other, i.e., the human being. The others, which lack reason, are perfect in their own natures but not really perfect. For in the final analysis the only thing which is perfect is that which is perfect in accordance with universal nature; and universal nature is rational. The other things can be perfect [only] in their own kind. **15.** And in this there cannot exist a happy life nor that which produces a happy life. But a happy life is produced by good things. In a dumb animal the happy life does not exist <nor does that by which a happy life> is produced; the good does not exist in a dumb animal.

16. A dumb animal grasps what is present by its senses; it remembers past events when it meets with something that reminds its senses, as a horse is reminded of the road when it is placed at its starting point. But when in the stable, it has no recollection of the road, no matter how often it has trodden it.

The third [part of] time, i.e., the future, does not apply to dumb animals. **17.** So, how can their nature seem to be perfect when they cannot make use of the past?[12] For time consists of three parts: past, present, and future. For animals the present is the briefest and most transitory time; they rarely recall the past and then only when it is occasioned by the occurrence of something in the present. **18.** Therefore, the good of a perfected nature cannot exist in an imperfect nature, or if such a nature has it, so do plants. I do not deny that dumb animals have great and powerful impulses toward achieving what is according to their natures, but they are disorderly and confused. But the good is never disorderly or confused. **19.** "What, then?" you say, "Are dumb animals moved in a thoroughly confused and disorganized fashion?" I would say that they are moved in a thoroughly confused and disorganized fashion if their nature were capable of orderliness; but as it is, each is moved according to his own nature. 'Disorganized' is [a term] reserved for those things which can sometimes move in a non-disorganized fashion, 'troubled' [a term reserved] for that which can be free of care. Nothing has a vice if it cannot have virtue; and such is the motion of dumb animals by their very nature. **20.** But to avoid detaining you any longer, there will be a kind of good in a dumb animal, a kind of virtue, and a kind of perfection; but there will not be good or virtue or perfection in an absolute sense since these properties apply only to rational animals, to whom it has been given to know why, to what extent, and how. So, nothing which does not have reason can possess the good. . . .

Epictetus

TEXT 138: Epictetus *Discourses* 1.1.10–13

10. But what does Zeus say? "Epictetus, if it had been possible I would have made both your body and your possessions free and unimpeded. **11.** As it is, do not overlook the fact that this body is not your own, but only some cleverly molded mud. **12.** But since I could not manage this, I have instead given you a part of myself, the power of impulse and rejection, of desire and avoidance, and, in a word, the power of using presentations. If you take care of this power and locate in it all that is your own then you will never be hindered, you will never be impeded, you will never groan, you will never blame anyone and never flatter anyone. **13.** Well? Do you think these are trivial gifts?" Far from it. "And so you are content with them?" I pray to the gods that I might be.

TEXT 139: Epictetus *Discourses* 1.4.18–29

18. Where is moral progress, then? If any of you abandons external things and turns to his own moral choice and works on it, laboring over it, so as to

---

12. "Past time" in Latin is *tempus perfectum*. The pun on "perfect" is not readily translated.

make it harmonious with nature, elevated, free, unhindered, unimpeded, trustworthy, and modest **19.** and has also learned that he who longs for or avoids what is not in his own power cannot be either trustworthy or free but will inevitably reverse himself and be tossed about along with those things, inevitably subordinating himself to those others who have the power to provide or prevent what they long for; **20.** and, moreover, if any of you preserves and lives by this knowledge when he rises in the morning, washing up like a trustworthy man, having breakfast like a modest man, and putting his principles into action in the various circumstances that come along, as a runner behaves like a runner and a voice coach behaves like a voice coach; **21.** *this* is the person who is genuinely making moral progress and *this* is the person [who] has not wasted his time coming to my school. **22.** But if any of you is focused on acquiring a bookish disposition and labors at this and traveled abroad for this purpose, then I say to him, "Go home right now and don't neglect matters there!" **23.** For his reasons for coming here are worthless. But what is not worthless is to work on eliminating from one's life grief and lamentation, the 'Woe is me!' and 'Alas, alack!' along with misfortune and bad luck, **24.** and to learn what death is, what exile is, what a prison is, what hemlock is, so that in prison one can say, "Oh, Crito, if it is the will of the gods so be it"[13] rather than "Woe is me, an aged man, is this what I lived so long for?" **25.** Who says this kind of thing? Do you think I'm going to tell you about some insignificant wretch? Isn't this what Priam says? Doesn't Oedipus say it? All the kings say it! **26.** For tragedies are nothing but the sufferings of people who are impressed by externals, performed in the right sort of meter.

27. For if it were necessary that someone be deceived into learning that nothing that is external or outside the range of our moral choice matters to us, then I for my part would welcome this deception, based on which I would be in a position to live with a smooth and undisturbed flow of life, and you folks could see to your preferences on your own. **28.** So what is it, then, that we get from Chrysippus? He says, "To learn that the beliefs which produce a smooth flow of life and freedom from passions really are true, **29.** pick up my books and you'll know that the doctrines which free me from passion accord with nature and are consistent with it." What great good fortune! What a benefactor, showing us the way!

TEXT 140: Epictetus *Discourses* 1.17

1. Since it is reasoning which analyzes and perfects all other things, and since it should not itself be unanalyzed, by what, then, should it be analyzed?

---

13. Plato *Crito* 43d (an almost exact quotation).

2. Clearly, either by itself or by something else. And that other thing is either reasoning or something more powerful than reasoning—but that is impossible. **3.** So if it is reasoning, then by what will *that* reasoning be analyzed in turn? And if it analyzes itself, then the initial reasoning can do so as well. If we need some further reasoning, then there will be infinite and unending regress.

4. "Yes, but therapy is even more urgent" [than logical analysis], etc. So, do you want to hear about those issues? Then listen. **5.** But if you say to me, "I don't know whether your discussion is true or false," and if I use an ambiguous term and you say to me, "Distinguish the senses," then I just won't put up with you anymore, but I'll say to you, "Yes, but this is even more urgent."

6. This, I think, is why they put logic first in the curriculum, just as we put the determination of the measure first when we are measuring wheat. **7.** And if we don't first determine what a bushel is and don't determine what a set of scales is, then how will we be able to measure or weigh? **8.** So in this case, if we haven't learned with precision the criterion for other things and how other things are learned, will we be able to learn anything else with precision? How could that be possible? **9.** "Yes, but the bushel is just wood and does not yield fruit." But it can measure grain. **10.** "And logic does not yield fruit." Well, we'll see about that. But even if that point is granted, it is enough that logic is able to discriminate about and investigate things—it can, so to speak, measure and weigh them. **11.** Who says this? Is it only Chrysippus and Zeno and Cleanthes? **12.** Doesn't Antisthenes say it? And who is it who wrote that the investigation of terms is the starting point for education? Doesn't Socrates say it?[14] Who was Xenophon writing about when he said that he began from the investigation of the meaning of individual terms?

13. "So, is this your great and wonderful achievement, to understand or interpret Chrysippus?" Who says that? **14.** "Then what is so wonderful?" To know the will of nature. "Well then, do you understand it all by yourself? What more do you need, then? For if it is true that all people err unwillingly and you have actually learned the truth, then you must already be performing [morally] perfect actions." **15.** But, by Zeus, I don't understand the will of nature! "So who interprets it?" They say that Chrysippus does. **16.** So I'll go and investigate what this interpreter of nature says. But at some point I begin to not understand what he is saying, so I look for someone to interpret him. "Look here, investigate what he is saying, as though it were in plain Latin."

17. So, what call is there for the interpreter to be arrogant in a case like this? Not even Chrysippus would be justified if all he does is interpret the will of nature but does not himself follow it. This applies all the more to the man who interprets Chrysippus. **18.** For we don't need Chrysippus for his own

14. See Xenophon *Memorabilia* 4.6.1; Plato *Phaedrus* 237b7–c5.

sake but only so that we can follow nature. And we don't even need the sacrificial diviner for his own sake but only because we think that through him we will learn future events as revealed by the gods. **19.** Nor do we need the entrails for their own sake, but only because they are the medium through which the signs are given; and we don't feel awe for the crow or the raven but rather for the god who uses them to give signs.

20. So I go to this interpreter and sacrificial diviner and I say, "Investigate the entrails for me and tell me what they mean." **21.** He takes them and lays them out and interprets them, saying, "Sir, you have a capacity for moral choice which by nature is immune to hindrance and compulsion. That is what is written here in the entrails. **22.** I will show this first in the domain of assent. Surely no one can compel you to reject the truth?" "No, no one can." "Surely no one can compel you to accept a falsehood?" "No, no one can." **23.** "Do you see that in this domain you have a capacity for moral choice which is free of hindrance, compulsion, and impediment? **24.** Come on, then, is it any different in the domain of desire or impulse? What can defeat an impulse except another impulse? What can defeat a desire or an aversion except another desire or aversion?"

25. "But," someone says, "if you threaten me with death, *that* compels me."

"It's not because you are threatened, but it's because you believe that it is better to do this or that rather than to die. **26.** So, once again it is your opinion that compelled you, that is, your moral choice compelled your moral choice. **27.** For if god made that part of himself which he broke off and gave to us subject to hindrance or compulsion, by himself or anyone else, then he wasn't a real god anymore and he wasn't taking care of us in the proper fashion. **28.** *This* is what I see in the sacred entrails," he says. "This is what the signs are saying to you. If you want, you are free. If you want, you will blame no one, you will criticize no one, everything will turn out according to the plan shared by you and god."

29. It is for this kind of prophecy that I go to this sacrificial diviner, this philosopher, not in awe of him because he is an interpreter but, rather, in awe of the content of his interpretation.

TEXT 141: Epictetus *Discourses* 1.22.1–4

1. Basic grasps are common to all human beings, and one basic grasp does not conflict with another; for who among us does not suppose that the good is advantageous and worth choosing and that one ought to go for it and pursue it in all circumstances? Who among us does not suppose that the good is honorable and fitting? So, where does the conflict come from? **2.** In the application of basic grasps to particular substances, **3.** as when someone says, "He did well and is brave!" [and someone else says,] "No, he is crazy." This is the source of the conflict between people. **4.** The conflict between the Jews and the Syrians and Egyptians and Romans is not about whether the sacred must be honored above all else and pursued in all instances but about whether this particular thing, eating pork, is sacred or unholy.

TEXT 142: Epictetus *Discourses* 2.5.24–26

24. So, what is meant by saying that some externals are according to nature and some contrary to nature? This is said to be so *as if* we were independent entities. For I'd say that it is according to nature for the foot to be clean; but if you take it as a foot and not as an independent entity it will be incumbent on it to walk in the mud and step on thorns and sometimes even to be chopped off, for the sake of the whole. Otherwise, it would not any longer be a foot. **25.** You should suppose that this is what it is like in our case too. What are you? A human being. If you look at yourself as an independent entity, it will be according to nature for you to live to old age, to be wealthy, to be healthy. But if you look at yourself as a human being and a part of some whole, then for the sake of that whole it is incumbent on you to get sick at one point, at another to take a dangerous voyage, at another to be impoverished, and sometimes to die prematurely. **26.** So, why do you complain? Don't you know that just as in the example it wouldn't even be a foot any longer, so too in our case you wouldn't be a human being any longer? For what is a human being? A part of a city, in the first instance a part of the city of gods and humans and secondarily a part of the city in the more narrow sense, which is a small-scale imitation of the former.

TEXT 143: Epictetus *Discourses* 2.6.6–10

6. "Go and salute Mr. So-and-so." "All right, I salute him." "How?" "Not in an abject fashion." "But you were shut out." "That's because I haven't learned how to enter through the window. And when I find the door shut [against me], I must either go away or enter through the window." **7.** "But speak with the man too!" "I do so." "How?" "Not in an abject fashion." **8.** "But you did not succeed."—Now surely that was not your business, but his. So, why do you encroach on what concerns someone else? If you always remember what is yours and what concerns someone else, you will never be disturbed. **9.** That's why Chrysippus was right to say, "As long as what comes next is non-evident to me, I always cling to what is better suited to getting what is in accordance with nature. For god himself made me such as to select those things. **10.** But if I knew for sure that it was fated for me now to be ill, I would even seek [illness]. For my foot, if it had brains, would seek to be muddied."

TEXT 144: Epictetus *Discourses* 2.10

1. Consider who you are. First of all a *human being,* and this means that you have nothing more authoritative than your power of moral choice and everything else is subordinate to it, but it itself is free and independent. **2.** Consider, then, what you are separate from in virtue of your rationality. You are separate from wild beasts and from sheep. **3.** And in addition you are a citizen of the cosmos and a part of it—not one of the servile parts but one of its principal parts. For you are able to follow the divine administration and figure out what comes next. **4.** So, what is the commitment of a citizen? To have no private advantage, not to deliberate about anything as though one were a separate part but just as if the hand or foot had reasoning power and were able to follow the arrangements of nature, they would never have sought or desired anything except after referring to the whole. **5.** That is why the philosophers are right to say that if the honorable and good person knew what was going to happen, he would even collaborate with disease and death and lameness, being aware that these things are dispensed by the arrangement of the whole and that the whole is more authoritative than the part and the state more authoritative than the citizen. **6.** But now, because we do not have this foreknowledge, it is appropriate for us to cling to what is better suited for selection since we are also born for this.

7. Next, remember that you are a *son.* What is the commitment made by this role? That he considers all that is his own as being under his father's sway, that he obeys him in all matters, never criticizes him to someone else, and neither says nor does anything to harm him, defers to him, and concedes to him on all occasions, cooperating with him as much as he can. **8.** Next, be aware of this as well, that you are a *brother.* This role too demands that you make concessions, be obedient, and speak properly to your brother; it never makes claims against him for any of the things not within the scope of moral choice but is happy to let him have those things so that you can have the advantage of him regarding things within the scope of moral choice. **9.** Just consider what it's like to acquire goodwill yourself, when compared to the value of a lettuce, for example, or a seat—that is how much you have the advantage over him.

10. Next, this point. If you are a *city councilor,* be aware that you are a city councilor. If a *young man,* be aware that you are young. If *an old man,* that you are old. If a *father,* that you are a father. **11.** If you take it into account in your deliberations, then each of these designations will outline the appropriate actions on each occasion.

12. But if you go around criticizing your brother, I say to you, "You have forgotten who you are and what your designation is." **13.** Further, if you were a metalworker and used your hammer ineffectively, you would be forgetting that you are a metalworker. And if you forgot that you are a brother and became an enemy instead of a brother, will you think that you have made a meaningless change? **14.** If instead of a human being, a tame and sociable animal, you have turned into a beast—harmful, scheming, and prone to bite—have you lost nothing? So, must you lose some spare change in the bargain for it to count as suffering damages? Will the loss of nothing else damage the human being? **15.** Further, if you lost grammatical or musical expertise you would consider the loss of the expertise as damage. Do you think it is nothing if you lose your modest demeanor, your dignity, and your gentleness? **16.** And yet, those things are lost as a result of some external cause, not in the realm of moral choice; but *these* losses are our own doing. Those things—having them is not honorable and losing them is not shameful. But losing or not having *these* things is shameful, blameworthy, a disaster! **17.** If someone submits to anal sex, what does he lose? Being masculine. And the one who does it to him? He loses many other things, but he too loses his masculinity just as much as the other. **18.** What does the adulterer lose? Being modest, self-controlled, orderly, a citizen, a neighbor. What does the angry person lose? Something else. The fearful person? Something else. **19.** No one is bad without some loss and damage.

But if you look for the damage in regard to spare change, then all of these people are free of harm, undamaged. If they are lucky, maybe they even get some benefit and profit when a bit of spare change comes their way due to one of these acts. **20.** Just consider whether you reduce *everything* to bits of spare change so that not even someone whose nose is cut off will have suffered harm. "Yes," he says, "for his body has been mutilated." **21.** Come on! Someone who has lost his sense of smell, has he lost nothing? So, is there no capacity of the soul such that whoever acquires it is benefited and whoever loses it is damaged? **22.** "What are you talking about?" Do we not have something that is by nature modest? "We do." Is the person who loses this not damaged? Is he not deprived of something? Does he not lose something that pertains to himself? **23.** Do we not have something that is naturally trustworthy, naturally affectionate, natural helpful, naturally inclined to refrain from other people's things? So, whoever sits and watches himself being damaged in these respects, is he to be unharmed and undamaged?

24. "What then? Shall I not harm the man who harmed me?" First, consider what harm is and remember what you have heard from the philosophers. **25.** For if the good consists in moral choice and the bad, similarly, consists in moral choice, consider whether what you are saying comes down to this: "What then? **26.** Since he has harmed himself by doing something unjust with respect to me, shall I not harm myself by doing something unjust with respect to him?" **27.** Why then don't we present the situation to ourselves in this light? Instead, where there is some reduction in our body or in our possessions, there we find damage, but where there is some reduction in our moral capacity, is there no harm? **28.** For someone who makes a mistake or commits an injustice does not get a headache or sore eyes or a sore hip, nor has he lost his farm. **29.** But we don't care about anything else. Whether we shall have a moral capacity that is modest and trustworthy or one that is shameless and untrustworthy, we scarcely even bother to disagree except in the petty argumentation of school debates. **30.** So anyway, we are making progress only in those petty arguments, but beyond that, not even the slightest progress.

TEXT 145: Epictetus *Discourses* 2.11.13–16

13. Consider the starting point of philosophy: a perception of the mutual conflict among people and a search for the cause of the conflict [plus] the rejection and distrust of mere opinion, an investigation of opinion to see if it is right, and the discovery of some canon, like scales which we invent for weighing things and the ruler for determining what is straight and crooked. **14.** Is this the starting point of philosophy? Are all the views held by all people right? And how is it possible that conflicting opinions are right? So, not all of them are right. **15.** But is it *our* opinions that are right? Why ours rather than those of the Syrians? Why ours rather than those of the Egyptians? Why *our* opinions rather than what *I* think or what any random person thinks? So, there is no reason to prefer one opinion to any other. So, each person's opinions don't suffice to establish what is the case. For in the case of weights and measures too, we are not satisfied with mere appearance; rather, we have found some canon for each. **16.** So, is there no canon here higher than mere opinion? But how is it possible for what is most vital to people to be undeterminable and undiscoverable?

TEXT 146: Epictetus *Discourses* 2.22.15–21

15. Don't be deceived. In general every animal has an affinity to nothing as much as to its own advantage. Whatever it thinks is standing in the way of its advantage, whether it is a brother or a father or a child or a beloved or a lover, this it hates and accuses and curses. **16.** For by nature it loves nothing so much as its own advantage. This is its father, its brother, its relations, its homeland, its god. **17.** So, when we think that the gods are standing in the way of our advantage, we revile even them and we tear down their statues and burn their temples, just as Alexander ordered that the temple of Asclepius be burned when his beloved died. **18.** It is for this reason that if someone places his own advantage alongside piety and what is honorable and his fatherland and his parents and his friends, then they are all secure. But if his advantage is placed on one side of the scales and his friends, fatherland, relatives, and justice itself are on the other, then all of them are ruined, outweighed by advantage. **19.** For wherever 'I' and 'mine' are located, that is where any animal necessarily inclines. If it is located in the flesh, that is where the decisive element lies. If it is found in moral choice, then that is where it is. If in external things, then it is there. **20.** So, if *I* am located where my moral choice is, it is in this way and this way alone that I will be the sort of friend, son, or father that I should be. For it will then be to my advantage to make sure that I remain a trustworthy person, a modest person, a tolerant person, an abstinent person, a cooperative person, and that I preserve my various social relationships. **21.** But if I locate *myself* on one side and the honorable on the other, then in this case Epicurus' theory wins, which holds that the honorable is either nothing or (if it is anything at all) merely opinion.

TEXT 147: Epictetus *Discourses* 3.2.1–5

1. There are three themes in which those who are to be virtuous must be trained. The theme dealing with desires and aversions trains them not to miss the object of their desire or to fall in with the object of their aversion. **2.** The theme dealing with impulses and rejections and, in general, with the appropriate trains them to act in an orderly, well-reasoned, and attentive manner. The third theme is the one dealing with avoiding deceptions and rash judgments and, in general, with the giving of assent. **3.** The most important and pressing of these is the theme dealing with the passions. For a passion occurs only if we do not attain the object of our desire or if we fall in with the object of our avoidance. . . . **4.** Next comes the theme which deals with the appropriate; for I should not be free of passions in the manner of a statue, but rather should attend to my social relationships both natural and acquired, such as those of a pious man, a son, a brother, a father, a citizen. **5.** The third theme applies only to those already making moral progress, and it is the one that deals with the stability of these very people, so that no one should let an unexamined presentation slip past him, even in his sleep or when drinking or when suffering from an excess of black bile.

TEXT 148: Epictetus *Discourses* 3.3.18–19

18. So, we ought to eliminate these pernicious opinions and to make every effort to do so. For what are lamentations and weeping? An opinion. What is misfortune? An opinion. What are civil strife, disagreements, reproaches, accusations, impiety, nonsense? **19.** All of these are opinions, nothing but opinions about things outside our moral choice, supposing that they are either good or bad. But just let someone transfer his opinions to matters that are within the scope of moral choice, and I guarantee you that he will be stable, no matter how his affairs turn out.

TEXT 149: Epictetus *Discourses* 3.24.83–94

83. . . . I am born to pursue my own goods and not born for what is bad. **84.** So, what is the training for this goal? First of all, the highest and most authoritative training, the one standing right at the gates, so to speak, is this: when you have an attachment to something, remember that you are attached to a thing which is not among those immune to loss but rather to something in the same category as a pot or a piece of glassware, so that when it gets broken you won't be upset. **85.** So too in real life, if you kiss your child or your brother or a friend, don't let your impressions go the distance and don't let your expansive feelings develop as far as they are inclined to do, but pull them back, slow them down, just like those who stand behind triumphal generals and remind them that they are [merely] human. **86.** You too should remind yourself in the same way, saying that what you love is mortal, that you don't love something that is truly your own; it has been given to you for the time being; it is not immune to loss, won't go the distance; it is like a fig, a bunch of grapes; it's available for a fixed season of the year, and if you long for it in winter then you are a fool. **87.** So too if you long for your son or your friend when he isn't available for you then you should realize that you are longing for figs in winter. For the entire set of circumstances in the cosmos is related to the things destroyed in accordance with it in the same way that winter is related to figs.

88. Furthermore, at the very moment when you are rejoicing in something, imagine the opposite state of affairs. What harm is done if right when you are kissing your child you whisper and say 'tomorrow you will die'? or if you say to a friend 'tomorrow you will go abroad—or I will—and we will never see each other again'? **89.** "But these are ill-omened words!" Yes, but so too are some incantations; but I don't mind because they do some good—just let them do some good! Do you label anything 'ill omened' except those words that indicate something bad? 'Cowardice' is ill omened, 'baseness' is ill omened, and so are 'grief', 'pain', [and] 'shamelessness'. **90.** These are ill-omened words, but still no one should hesitate to utter them in order to ward off the things themselves. **91.** Do you mean to tell me that a word that indicates some natural state of affairs is ill omened? Go ahead and tell me that 'harvesting the grain' is ill omened—after all, it indicates the destruction of the grain, but not the destruction of the cosmos. Tell me that the falling of leaves is ill omened or the conversion of figs into dried figs or of grapes into raisins. **92.** For all of these are the changes of what was there previously into something different. It isn't a destruction, but just an orderly management and administration of things. **93.** And that is all that a journey abroad is, just a small change. This is what death is, a somewhat larger change from what now exists *not* to what doesn't exist but merely to what doesn't exist right now.

94. "So, will I no longer exist?" No, you won't. But there will be something else, something which the cosmos now needs. After all, you weren't born when you wanted to be born, but rather when the cosmos needed you to be born.

TEXT 150: Epictetus *Discourses* 4.1.128–31

128. Come, then, let us go back over what we have agreed on. The unhindered person is free and things are ready to hand for him just as he wants them. If someone can be hindered or compelled or impeded or thrust into something against his will, then he is a slave. **129.** Who is unhindered? The person who desires nothing that is not his own. Which things are not one's own? Those that it is not in our power to have or not to have, either in their own nature or in relation to other things. **130.** So, the body is not our own and its parts are not our own and our possessions are not our own. Therefore, if you are attached to any of these as though it were your own, then you will pay the penalty that is appropriate for someone who desires what is not his own.

131. This is the path that leads to freedom, this is the only way to escape from slavery: being able to say with all your heart,

> Lead me, O Zeus, and you O Fate,
> to whatever place you have assigned me.[15]

---

15. From Cleanthes' *Hymn to Zeus*.

Glossary

We trust the reader to find compound words and negations by looking under the main root. For example, the explanation for the term 'ungraspable' is found by reading the entry on **grasp.**

abolish (*anairein*): to show by argument that something is untrue or non-existent; the use of the word does not necessarily indicate that the author regards the argument as successful; also, undermine, deny.

accident (*sumbebēkos*): Accidents can include permanent attributes of a thing; the technical meaning of the term is very broad.

administered (*dioikeisthai*): ordered and guided by a rational power.

affinity, etc. (*oikeios, oikeiōsis*): This refers to an animal's relationship with something that is compatible with or promotes its health, well-being, constitution, or interests; opposite: **alien, alienation** (*allotrios, allotriotēs*). Affinity is the objective relationship between an animal and things that have an affinity for it, not a subjective disposition or attitude. *Allotrios* is sometimes translated as "not one's own" and *oikeios* as "one's own."

ailment (*arrostēma*): a sickness in the soul, a moral and intellectual weakness founded on error.

alienation (*allotriotēs*): see **affinity**.

alive, animate (*empsuchos*): Etymologically the term means "having a soul within," "ensouled."

alteration (*alloiōsis, heteroiōsis*): used particularly for qualitative change.

appropriate (acts) (*kathēkonta*): actions that are reasonable for an agent to perform in view of his or her nature and the circumstances. An appropriate action can be performed by anyone, but only a **wise man** can perform a (morally) perfect action, which is a form of appropriate action.

assent (*sunkatathesis*): agreeing or committing oneself to the truth of a proposition or to the doing of an action.

atom, atomic (*atomos*): literally means "uncuttable."

avoid (*ekklinein*): In Stoicism, avoidance is appropriate for something that is rejected or contrary to nature.

bad (*kakos*): in Stoicism, morally bad.

base (*phaulos*): in Stoicism, the standard term for foolish, and therefore non-virtuous people.

beautiful (*kalos*): The same term is usually translated as "**honorable**" (q.v.).

benefit (*ōpheleia*): In Stoicism, benefit is narrowly defined in terms of the attainment or preservation of a virtuous state of one's soul.

canon (*kanōn*): standard of judgment; reference point for decision; criterion.

cause (*aition*): usually in a narrower sense than that which applies to the four Aristotelian causes (or forms of causal explanation): formal, final, material, and efficient. In Stoic thought, the term 'cause' indicates the active principle that brings about some other event, object, or state of affairs; closer to the familiar modern concept of cause than Aristotle's notion, but often roughly equivalent to Aristotle's efficient cause.

caution (*eulabeia*): the rational and correct avoidance of something bad; the virtuous counterpart of fear, which is a passion.

choice (*hairesis*), **choose** (*haireisthai*): rational or deliberative desire; in Stoicism, rational desire for the good; hence, what is to be chosen (*hairēteon*); worth choosing (*haireton*).

clarity, clear (fact) (*enargeia, enargēma*): an originally Epicurean term for a **presentation** (q.v.) obtained directly by the senses or the intellect without interpretive additions. See also **self-evident**.

complete (*teleios*): also, **perfect**.

condition (*hexis*): a state or alteration of the *pneuma* that constitutes something; hence, a quality or (non-permanent) attribute of something.

conflagration (*ekpurōsis*): in Stoic physics, the periodic dissolution of the universe into fire.

constitution (*status, sustasis*): the basic structure and characteristics of a thing that make it what it is.

cosmos, pl. **cosmoi** (*kosmos*): world; the organized and structured portion of the universe.

daimōn: a supernatural power; the term often includes gods, but it is not limited to them.

demonstration (*apodeixis*): a technical term for an argument in syllogistic form that reveals something non-evident.

desire (*epithumia*): irrational striving, one of the four passions in Stoicism. Desire (*orexis*) is also used in a more general sense.

differentiated thing (*to kata diaphoran*): something that exists and can be known all on its own, something non-relative; it is distinct (differentiated) from other things.

disagreement (*diaphōnia*): conflict or inconsistency between objects, theories, or hypotheses.

disease (*nosēma*): in Stoicism, a sickness of the soul.

disjunction, disjunctive (*diazeugmenon*): In Stoic logic, the term refers to exclusive disjunction.

disposition (*diathesis*): In Stoicism, the term has a special sense: a firm and unchangeable condition (*hexis*).

disposition (*pōs echon*): in Stoic category theory, a thing in a certain state.

disvalue (*apaxia*): negative value; the property of being disadvantageous or contrary to one's health, well-being, moral progress, etc.

dogma (*dogma*): Owing to skeptical attacks, this term has come to be used in a pejorative sense. In a non-polemical context, however, it is simply the content of a belief.

doubt (*aporia*): an argument or state of mind that prevents understanding; also, puzzlement, impasse, problem. Hence, dubitative (*aporētikos*).

element (*stoicheion*): one of the basic forms of matter: earth, air, fire, and water.

essence (*logos*): *Logos* usually refers to the statement of the essence but is sometimes used of the essence itself.

fact, object (*pragma*): generally, a thing. The term is extended in Stoicism to include *lekta* (things said) and states of affairs (*pragmata*).

fate (*heimarmenē*): Stoic term for the causal connections in nature.

freedom from passion (*apatheia*): in Stoicism, absence of or freedom from the irrational passions of the soul, namely, pleasure, pain, fear, and desire.

fresh (*prosphaton*): in Stoicism, stimulative of irrational contraction or elation.

goal (*telos*): the final aim or purpose of a thing, particularly of a human life. Greek philosophers hold that **happiness** (q.v.) is the goal of life.

good state (of the soul) (*eupatheia*): in Stoicism, a virtuous reaction by the soul; good states are joy, caution, and wish, which correspond to the passions pleasure, fear, and desire. The fourth passion, pain, has no rational counterpart since the **wise man** is not pained (in his soul) by anything that happens in the rational universe.

grasp: a family of terms (nouns and verbs) built on the Greek root that literally means grasping with one's hand. *Antilambanō* and its congeners are the most general in meaning and are used by all schools in the Hellenistic period for an intellectual or perceptual awareness of something real. The verb *dialambanō* has the sense of distinguishing clearly between things, grasping the distinctions among things. *Katalambanō* and its congeners (*katalēpsis, katalēpton, katalēptikon*) are used specifically in Stoicism to indicate the firm grasp that is the foundation for all other knowledge.

happiness (*eudaimonia*): the state of a human being in which it is in the best possible condition relative to its nature; flourishing. It is not a subjective state of personal contentment but an objective fact about the condition of the human being.

harm (*blaptō, blamma*): in Stoicism, restricted to moral harm, things that hinder the life according to virtue.

honorable (*honestum, kalon*): in Stoicism, morally good. The Stoic doctrine is that only what is honorable is really good; all other kinds of value are 'good' in the sense of being **preferred** (q.v.).

hormetic (*hormētikon*): of or concerned with an impulse (*hormē*), as a hormetic condition, the disposition to have a certain impulse.

impulse (*hormē*): the action of the soul in setting the agent in action, usually to get or avoid something. In a rational agent, it is always the result of an act of **assent,** either conscious or implicit.

inaction (*apraxia*): the state of not being able to act. The Stoics maintained that if, following the skeptics, one made no judgments, it would be impossible to do anything at all, since actions required assent and judgment. The argument from inaction was held to be a pragmatic refutation of skepticism, since it is manifest that people do act.

indicative (*endeiktikon*): of signs, revealing to us something not previously perceived.

indifference, indifferent (*adiaphoria, adiaphoron*): An indifferent thing, in Stoic ethics, is something that does not contribute to happiness or unhappiness; in another sense, it is what makes no difference at all in ethics.

individual quality (*idiōs poion*): the particular quality that makes an individual thing exactly what it is; thus Socrates is Socrates by virtue of his individual quality but is a man by virtue of his common quality.

infinite (*apeiron*): having no limit; also translated as "unlimited."

intellect (*dianoia*): cognitive activity that is not limited to the activities of one or more of the five senses; the faculty that governs this activity.

internal (*endiathetos*): In Stoicism, internal reason is the (capacity for) thought or mental discourse; opposite: verbalized reason, i.e., speech.

investigate, investigation (*zēteō, zētēsis*): inquiry into something non-evident.

joy (*chara*): In Stoicism, joy is the rational and morally correct form of pleasure that only the **wise man** can have.

lack of self-control (*akrasia*): the inability to control desires deemed undesirable or irrational.

leading part of the soul (*hēgemonikon*): in Stoicism, the dominant and controlling part of the soul. In an adult human it is totally rational. All the other parts and functions of the soul operate as ancillary to the leading part of the soul. It is almost the equivalent of the term 'mind' (*nous*).

living and breathing (*empnous*): endowed with soul and breath (*pneuma*).

mode (*tropos*): in skepticism, a dialectical move or type of argument.

moral choice (*prohairesis*): in the work of the Stoic Epictetus, moral choice is something more than a decision. It is the moral personality of the agent, virtually the same thing as the **leading part of the soul** (*hēgemonikon*).

[moral] mistake, [moral] error (*hamartēma*): Stoic term for a disposition to act other than according to reason or the action itself. All actions, except those of wise men, were held by the Stoics to be moral errors.

[moral] progress (*prokopē*): in Stoic ethics, development toward a fully rational and virtuous life; someone making moral progress is still considered to be vicious.

[morally] perfect action (*katorthōma*): an appropriate action that is perfect and (by definition) guaranteed to be correct. Only the virtuous **wise man** can perform such an action, and all of his or her actions are like this.

natural things (*ta kata phusin*): things that promote or preserve the basic nature of an organism.

nature (*phusis*): The meaning of this term is just as wide in Hellenistic thought as it is in Greek philosophy generally. It can refer to nature in general, the specific nature of one object, or one particular object or kind of object; it might in places also be translated as "entity," as in the Epicurean definition of void as an intangible nature.

non-evident (*adēlon*): not subject to direct observation; unclear; unobservable.

opinion (*doxa*): a cognitive state distinct from a more rigorous form of cognition (knowledge) that does not admit of falsity.

organization (*diakosmēsis*): the basic, rational ordering of the cosmos.

outline [definition] (*hupographē*): a rough sketch of the meaning of a term, which falls short of the precision of a true definition.

passion (*pathos*): in Stoic ethics, a vicious state or motion in the soul. The four passions are pleasure, pain, fear, and desire.

perceive (*percipere*): sometimes used, especially in Cicero, in the sense of a firm and true perception, i.e., a **grasp**.

perfect (*teleios*): also, **complete**.

pneuma: in Greek generally, breath or wind. In Stoic texts, designates a special material compound that is fundamental to Stoic physics, being a breathlike mixture of fire and air (or the fiery and the airy). God, soul, and conditions (*hexeis*) are all forms of *pneuma*. The specific substance of each thing is determined by its inborn *pneuma*.

predisposition (*euemptōsia*): in Stoic ethics, a tendency to have a passion.

preferred (*proēgmenon*): In Stoicism, an **indifferent** thing (q.v.) that has value for the life according to nature is said to be preferred.

presentation (*phantasia*): an intentional state of the soul ultimately caused by an external object or state of affairs, which by itself indicates both itself and its cause.

principle (*archē*): the starting point for an argument or theory; may be a definition, axiom, etc. In Stoic physics, the two basic principles are god (active) and prime matter (passive).

proposition (*axiōma*): a statement with truth value. In Stoicism, an *axiōma* is a form of **thing said** (q.v.).

providence (*pronoia*): in Stoicism, equivalent to the rational, causal order of nature.

prudence (*phronēsis*): the highest rational virtue; the flawless use of reason to guide life and so produce happiness.

reason (*logos*): also, statement, argumentative procedure, argument, theory, rational discourse, account, rational principle; hence, 'which reason can contemplate' (*logōi theorēton*): not amenable to sense-perception; graspable only by the reason or rational inference. Such things are not necessarily incorporeal, since there are (at least in Epicureanism and Stoicism) material entities that cannot be directly perceived. See also **essence**.

rejected (*apoproēgmenon*): In Stoicism, an **indifferent** thing (q.v.) that has **disvalue** with respect to the life according to nature is said to be rejected.

rejection (*apeklogē*): in Stoicism, the decision to avoid or flee from something that has disvalue or is contrary to nature.

right reason (*orthos logos*): a term in ethics indicating correct use of reason in matching up means and ends or in determining what is right. In Stoicism, right reason is also one of the descriptions of god.

seed (*sperma*): often used in an extended sense for any generative principle.

selection (*eklogē*): in Stoicism, the choice of something that is preferred or according to nature; rational choice of something that is not morally good.

self-control (*enkrateia*): the ability to control desires deemed undesirable or irrational.

self-evident (*prodēlos*): something evident that does not depend on something else for its truth or knowability.

self-sufficiency (*autarkeia*): autonomy; the state of not needing anything external. Virtue is said to be self-sufficient for happiness by the Stoics since they hold that the virtuous person is happy no matter what external circumstances he or she is in. Self-sufficiency in some sense is a goal in most of Greek ethics.

sense-perception (*aisthēsis*): the use of one or more of our five senses; also 'sense', 'sense-organ'.

sensible (*aisthēton*): the direct object of one of the five senses.

shame(ful) (*aischron, aischunē, aischos*): In Stoic ethics in particular, this term indicates the opposite of what is **honorable**.

sorites (*soritēs*): a paradox formed of a complex of linked syllogisms.

sound (*hugiēs*): of conditional inferences, one that does not infer from a truth to a falsehood.

spermatic principle (*spermatikos logos*): in Stoicism, the organic bearer of the rational principle of the universe or its contents.

state (*pathos*): condition, experience, feeling, modification. See also **passion**.

subsist (*huphistasthai*): In Stoicism, the term indicates the dependent mode of existence that characterizes incorporeals, such as a **thing said** (q.v.).

substance (*hupokeimenon*): also, *hupostasis, ousia;* genuine entity or real thing. In Stoic category theory, it is an underlying primary object and always corporeal.

supervene (*epigignesthai*): to exist or occur as temporally, metaphysically, or logically subsequent to something else on which it is dependent.

symmetry (*summetria*): balance and harmony; frequently used by Chrysippus and other Stoics in an extended sense.

sympathy (*sumpnoia, sumpatheia*): in Stoic physics, the state of sharing the same *pneuma* with something, being organically bound up with it.

thing said (*lekton*): the content of propositions and meaningful phrases mediating between the words used and the objects or states of affairs denoted by them.

unaffected, impassible (*apathes*): not subject to change or alteration.

undecidable (*anepikritos*): something that cannot be settled because of its intrinsic obscurity or the equally balanced arguments for and against it.

unnatural things (*ta para phusin*): things that impede or oppose the basic nature of an organism.

unqualified substance (*apoios ousia*): prime matter; the passive **principle** in Stoic physics; material stuff with no qualities. Unqualified substance must be shaped by rational principles before it can have qualities; it is prior to the four **element**s (earth, air, fire, and water), which are modifications of it.

value (*axia*): in Stoicism, worth that is significant in ethics. There are two kinds of value: moral value, which is coextensive with virtue and suffices to produce a happy life, and so-called 'natural' value, which contributes to a life according to the specific nature of the species in question. Health has natural value but no moral value.

vice (*kakia*): moral badness.

virtue (*aretē*): excellence of soul, in particular moral excellence, but also intellectual and other excellences. In Stoicism, only the virtuous man (*asteios, spoudaios*) is a **wise man**.

void (*kenon*): containing nothing; having nothing real corresponding to it. In Stoic physics, the void is incorporeal and surrounds the organized cosmos.

way of life (*bios*): a broad term for a pattern of activity over an entire life.

wise man (*sophos, sapiens*): the ideally virtuous person according to Stoic theory, which held that wise men were extremely rare; possibly only Socrates qualified.

wish (*boulēsis*): fully rational desire.

yielding (*eixis*): in Stoicism, the concession of the mind (usually an animal's) to some presentation, without rational assent.

Philosophers and Philosophical Sources

Achilles Tatius: mid- to late second century A.D.; Stoic philosopher, author of an introduction to Aratus' *Phaenomena.*

Aëtius: probably first century A.D.; philosopher and doxographer.

Alexander of Aphrodisias: late second to early third centuries A.D.; Peripatetic philosopher and scholar.

Ammonius of Alexandria: fifth and sixth century A.D.; a Platonist from Alexandria, he wrote commentaries on Aristotle.

Anaxagoras of Clazomenae: fifth century B.C.; pluralist philosopher.

Antigonus of Carystas: third century B.C.; wrote *Lives of the Philosophers,* source for Diogenes Laërtius.

Antiochus of Ascalon: c. 130/120–? B.C.; pupil of Philo of Larissa and initiator of a dogmatic form of Academic philosophy.

Antipater of Tarsus: second century B.C.; successor to Diogenes of Babylon as head of the Stoic school and teacher of Panaetius.

Antipater of Tyre: first century B.C.; Stoic philosopher.

Apollodorus of Seleucia: second century B.C.; Stoic philosopher and pupil of Diogenes of Babylon; attempted to reconcile Stoicism and Cynicism.

Apollonius of Tyre: first century B.C.; Stoic philosopher.

Aratus of Soli: third century B.C.; Stoic poet and author of the *Phaenomena.*

Arcesilaus: 316/315–242/241 B.C.; head of the Academy in the mid-third century and originator of its skeptical turn.

Archedemus of Tarsus: second century B.C.; Stoic philosopher, founder of a school of Stoicism in Babylon.

Aristippus of Cyrene: late fifth century B.C.; Hedonist and acquaintance of Socrates. The Cyrenaic school was founded by his grandson of the same name.

Aristocles of Messene: first or second century A.D.; Peripatetic philosopher.

Ariston of Chios: mid-third century B.C.; Stoic follower of Zeno of Citium and founder of an independent branch of the Stoic school.

Aristotle: 389–322 B.C.; pupil of Plato and founder of the Peripatetic school.

Athenodorus of Tarsus: early to mid-first century B.C.; Stoic philosopher and keeper of the library at Pergamum.

Augustine of Hippo, Saint: A.D. 354–430; Christian philosopher and theologian.

Aulus Gellius: second century A.D.; Roman author and grammarian; wrote a long compilation of notes on many branches of knowledge, including philosophy.

Boethus of Sidon: second century B.C.; unorthodox Stoic and a pupil of Diogenes of Babylon.

Calcidius: late third and early fourth centuries A.D.; Platonic philosopher; wrote a Latin commentary on Plato's *Timaeus.*

Carneades: 214/213–129/128 B.C.; most famous head of the skeptical Academy.

Cassius: late fourth and early third centuries B.C.; skeptic philosopher who criticized Zeno of Citium.

Celsus: early to mid-second century A.D.; Epicurean and opponent of Christianity.

Chrysippus of Soli: c. 280–207 B.C.; successor of Cleanthes as head of the Stoic school.

Cicero: 106–43 B.C.; Roman statesman, orator, and Academic philosopher.

Cleanthes of Assos: 331–232 B.C.; pupil of Zeno and his successor as head of the Stoic school (263–232).

Clement of Alexandria: late second and early third centuries A.D.; Platonist and Christian philosopher; head of the Catechetical School of Alexandria and succeeded by Origen.

Clitomachus: 187/186–110/109 B.C.; successor to Carneades as head of the Academy.

Colotes of Lampsacus: fourth through third centuries B.C.; pupil and devotee of Epicurus.

Crantor: c. 335–275 B.C.; pupil of Xenocrates and Academic philosopher.

Crates of Thebes: 365–285 B.C.; Cynic philosopher, follower of Diogenes of Sinope.

Critias: late fifth century B.C.; Athenian aristocrat and intellectual.

Demetrius of Magnesia: first century B.C.; contemporary of Cicero; wrote a book *Men of the Same Name.*

Democritus of Abdera: c. 470/457–c. 360 B.C.; along with Leucippus the founder of atomism.

Diocles of Magnesia: Hellenistic doxographer of uncertain date, important source for Diogenes Laërtius.

Diodorus Cronus: c. 300 B.C.; founder of the Megarian dialectical school; Zeno of Citium and Arcesilaus were among his pupils.

Diogenes Laërtius: early third century A.D.; doxographer and biographer; wrote *Lives of the Philosophers,* an important source for the development of Greek philosophy.

Diogenes of Babylon: c. 240–152 B.C.; pupil of Chrysippus and successor of Zeno of Tarsus as head of the Stoic school.

Diogenes of Sinope: c. 400–c. 325; founder of the Cynic school.

Dionysius of Heraclea: c. 328–248 B.C.; follower of Zeno of Citium, who later converted to hedonism.

Diphilus: second century B.C.; pupil of Panaetius of Rhodes.

Empedocles of Acragas: fifth century B.C.; pluralist philosopher.

Epictetus: c. A.D. 55 to 135; Stoic philosopher active in Rome as well as Greece.

Epicurus: 341–270 B.C.; founder of the Epicurean school.

Euboulides of Miletus: mid-fourth century B.C.; dialectician with links to the Megarian school.

Eusebius: c. A.D. 265–339; Christian theologian and admirer of Origen.

Galen of Pergamum: second century A.D.; physician and Platonic philosopher.

Heraclitus of Ephesus: c. 500 B.C.; Ionian philosopher.

Herillus of Carthage: mid- to late third century B.C.; pupil of Zeno of Citium and founder of an independent school.

Hermippus of Smyrna: third century B.C.; Peripatetic philosopher and biographer.

Hieronymus of Rhodes: c. 290–230 B.C.; trained in the Peripatetic school, he later left to found his own school.

Hippobotus: second century B.C.; historian of philosophers and philosophical schools.

Hippolytus of Rome, Saint: early to mid-second century A.D.; prolific writer, polemicist, and theologian.

Marcus Aurelius: A.D. 121–180; Roman emperor and philosophical writer; his *To Himself* or *Meditations* draws heavily on his Stoic convictions as well as influences from other philosophical schools.

Metrodorus of Stratonicea: late second century B.C.; Academic philosopher; former Epicurean and then pupil of Carneades.

Miltiades: third century B.C.; pupil of Ariston of Chios; also the name of Ariston's father.

Mnesarchus: c. 160–c. 85 B.C.; Stoic philosopher, pupil of Diogenes of Babylon.

Musonius Rufus: mid-first century A.D.; Roman Stoic philosopher, teacher of Epictetus.

Nemesius: end of fourth century A.D.; Christian philosopher and author of *On Human Nature.*

Numenius of Apamea: second century A.D.; Neopythagorean and Platonist philosopher.

Origen: c. A.D. 185–c. 254; early Christian scholar and theologian.

Panaetius of Rhodes: c. 185–109 B.C.; Stoic philosopher who succeeded Antipater as head of the school.

Parmenides of Elea: early fifth century B.C.; founder of the Eleatic school.

Persaeus of Citium: c. 306–c. 243 B.C.; Stoic and pupil of Zeno of Citium.

Philo of Alexandria: c. 25 B.C.–c. A.D. 50; Jewish philosopher of mostly Platonic leanings.

Philo of Larissa: first century B.C.; successor to Clitomachus as head of the Academy.

Philo the Dialectician: late fourth and early third centuries B.C.; a logician and pupil of Diodorus Cronus.

Plato: 427–347 B.C.; founder of the Academy and pupil of Socrates.

Plotinus: A.D. 204–270; Platonist philosopher, author of the *Enneads.*

Plutarch: A.D. 46–after 120; Academic philosopher and biographer; author of works of Platonism and criticisms of other schools.

Polemo: ?–270 B.C.; head of the Academy after Xenocrates.

Porphyry: third century A.D.; pupil of Plotinus and Platonic philosopher.

Posidonius: c. 135–c. 50 B.C.; Stoic philosopher, pupil of Panaetius.

Prodicus of Ceos: fifth century B.C.; sophist and contemporary of Socrates.

Protagoras of Abdera: c. 450 B.C.; most famous of the sophists.

Pyrrho: 365/360–275/270 B.C.; founder of Greek skepticism.

Pythagoras of Samos: sixth century B.C.; mathematical and religious philosopher.

Seneca: c. 1 B.C.– A.D. 65; Roman politician, playwright, and Stoic philosopher.

Sextus Empiricus: c. A.D. 200; physician and skeptic, major source for ancient skepticism.

Simplicius: sixth century A.D.; Platonist philosopher and author of commentaries on Aristotle.

Socrates: 469–399 B.C.; the teacher of Plato.

Sotion of Alexandria: early second century B.C.; Greek doxographer and biographer, an important source for Diogenes Laërtius.

Sphaerus of Borysthenes: c. 285/265–c. 221 B.C.; pupil of Zeno of Citium and then of Cleanthes.

Stilpo: c. 380–300 B.C.; third head of the Megarian school.

Stobaeus: late fourth to early fifth centuries A.D.; excerpter and anthologist.

Syrianus: fifth century A.D.; Platonist philosopher and head of Plato's Academy in Athens (431/2).

Tertullian: c. A.D. 160–c. 225; early Christian writer and opponent of Greek philosophy.

Theodoretus: c. A.D. 393–c. 457; Christian theologian.

Xenocrates: 396–314 B.C.; pupil of Plato and head of the Academy after Speusippus (339–314).

Xenophon: c. 431–355 B.C.; contemporary and admirer of Socrates; historian and writer of Socratic dialogues.

Zeno of Citium: 335–263 B.C.; founder of the Stoic school.

Zeno of Sidon: third century B.C.; Stoic pupil of Zeno of Citium and also of Diodorus Cronus.

Zeno of Tarsus: late third and early second centuries B.C.; Stoic philosopher and successor to Chrysippus as head of the Stoic school in 204 B.C.

Index of Passages Translated

Index